A LITTLE CIRCLE OF KINDRED MINDS

A LITTLE CIRCLE OF KINDRED MINDS

JOYCE IN PARIS

CONOR FENNELL

Green Lamp Editions
Glasthule, Dublin, 2011

Green Lamp Editions

This first edition was published in 2011

A Little Circle of Kindred Minds: Joyce In Paris

Copyright © Conor Fennell, 2011

ISBN: 978-1-907694-98-1

Publisher: Eoin Purcell
Cover Design by Ciara Panacchia

A digital edition of this book is available through
Amazon.com and Amazon.co.uk

For more information on Green Lamp Editions
visit our website www.greenlampmedia.com

He could not sway the crowd, but he might appeal to a little circle of kindred minds.

A Little Cloud, *Dubliners*.

Contents

A Little Circle Of Kindred Minds

Acknowledgments

I am grateful to Professor Declan Kiberd of UCD for his encouragement and generosity of time, and for the advice of Dr Clíona Ní Ríordáin of the Université Sorbonne Nouvelle Paris 3. Margaret Farrington, niece of Thomas MacGreevy, has been most helpful as has Gerry O'Flaherty and Dardis Clarke. Friends and former colleagues also kept me going with their kind words, none more so than Véronique Didon who urged me to start the project, and Seamus Hosey, Michelle McCaughren, Sharon Geoghegan and Sue Murray of RTÉ who kept at me to finish it. I am also grateful to Eoin Purcell of Green Lamp Editions for bringing this long-gestating baby into the world.

I have been fortunate to be on the receiving end of the sound guidance and encouragement of the author Patricia O'Reilly and the literary consultant Emma Walsh.

I feel compelled to express here my appreciation of the achievements of others. Anyone who has written about Joyce owes an immeasurable debt to that doyen of biographers, Richard Ellmann. Noel Riley Fitch's superb book *Sylvia Beach and the Lost Generation* provides an exciting link between Joyce and Literary Paris. I have also been helped by Susan Schreibman's extensive research into the life and works of Thomas MacGreevy, Adrian Frazier's biography of George Moore and Patrick J Murphy's study of the artist Patrick Tuohy.

The memoirs of those who knew Joyce in Paris, such as those written by Arthur Power and by Padraic and Mary Colum, provide an intimate picture of the man and his relationship with those around him. Equally, the memoirs of Ernest Hemingway and Robert McAlmon paint atmospheric pictures of Paris and its writers in the 1920s, even though parts of their accounts should be taken with several grains of salt.

The award for forbearance must go to my wife, Penny, for putting up with my long absences at libraries and at the keyboard.

My research was helped considerably by the efficiency and kindness of staff at the National Library of Ireland, UCD Archives, the Manuscripts and Research Library at Trinity College Dublin, and the Bibliothèque Nationale de France in Paris. Much credit is due to the Irish public library service, which is often the first port of call for any Irish writer.

Writing is a lonely occupation and I would not have finished this book without the encouragement of many people. I thank them wholeheartedly.

Introduction
The Revolution Of The
Word

Legend has it that it was the taxis that saved Paris. On 6
September, 1914, as the German guns came within 30
miles of the city, its defenders – French and British
troops stationed along the Marne – were badly in need of
reinforcement. French reserve troops were available in
Paris but there was a shortage of motor vehicles and
drivers to transport them. So the city's taxis were
assembled and 600 vehicles, each carrying five soldiers,
made two journeys eastwards. Two days later 6,000
troops had been ferried to the front. The ensuing Battle
of the Marne resulted in stalemate and both sides dug in
for the trench warfare that would last for years.

Paris was spared. What might have been destroyed in an
attack must remain conjectural. But given not just the
splendour of Haussmann's boulevards, but also the
historic and cultural aspects of the city, its monuments
and museums, its art, its books, its archives, one can only
express enormous relief.

It could so easily have been otherwise. The government
had deserted the city for Bordeaux and almost a million
Parisians fled to other parts of France.

For those who stayed on, the custom of people watching
was temporarily abandoned as the café terraces were
closed and customers had to sit inside at the zinc counters
of those few that remained open. Theatres and music

halls were also shut down. The City of Light became a city of darkness.

As men were mobilised, women did what they could to keep the wheels of the economy moving and to help the war effort. And not just the French: Dolly Wilde, niece of Oscar, went to Paris to join a group of women ambulance drivers on their way to the front. Eileen Gray, the Irish designer, became one of the first women in Paris to acquire a driving license; she bought her own car for use as an ambulance on condition she would be the only driver (she claimed it was the fastest ambulance in town). Gertrude Stein and her partner Alice B Toklas acquired a Ford, which they called affectionately 'Auntie.' Stein learned to drive and they carried supplies to French hospitals.

With the peace in November 1918, the city threw open its doors again, especially to the Americans who had helped win the war.[1] Paris was open for business. The Germans had been repelled. But now the city was to see an invasion of a very different kind.

Within a year a wave of writers, artists and musicians began to arrive and for most of the 1920s their numbers steadily increased from a trickle to a flood. Many of them were intellectual refugees fleeing from a climate of conservatism and prejudice in their own countries. For those whose ambition was to write or paint or compose, Paris offered them creative freedom and a tolerance in which they could explore and develop their art and bring it forward into the rest of the century whose early years had been so savagely interrupted by war.

Unknowingly they were participants in a revolution, what one of them – Eugene Jolas, founder of the literary magazine *transition* – called the Revolution of the Word.

Revolution was not new to Paris. But the quiet revolution that started in the cafés and bars of Montparnasse in the aftermath of the Great War had an impact well beyond France and its reverberations are likely to be felt well into the 21st century.

Many of them were influenced by the presence in the city of painters such as Pablo Picasso, composers like Igor Stravinsky and writers like Stein who had begun to break away from the old, established values of their art. But now there was another attraction: the city had become more affordable as the post-war franc fell in value against sterling and the dollar.

Among the first of these to arrive – in July 1920 - was an Irishman who had no intention of putting down roots in Paris. James Joyce was on his way from Trieste to London and Dublin where he would finish writing *Ulysses* in 'a quiet place.'[2] He stopped off in Paris to see about French translations of *A Portrait of the Artist as a Young Man* and *Dubliners*. Crucially, he was invited to do so by the American poet Ezra Pound who had been secretary to William Butler Yeats (Yeats had introduced Pound to Joyce). Joyce intended to stay no longer than a week. Instead he stayed for 20 years, during which time he completed *Ulysses* and wrote *Finnegans Wake*.

Joyce regarded himself as an exile. But in a sense he was as much an expatriate as others who made Paris their home.[3] And he was far from unique among the Irish writers of the time. In 1931, Daniel Corkery wrote that there were more Irish writers overseas than at home. 'Where today are those wild geese of the pen?' he asked, going on to name over 30 people, among them Padraic Colum, Frank Harris, Thomas MacGreevy, Austin Clarke, James Joyce, James Stephens, George Moore and Liam O'Flaherty. 'It would be impossible to make a list quarter as long of home-staying writers.'[4]

Expatriate or not, Joyce was surely a patriot, for he was among those who, as Malcolm Cowley put it, 'had fled in despair from their own country, but still they wanted to redeem it.'[5] Joyce would seek to redeem his country through his writing.

Whatever way Joyce preferred to define himself, his main concern was to finish writing *Ulysses*. Within three days of his arrival he met an American expatriate who was to have an enormous effect on his work. Sylvia Beach, the owner of a bookshop called Shakespeare and Company, would soon become his publisher. Thanks to Pound's encouragement and Beach's practical support, the outline of a Joyce circle began to form, which would come into sharper focus as others befriended the Irish writer and offered their help. Joyce particularly enjoyed the friendship of writers from Ireland who provided him with an opportunity to keep up to date with events in Dublin. But he was not slow to exploit them. He was frank about it too. He told Arthur Power: 'I'm always friends with a person for a purpose.'[6]

The publication of *Ulysses* in February 1922 was a revolutionary milestone of the period. The novel, according to Malcolm Cowley, 'came to be revered by the new writers almost as the Bible was by Primitive Methodists.' Joyce, he wrote, was the paramount hero of the age.[7]

Joyce's presence in Paris, together with Pound and Stein, made the city the centre of English-language Modernism. In the years immediately following Joyce's arrival, scores of writers and others made their way there to see if they too could hone their skills and expand their art.

Robert McAlmon arrived in autumn 1921. Ernest Hemingway followed in December. Djuna Barnes and Ford Madox Ford arrived in 1922. F Scott Fitzgerald and his wife Zelda visited the city in 1921, and stayed for longer in subsequent years. TS Eliot came and went, as did Wyndham Lewis.

Of the Irish, George Moore had a long-lasting flirtation

with the city. Padraic and Mary Colum were regular
visitors and James Stephens, who owned an apartment in
the city, regarded Paris as his second home. Thomas
MacGreevy came in 1927 and Samuel Beckett a year
later. All this time many Irish artists were studying or
working in Paris. Evie Hone and Mainie Jellett spent
much of the 1920s there and Eileen Gray had her own
gallery at Faubourg Saint-Honoré (she called one of her
rugs 'Ulysses' in homage to Joyce who was one of her
clients).

This book is an attempt to describe some of those who
came to Paris and who became part of the Joyce circle. It
is not exhaustive; its emphasis is on Irish writers and
those of Irish extraction. The Joyce circle was constantly
changing as people came and went and as they moved in
and out of favour.

Joyce attracted people like a magnet and as they got
closer he energised them. He also exploited them
shamelessly. Such was their devotion that they let him.
They took his dictation, typed his manuscripts, wrote
articles in praise of his work and provided prefaces for his
books. Perhaps, most important of all, they listened to
him and talked to him about Dublin and Ireland, Greece
and Rome, history and geography. They had
conversations that triggered in Joyce's mind words and
ideas that ultimately found their way into *Finnegans
Wake.*

They so admired Joyce that they put up with his foibles
and his moods. Depending on the company he was in,
Joyce could be witty or shy, loquacious or silent. He did
not like being asked about anything and particularly
resented journalists who questioned him about his sight.
But the gregarious side of his nature emerged in the
evening, either dining out at an expensive restaurant (for
he lived well on the vast sums he got in patronage) or
during soirées at home among family and friends when he

would sing, play the piano and dance.

In looking at those who befriended Joyce and helped him, much is revealed about the man himself. And one thing becomes clear: in the Joyce circle it was always Joyce who was in control.

---

[1] In 1918 Parisians celebrated the Fourth as well as 14 July with a parade down the Champs-Elysées.

[2] Letter to Ezra Pound, 5 June, 1920, from Trieste: 'I live in a flat with eleven other people... I spend a great part of my time sprawled across two beds surrounded by mountains of notes... So I propose to pass three months in Ireland in order to write *Circe* and the close of the book. I shall return here with my family in October.'

[3] Joyce biographer Anthony Burgess described him as 'a chronic exile, no mere expatriate.' The writer Sisley Huddleston wondered if the word was 'meant as a reproach or as a compliment?'

[4] Corkery: *Synge and Anglo-Irish Literature* 4.

[5] Cowley: *A Second Flowering* 16.

[6] Power: *From an Old Waterford House* 67.

[7] Cowley: *A Second Flowering* 16.

Chapter One
The City of Light

The literary beacon that attracted so many English-speaking writers and others to Paris in the 1920s had been shining for centuries. The city was renowned as the ultimate capital of culture and for anyone interested in the arts it was the place to be.

But there was something else that lay behind the movement of such vast numbers across the Atlantic, the Irish Sea and the English Channel and that was the state of culture in their home countries. In the United States, a new Puritanism, even bigotry, was stifling the arts. The mere mention of the name of Gertrude Stein would invite ridicule, not just because of her experimental writing but also because of her sexual proclivity. A similar culture existed in the newly independent Ireland where the Free State government was pre-occupied with tackling poverty and militant republicanism and where the Catholic Church kept its flock under strict control. To refer in conversation to James Joyce would result in sniggers about a writer of dirty books.

For Americans, travel to France had become easier after the war, thanks to a surplus of merchant ships. Many of these were converted into passenger liners by Cunard and Ellerman and carried thousands across the Atlantic for only $80. It was different for the Irish whose route to Paris brought them through England and the Channel ports. It would have been as easy to go to London.

The reason they chose Paris over London seems to be bound up in their perception of the two cities. Around the turn of the 20th century, according to the writer and scholar Declan Kiberd, many Irish writers – Tom Kettle and Joyce among them – saw the country as belonging to the European mainstream. England had become provincial; Oscar Wilde's *Salomé* was banned in London and had to be staged in Paris. Besides, London was not the place to go because of the stereotype of the Irish there.

> *That is why the debate in Joyce's great story* The Dead *is about whether the Irish person of the future will recreate themselves on Aran or on the Continent. All of a sudden England is a bore.*[1]

Many Irish writers of the period reached beyond Britain for their mentors. Rather than look eastwards, Joyce looked north to Scandinavia (Henrik Ibsen) and Beckett looked south to France (Marcel Proust).

One wonders if Britain even existed. Talking in Paris to the poet Austin Clarke (another ex-Belvedere man), Joyce said that Dublin was the nearest city to the continent. 'Places here in Paris on a Saturday night are like Capel Street and Thomas Street. There's the same joy and excitement, as though bargaining for Sunday's dinner was a holiday. The very faces I see seem to be the same.'[2]

Irish politicians (perhaps more mindful of history) also looked beyond Britain for their ideas and philosophy. Arthur Griffith's advocacy of 'economic nationalism' was based on the German Friedrich List. And he took his views on a dual monarchy from the history of Austria and Hungary. According to one of his biographers, 'Griffith was a Europhile long before the idea of close European co-operation gained currency, this while espousing a nationalism which has often been stigmatised as inward-looking.'[3]

Some writers looked to Europe as a means of escape from

the 'old enemy' that was subordinating them. Mary
Colum, looking back on that period, wrote: 'The truth, as
I now see it, is that the country's writers were not
economically independent of England and consequently
not intellectually independent.'[4]

Paris was 'a free space beyond Anglocentric images of
Ireland.'[5] It stood for independence and liberty. Besides,
France was no stranger to the Irish. Thousands of
Irishmen had fought in France's wars and its navy had
responded to calls for help, resulting in abortive attempts
to land at Bantry and elsewhere. Over three centuries,
innumerable Irishmen studied at the seminary of the Irish
College in Paris. Paris was where, in 1833, Harriet
Smithson, an actress from Co Clare, met and married
Hector Berlioz, inspiring his *Symphony Fantastique*.[6] It
was where Fenians lived in exile and where Maud Gonne
founded a branch of the Young Ireland Society
(*L'Association Irlandaise*) and a newspaper (*L'Irlande
Libre*). Paris was where John Millington Synge wrote
articles for French magazines about the Irish language
revival. Paris was where WB Yeats met Synge, telling
him to go to the Aran Islands. Paris was where Synge met
Joyce.

In the 1870s, Henry James had acclaimed Paris as the
'great literary workshop of Europe.' Yet until the Great
War, American writers were more likely to go to London
and composers to Germany. By and large it was only
painters who gravitated towards France. All that changed
after the war. Malcolm Cowley wrote of Paris in the
1920s: 'There was no second centre for a dozen years
after the war; almost every aspirant in every art spent
more or less time in Paris.'[7]

Cowley was one of many young American men who had
spent wartime service in Europe and found the city
irresistible. Typically, they had served in the ambulance
corps of the Red Cross. They included young writers such

as Ernest Hemingway, John Dos Passos, Archibald
MacLeish and EE Cummings – men whose senses were
sharpened, as Cowley put it, by the thought of dying the
next day. Some of them passed through Paris on their
way home after the war, losing their virginity *en route*,
determined to make the most of their young lives having
seen death and devastation up close.

The France they were leaving was tolerant, a country
where private space was not intruded upon and where
sexual morality was not an issue; and they were returning
to an America where religious conservatism and social
narrow-mindedness were prevalent. And just as a new
form of popular music called jazz was spreading from
New Orleans to Chicago and New York, bringing with it a
new sense of freedom and excitement, just as women
were liberating themselves from the shackles of
Edwardian society, just as America was emerging as a
potent force of progress and modernity, Congress
legislated to ban the sale of alcohol. This was, for many,
the final straw. As one writer put it, a government that
could pass the Eighteenth Amendment would probably do
a lot of things to make life as stuffy and as bigoted as
possible.[8]

Stein believed her country had gone back in time:

> '*America is the mother of Twentieth Century*
> *civilisation, but she is now early Victorian.*'[9]
> *Another writer referred to the erosion of liberty in*
> *the land of the free:* '*Many an American who*
> *feels outraged at living under a government*
> *which treats its subjects like a set of naughty*
> *children, who shall be told what to drink, to read,*
> *to wear, and to see at the theatre, prefers to go*
> *into exile.*'[10]

It was difficult to live life to the full in conservative
middle-America. If you expressed interest in the arts, you

would likely be regarded as neurotic or effeminate. There was widespread hostility towards African-Americans and Jews. The United States Post Office had power to intercept mail they believed to be salacious or dangerous (copies of *Ulysses* had to be smuggled into the country). Sexual liberation was still a long way off, even though condoms had become generally available (they had been issued to soldiers during the war to prevent the spread of venereal disease) and couples of the same sex felt compelled to hide their relationships.

Political power in the United States was moving into the hands of big business and profit was everything; Cummings called it 'the age of dollars and no sense.' He was one of many who could not abide the new philosophy of greed. According to Samuel Putnam, 'the conclusion was that life must somehow be spiritualised... and it seemed that this could be done only in Europe.'[11]

Many of the former conscripts got jobs as newspaper reporters. With the shortage of newsprint no longer an issue, the bigger US papers opened Paris bureaux. Newspapers in Chicago and New York launched English language editions in Paris and journalists and would-be novelists were attracted to work for them. In time, some of these writers moved away from hard news to set up literary journals. Although their circulation figures were small, the influence of these 'little magazines' was enormous since they provided a platform for many writers, among them Joyce, Hemingway and Stein.

In Britain, life was not much better than in the US. The country had lost 700,000 soldiers in the war and there had been over two million casualties. They included many prose writers and poets who had been conscripted after the casualty figures among the regular soldiers had reached alarming proportions. Post-war government promises of a better society and a higher standard of living were not fulfilled and there was mass unemployment. Both Stein and Natalie Barney found London depressingly unsympathetic to women. Dolly Wilde regarded the city as sexually stifling (it was not that long since her Uncle Oscar's trial). TS Eliot, in 1920, wrote that 'Paris was a great relief after many months of London.'[12] In the same year Ezra Pound, who had spent twelve years in England where he was associated with several literary magazines, eventually decided that everything of importance in modern literature was happening in Paris. 'There is no longer an intellectual life in England,' he wrote.

In Ireland, those who had fought in the war returned in silence. Public opinion had changed dramatically while they had been away. Proud to fight for king and country when they left, they came back to a society whose mood had shifted, in the aftermath of the Easter Rising in 1916, away from thoughts of Home Rule and towards a more militant demand for full independence from the country on whose side they had fought. Caught in this surge of nationalism, many ex-soldiers never spoke about the war, even to their own families, for the rest of their lives. (In an awful irony, some of the returned soldiers joined the new Free State army only to find themselves fighting a civil war against their own).

As happened elsewhere, economic difficulties beset the Free State that emerged painfully in 1922, exacerbating the slow but relentless haemorrhaging of its population that had started with the Famine 80 years earlier. The poor and the jobless had few on their side for the Left had little influence. The Irish were reluctant to embrace either communism or fascism to any significant degree, believing instead that the more important 'ism' was nationalism.[13]

Since the new State promoted Gaelic culture above all else, the Literary Renaissance was seen as Anglo-Irish and therefore not quite Irish.[14] The old enemy, England, was to an extent replaced by the enemy within as the new government felt obliged to make its presence felt in exercising law and order. Parallel to this – and often in collusion with it – the Catholic bishops exercised crosier-belting authority over their flock. This combination of state and religious conservatism compelled many of the country's writers and artists to leave.

Joyce, who while in exile kept in touch with his native country, noted how it had changed with independence: whereas under British rule anyone could say what they felt, independence brought responsibility and cautiousness.[15] Kiberd has described 1920s Ireland as a 'far-from-free state' where 'war and civil war appeared to have drained all energy and imagination away.'[16]

The new state introduced film censorship as early as 1923. When it came under increasing pressure to introduce further censorship it set up a Committee on Evil Literature in 1926 to consider if it was necessary to ban certain publications. It urged the banning of several British newspapers[17] and recommended the establishment of a censorship board. Contrary to popular belief, *Ulysses* was never banned in Ireland although it was banned in Britain from its publication until 1936.

Sex was a major preoccupation of the Free State at this time. Historian Diarmaid Ferriter notes: 'It was frequently maintained that sexual morality was in decline and that perceived moral failings needed to be tackled by a joint alliance of state, Catholic church and voluntary lay Catholic groups in an effort to recover a historic (or mythical) Irish chasteness.'[18]

It was not only writers and artists who found it difficult to stay at home. Erskine Childers, a future president of Ireland, could not live in a country whose governing party had executed his father. Having completed his studies at Cambridge, he moved to Paris in 1927 where he worked for a travel agency whose limousine taxis carried, among others, James Joyce.[19] (The writer was very generous with his tips as a result of which, according to Thomas MacGreevy, 'like the attendants at the opera, pretty well every taxi-driver in Paris knew Joyce and took care of him').[20]

By comparison with Dublin, London and New York, Paris after the war was liberal rather than conservative, colourful rather than grey, innovative rather than stagnant. True, there were economic difficulties and industrial unrest in France too, and as Joyce was arriving in July 1920 its legislature outlawed abortion and banned the sale of contraceptives – but this was seen partly as a response to the need for an increase in the birth rate following the devastation of the war in which almost one and a half million Frenchmen had died and four times that number had been wounded.

By 1920 the city's artistic centre had changed from Montmartre to Montparnasse where it was cheaper to rent a studio; the Left Bank *quartier* became the new focus for the city's painters and writers, its bistros and cafés the centre of their intellectual lives. This was where most of the new expatriates settled. As the war had left the French currency at a very low exchange rate, they could afford to stay in hotels and spend much of their time on the café terraces. The American journalist Janet Flanner's hotel room cost her $1 a day (about $10 in today's money).

They arrived in a society that admired American popular culture and was open to ideas and trends coming across the Atlantic. Parisians organised Fourth of July parades as well as their own *quatorze juillet*. The French were quick to adapt outdoor advertising to their street kiosks and embraced wholeheartedly America's latest export, jazz.

The city had changed enormously since the war. Duelling

was no longer acceptable. Taxis had replaced fiacres. *Flaneurs* still walked the boulevards but they had to be more careful when crossing the street. Skirts rose and social barriers fell so that few cared about one's sexual inclination. The Americans brought with them the cocktail and there were discussions in French academic circles as to whether it should be spelt *coquetèle*.[21] (The cocktail hour encroached on the *cinq a sept*, a more generous period set aside for the Frenchman's liaison with his lover before going home to his wife for dinner).

By 1923, Paris had become the new cultural centre of the United States, with Montparnasse replacing Greenwich Village.[22] The heart of expatriate social activity in that *quartier* was the junction where Boulevard du Montparnasse meets Boulevard Raspail, where the cafés of the Rotonde and the Dome face each other. Each had its own clientele. The Dome attracted British, Americans, Irish and Scandinavians; the Rotonde Italians, Spanish and Russians. Poles drank at the Closerie des Lilas, Germans at the Coupole. The Irish-American writer Robert McAlmon recalled that, as early as the summer of 1921, before the throngs arrived in the following years, 'crossing and recrossing between the Dome and the Rotonde of an evening... anybody from the writing or art world of any country was apt to appear and quite as apt to be dead drunk or mildly intoxicated.'[23]

Joyce, however, was a family man who shunned the bistros and bars of the Left Bank (although he did fall by the wayside on occasions, much to his wife's annoyance). Several expatriates crossed his path and became intimate friends. Hemingway was one of the early arrivals, having been encouraged by Sherwood Anderson who gave him a letter of introduction to Joyce. He became a frequent visitor to the Joyce home and was much admired by the Irish writer. Hemingway rowed with almost everyone, notably with F Scott Fitzgerald (who also got to know Joyce) and McAlmon, who undertook secretarial work for Joyce and provided him with a regular income. Joyce never fell out publicly with any of them (although he later became estranged from women like Sylvia Beach and Harriet Weaver who had helped him so much financially and in kind) and he frequently took advantage of them to promote his writing.

But it was those coming from Ireland who had a special place in Joyce's heart. If they came from Dublin, he was eager to glean from them the latest happenings in the city he was writing about and to recall the name of a certain shop or the precise location of a landmark. He became friendly with Beckett – who made Paris his permanent home - through the Kerry poet Thomas MacGreevy to whom Joyce and his family became particularly attached. Other visitors, such as Padraic Colum, he had known from his younger days at the Royal University in Dublin. He had met James Stephens during his last and final visit to Dublin in 1912 when they were both having rows with a Dublin publisher; in Paris he asked Stephens would he finish writing *Finnegans Wake* if he was unable to complete it. Joyce developed a lasting friendship with the writer and artist Arthur Power who was among the first of the Irish he met in Paris; and he got to know the irascible painter Patrick Tuohy after he had done a portrait of his father. Most strangely of all, Joyce developed an obsession with the career of the Irish tenor John Sullivan and persuaded his friends to campaign publicly on the singer's behalf.

Joyce's exceptional linguistic ability as well as his deep interest in European literature meant that, unlike many of his American and British counterparts, he became friendly with many French writers. While he is reputed to have talked to the reclusive Proust for only seconds, he developed long-lasting friendships with Paul Valéry, Léon-Paul Fargue, Philippe Soupault and Valery Larbaud.

After Pound, the person who had the biggest influence on

Joyce staying in Paris was Beach. Shakespeare and
Company became more than the publisher of *Ulysses*. It
was, in effect, the *poste restante* for Joyce, for the family
moved home 19 times during their 20 years in the city.
For many years it was the bookshop rather than the man
himself that became the centre of the Joyce circle. It was
the information and communications base for friends and
acquaintances of Joyce, among them writers from
Ireland, Britain, the United States and France itself.[24]

It was to Shakespeare and Company that Hemingway
went when he wanted to meet Joyce. McAlmon used the
shop as a post office and as a storehouse for unsold books
left over from his publishing business. Fitzgerald was too
shy to approach Joyce, so he persuaded Beach to
introduce him. Padraic Colum always made the bookshop
his first port of call when he came to the city. And it was
at Shakespeare and Company that Beach introduced
Joyce to Larbaud who would be highly influential in
promoting his work. Larbaud praised Beach as one who
'assembles the elite among the young English, Irish and
Americans who are temporarily in Paris.'[25] Without her
there might never had been a Joyce circle.

Across the road from Shakespeare and Company – when
the shop moved to rue de l'Odéon - was a French
bookshop, La Maison des Amis des Livres, run by
Adrienne Monnier. The shops complemented each other.
Far from being business rivals, the two women became
lovers and they played vital roles in literary Paris and in
the life of Joyce in particular. They introduced French
and English writers to one another. As one writer put it:
'... the French and Anglo-American circles that
frequented the rue de l'Odéon were sometimes
concentric.'[26]

This cross-fertilisation of literary language and culture in
one Parisian street benefited the French as well as the
Anglo-Irish-Americans. Simone de Beauvoir, then a

young student at the Sorbonne, devoured books at Monnier's shop. 'After a monumental *Ulysses* appeared in French,' she recalled, 'a door opened for us to a new world of foreign writers.' It was at Monnier's that she saw those writers, among them Joyce, 'the most remote and inaccessible of them all.'[27]

Although living in Paris, the expatriate writer's mind was at home; Stein wrote about America, Hemingway about Americans and the Midwest, Joyce about Dublin.

'There are exiles – expatriates as they prefer to call themselves – in Paris who know more about the United States, about Ireland, about England, than anybody who lives in those countries,' wrote Sisley Huddleston.[28] Paris, he said, will 'take the provincialism from the majority of writers.'

Another circle revolved around the American writer Stein. She kept a literary salon at the home she shared with Alice B Toklas at 27 rue de Fleurus. She had come to Paris in 1903 and went on to live at the same address (except for wartime interludes) for 35 years. About all that Stein and Joyce had in common was that both experimented with language, albeit in different ways.

Stein often visited Shakespeare and Company to borrow books, although she and Joyce never met there. Neither acknowledged the other's existence. Hemingway, who got on well with both, felt it unwise to mention one to the other.

Beach frequently went to the Saturday evening salons run by Stein, and she introduced many American writers to the often-difficult and overpowering hostess. Joyce never attended Stein's salons. She, on the other hand, frequently went to the Friday salons run by a fellow American writer and lesbian Natalie Barney. Joyce, too, was known to have visited Barney's salon at rue Jacob, though probably not more than once.[29] Unlike Stein, who had a long-term relationship (she called it a marriage) with Toklas, Barney was renowned for her promiscuity. She was extrovertly lesbian and feminist (her home featured a *Temple a l'Amitié* in praise of women) and among her lovers were Dolly Wilde and the American painter Romaine Brooks. She was a writer, intellectual and linguist and her salon was one of the liveliest in Paris, attracting an eclectic mix of writers and raconteurs, French and English-speaking. Some of the best-known French figures of the period could be seen there, among them Sidonie-Gabrielle Colette, Paul Valery, André Gide, Jean Cocteau and Louis Aragon. Frequent English-speaking visitors included Stein, Djuna Barnes, Pound and Ford Madox Ford. Occasionally one might see Eliot or the American composer George Antheil or the heiresses Nancy Cunard and Peggy Guggenheim.

The literary circles of Barney, Stein, Pound and Joyce were far from being mutually exclusive. They overlapped and, like the effect of several stones cast into a pond, they opened into one another, merging and interrelating, the better to spread Eugene Jolas's 'Revolution of the Word.'

---

[1] Prof. Declan Kiberd in a UCD lecture on *Ireland – Dependence and Independence* broadcast on RTE 15 February, 1984.

[2] Clarke: *Twice Round the Black Church* 27.

[3] Maye: *Arthur Griffith* 4.

[4] Mary Colum: *Life and the Dream* 80.

[5] Prof. Declan Kiberd in conversation.

[6] Berlioz also put music to poems by Thomas Moore.

[7] Cowley: *A Second Flowering* 53.

[8] Calvin Tomkins: *Living Well is the Best Revenge.*

[9] *Paris Tribune,* 26 October 1928.

[10] Alex Small, *Paris Tribune,* 20 September 1929.

[11] Samuel Putnam: *Paris was our Mistress* 28.

[12] Eliot to Sydney Schiff, 22 August, 1920. (Valerie Eliot, ed., *The Letters of T. S. Eliot Vol. 1*, 402).

[13] The writer Liam O'Flaherty got little support when, in January 1922, he took over the Rotunda concert hall in Dublin along with 200 unemployed people on behalf of the communist party. Many resented the red flag flying over the building. In 1928 there were just 90 communists in Ireland (Maurice Curtis: *A Challenge to Democracy:* The History Press, Dublin, 2010).

[14] Kiberd: *Inventing Ireland.*

[15] Idem. 265.

[16] Idem. 263.

[17] Mainly because they carried advertisements advocating contraception. Censorship in Ireland was overwhelmingly concerned with 'race suicide' (contraception) and 'indecency.'

[18] Diarmaid Ferriter: *Occasions of Sin* 100.

[19] John Young: *Erskine H Childers, President of Ireland* 63.

[20] MacGreevy memoir in *Thomas MacGreevy and Joyce* by Hugh J. Dawson, James Joyce Quarterly, spring 1988. Also the *Thomas MacGreevy Archive* online.

[21] Sisley Huddleston: *Paris Salons, Cafés, Studios* 20.

[22] Bernard J. Poli: *Ford Madox Ford and the Transatlantic Review* 18.

[23] McAlmon: *Being Geniuses Together* 24.

[24] Noel Riley Fitch: *Sylvia Beach and the Lost Generation* 16.

[25] Article in *Revue de France.*

[26] William Wiser : *The Crazy Years* 46.

[27] In a Preface to *James Joyce in Paris* by Giséle Freund and V. B. Carleton.

[28] Huddleston: *Paris Salons, Cafés, Studios.*

[29] Joyce went to Barney's salon (accompanied by Paul Valéry) to try to promote the staging of his play *Exiles*. But he had an altercation with Natalie in a discussion about French literature.

Chapter Two
Meeting Mr Joyce

Like many of the expatriates, Arthur Power felt he had
to get away from the stifling social and political
atmosphere in his own country. Having been invalided
out of the British Army with exposure to gas in the
trenches of Flanders, he returned to Dublin in 1916 only
to be shot at by republican rebels. Unlike many of his
compatriots who had returned from the war, Power was a
man of independent means and could well afford to
travel. He chose Paris because of his deep interest in art
and the opportunity it provided him to lead a bohemian
existence.

Involving himself in the city's literary scene was not on
his agenda and meeting James Joyce was the last thing on
his mind. Yet he was to become a close friend and
confidant of Joyce and his family and friends with whom
he frequently attended Irish parlour-style singsongs.

The two men met by accident in a dance hall in
Montparnasse.[1] It was an evening in early April 1921.
Power had arranged to meet a young French woman but
she failed to turn up. Wandering through the dance hall in
search of a substitute, he saw a familiar face – a woman
seated at a table with a group deep in conversation. He
tried to avoid her, for he just wanted to enjoy himself.
But eventually she called him over and introduced him to
the others. Among them was a slightly built man with a
small pointed beard who wore thick-lensed glasses.

Power was taken aback. He had never met Joyce and he

had heard the writer was living in Switzerland. Now here he was shaking his hand in a noisy dance hall in Montparnasse.

It was the start of a friendship that would remain close for the next decade. Even after Joyce's death in 1941, Power kept in touch with his wife, Nora.

Appropriately for a man who was passionate about French culture, he had been born midway between the two countries – in the island of Guernsey – and brought up near New Ross in the southeast of Ireland in a mansion that resembled a chateau. His grandmother, who had been reared in France, had filled the house – 'Bellevue' – with French tapestries and furniture.[2]

Arthur's was a privileged upbringing with gracious dinner parties and croquet on the lawn that swept down to the River Suir. In common with other children of the Irish rural gentry he was sent to a boarding school in England. There he got his first taste of things French. On the day he made his First Communion, his young French teacher planted a kiss on his lips to thank him for helping out in the organ loft. It was a moment he would always remember.

It was inevitable that, like his father, Power should join the army. He carried the rank of lieutenant when the Great War broke out and he was sent to the trenches of Flanders. After eight months at the front he was badly gassed and invalided out, a nervous and physical wreck.

Following hospitalisation in England, he returned home in 1916 only to experience some of the drama of the Easter Rising. Having come to Dublin for a medical check-up, he decided to stay over the Easter weekend and his car was shot at as he left the city for the races at Fairyhouse on Easter Monday. He also witnessed the battle of Mount Street Bridge between the rebels under the command of Eamon de Valera and British Army reinforcements. Power, who deplored all violence, had no sympathy for the republican cause, even after the execution of its leaders.

Like many of his former comrades, Power found himself in a different kind of 'no man's land' – having no time for an increasingly nationalist Ireland and blaming his parents' generation for the war which had traumatised him. But he differed from many others in that he had the financial independence to do something about his predicament.

He did not need persuading to leave Ireland, wanting to escape from what he later described as 'the clogging intellectual atmosphere' of his own country.

While in Dublin he had met the painter Paul Henry who had moved there from Achill. Henry had lived in Paris and the two men often discussed French art, thus influencing Power's move to France.

In his search for artists in Paris, he went first to Montmartre, unaware that the rising cost of renting studios was forcing the local painters to relocate to cheaper lodgings around Montparnasse. He too moved to the Left Bank, booking into a hotel at Place de la Sorbonne.

His first encounter with an artist was with the young Russian sculptor Ossip Zadkine[3] with whom he got talking in a café. Shortly afterwards, the Russian set off for a period of sculpting in Savoy, arranging for Power to rent his studio.

Power then made contact with the American sculptor Jo Davidson[4] whom he had met while recuperating in London. A man of considerable charm and influence, Davidson got Power a job writing a column for the *New*

York Herald on the artistic life of Paris. The column was called *Around the Studios* and it brought Power into direct contact with many of the city's painters and sculptors. He took to the task with enthusiasm, even taking classes at the Académie Colarossi in the rue de la Grande Chaumière where many artists had their studios.[5] Power took a studio there himself – next to that of Amedeo Modigliani.[6]

Unlike many of the artists he was writing about, Power lived alone. He was now 30 years of age. He became friendly, however, with the young woman who called to his studio once a week to look after his laundry. Her name was Annette and she told him she went dancing every Saturday. Power was attracted to her and they agreed to meet at the Bal Bullier, a popular dancehall on the boulevard St-Michel near avenue de l'Observatoire.

That weekend the Bal Bullier was, as usual, teeming with young men and women who worked in the shops and cafés of Montparnasse. They were attracted as much by the cheap drink as the opportunity to dance and socialise. But there was another type of person who liked to come here. They were the more serious and mature ones who were tiring of the cafés where increasing numbers of expatriates seemed to be taking over the terraces.

Joyce was in one such group that evening. At first, Power felt uncomfortable, for he had read *Dubliners* and *A Portrait of the Artist as a Young Man*, but they had left little impression on him.

Now another book of Joyce's was about to make its appearance, and this was the cause of the evening's celebration. The book was *Ulysses* and one of those at the table had agreed to publish it. Sylvia Beach was a diminutive young American and proprietor of Shakespeare and Company, a bookshop and lending library on rue Dupuytren near Odéon. Just that day she had finalised arrangements with a printer in Dijon, Maurice Darantière, for a limited edition of 1,000 copies of *Ulysses*. Under the agreement, Joyce would receive an exceptionally large royalty of 66 per cent of the net profit.

Joyce loved to celebrate and would do so at the drop of a hat. On this occasion, he had particularly good reason: he had devoted more than seven years to writing his novel and eventually he had found someone who would publish it. He was still working on the book and not without difficulties. The previous day, the husband of the woman who was typing the last pages of *Circe* read some of the manuscript and, believing it to be indecent, burned it. Joyce had to ask John Quinn – the Irish-American lawyer to whom he had sent a copy of the chapter – to return it.

Sitting next to this writer whose works he did not think much of, Power found himself being pumped for information about Dublin and the people he knew there. Power had come to Paris to forget about Ireland but it seemed his new acquaintance was not going to let him. He soon warmed to him, however. He found him sympathetic rather than friendly and enjoyed his old-fashioned politeness. But he was surprised to be asked if he was a 'man of letters.'

Embarrassed by the question, Power admitted to at least being interested. He was ill prepared, however, for the direct questioning that followed.

'What do you want to write?' asked Joyce.

Recalling his own interest in literature, Power replied: 'Something on the model of the French satirists.'

'You'll never do it. You are an Irishman and you must write in your own tradition. Borrowed styles are no good. You must write what is in your blood and not what is in your brain.'

Power insisted that he wanted to be international, like all the great writers.

'They were national first,' responded Joyce, 'and it was the intensity of their own nationalism which made them international in the end, as in the case of Turgenev [Ivan Turgenev]. You remember his *Sportsman's Notebook*? - How local it was - and yet out of that germ he became a great international writer. For myself, I always write about Dublin, because if I can get to the heart of Dublin I can get to the heart of all the cities of the world.'

At that moment, one of the bands struck up. It was fashionable in the Bal Bullier for two small orchestras - one string and one brass - to play at opposite ends of the dance floor. Usually, neither was of a particularly high standard and their sound could verge on the cacophonous - but at least they played alternately.

Attracted to a pretty young French woman nearby, Power asked her to dance. As they waltzed out into the centre of the floor, Power felt distracted by the brief conversation he had just had. Sensing his inattention, his dancing partner wandered off when the music stopped. Power, though, was happy to rejoin Joyce's table and to resume his conversation.

'How do you feel about being Irish?' he asked Joyce.

'I regret it,' said Joyce, 'for the temperament it has given me.'

At that point Beach interrupted to propose a toast to the success of *Ulysses*.

As they were leaving, Joyce suggested, in the time-honoured Irish way, that Power join them for a last drink at the Closerie des Lilas across the road.

Power's unexpected encounter with the author of *Ulysses*

was the start of a long friendship. The two men would often meet, in restaurants or in Joyce's apartment, to argue over literature and talk about Dublin.

At the time of their meeting at the Bal Bullier, Power's perception of Joyce was limited to hearsay and to his own assumptions about the writer. He was to be proven very wrong. He had heard accounts from Trieste of Joyce being found lying in the gutter the morning after a drinking session. But the man he had met struck him as quite bourgeois – a feature that disappointed Power who felt that an artist should be more bohemian.

The assumption that there was any bohemian element in Joyce's make-up threatened Power's friendship with Joyce when it had barely begun.

Shortly after their first encounter, he decided to call on the Joyces at their apartment at 5 boulevard Raspail. It was a large flat, dark and forbidding, and it was costing Joyce more than he could afford. But it was furnished and included a piano, which pleased him. A large red lampshade dominated the living room. Joyce called it 'my damn brothel.'

Power dropped in on his way to a party being thrown by some artist friends in the studio of a Russian painter. He thought he would ask Joyce if he would like to come along. He thought Joyce's life was too settled and restricted and that he would benefit from a party where he might, as he put it, 'have a drink and talk with the girls.'

Tactlessly, Power arrived at the Joyce apartment his pockets bulging with bottles. Unsurprisingly, he was not well received by the family. Joyce was going through a difficult time with his eyes and had been forbidden to drink. Power was perceived as the proverbial drunken Irishman luring Joyce away from home for a wild night on the town.

Georgio Joyce, now a tall youth of 16, stood over Power's chair, legs apart, as much as to say: 'When are you going to leave?'

Joyce having declined his invitation, Power was glad to escape from what had become a charged atmosphere. Joyce accompanied him to the door of the apartment where, in a plaintive but amused voice, he told his visitor: 'You know I am an intelligent man, but I have to put up with this sort of thing - however, we will meet again soon.'[7]

Shortly afterwards, the two met in the street and Joyce invited Power back to his flat. Over a meal, Power was amazed at the frequency with which Joyce talked about Dublin. While Power had left his native land to become more cosmopolitan, Joyce seemed to have left it to sharpen his Irish consciousness.

Power got on well with all the family, especially Nora who, he felt, now realised that he had no intention of leading her husband astray and that in fact he disliked drinking to excess. He also met Giorgio's 14-year-old sister Lucia who seemed hypersensitive, possibly showing early signs of what would later be diagnosed as schizophrenia.

Power reciprocated by inviting Joyce and Nora to his studio at rue de la Grande Chaumière. He was having a party to which he had also invited Jo Davidson and his wife Yvonne. They brought along an American journalist who was staying with them.

Lincoln Steffens, a Californian, was probably the first campaigning journalist, having exposed corruption in public authorities in the States. He had come to Paris at the time of the Armistice in November 1918. He later covered post-war peace and economic conferences in Europe alongside Hemingway and the two became good friends. Following a visit to Bolshevik Russia, he had become radicalised, declaring: 'I have been over into the future and it works.'

As soon as Steffens arrived, Power sensed he had an agenda, as if he were out to expose artistic Paris as some kind of sham. Since Davidson knew Joyce (probably through Beach who was very fond of the American artist), Power left him to introduce Joyce to the others while he went about bringing food and drink from the kitchen. Joyce made little effort to socialise, however, and seemed to Power to be either shy or simply bored by his fellow-guests. Nora, he noticed, was far chattier.

There was a knock on the door. It was Annette, his young blanchisseuse, calling to explain why she had failed to turn up at the dancehall. As she was in her working clothes, Power ushered her into the kitchen. There was a pause in the conversation outside, his guests assuming there was a relationship between their host and the young woman. An embarrassed Power returned to offer cakes to those present. When he got back to the kitchen the young woman had disappeared.

Power was talking to Joyce when Steffens came over. The journalist looked determined to establish if this was indeed the same James Joyce whom literary Paris was talking about. Power politely left the men to their conversation but observed that Joyce was refusing to answer questions. Afterwards, Power talked to the journalist, who was clearly disappointed. 'There is nothing left in him,' Steffens told him, quoting Joyce. 'It has all gone into his book.'

After that Power saw Joyce and his family virtually every day, becoming Joyce's closest friend at the time. Joyce had many acquaintances, especially those who could be useful to him and his writing. He enjoyed the company of people who could talk to him about Dublin and if they could be useful to him in other ways, such as promoting his work or funding it, so much the better.

For the moment Power satisfied the first of these. Although nine years younger than Joyce, he was an affable young man with literary interests that appealed to Joyce; and the fact that he got on well with Nora and the children was important.

Power became a regular visitor to the Joyces wherever they lived, for they never seemed to stay long in the one place.[8] In June 1921 they moved to their fifth home in the eleven months since they had arrived in Paris – an apartment at 71 rue du Cardinal Lemoine[9] borrowed from the French writer Valery Larbaud. By the end of that year, Joyce had moved again, to Hotel Lenox at rue de l'Université (where he was living when *Ulysses* was published in February 1922). Towards the end of that year, the family moved to a bright apartment at 26 avenue Charles Floquet near the Eiffel Tower.

By then the idea for a new book was forming in Joyce's mind. He kept its title, *Finnegans Wake*, a secret, telling only Nora. To everyone else he called it his Work in Progress. Despite difficulties with his eyes, Joyce worked away on its early drafts. He spent much of his time with blinds drawn and joked that he was waiting for Ireland's Eye to do its duty.

Joyce had good reason to fear losing his sight. He suffered from iritis and glaucoma and between 1918 and 1932 he had over a dozen operations for these and to remove cataracts. Between operations he underwent painful treatment, which was alleviated by morphine and cocaine. Sometimes leeches were applied to his eyes, which looked red much of the time. As his sight deteriorated his hearing improved and he was able to recognise friends by their voices.

Power took care not to arrive before late afternoon when he called on Joyce, to be sure that he had finished his work for the day. Then, the writer would leave his study and come into the living room, dressed in a short white working jacket rather like a dentist's, collapsing into an armchair. Often Nora would scold her husband: 'For God's sake, Jim, take that coat off you!'[10]

Sometimes Power would accompany Joyce in a taxi to his doctor on rue de la Paix. Dr Louis Borsch's consulting rooms were small and drab and as often as not he would, after examination, ask Joyce to come back in a couple of days. The two would then catch a taxi to the Café Francis, Joyce's latest haunt overlooking the Seine by the Pont de l'Alma.

Drinking his favourite tipple at the time, a Cinzano with water, Joyce would discuss literature, Dublin and what Power called the 'disadvantages of possessing a Celtic temperament.' Then the two would return to the flat and an excellent dinner cooked by Nora.

Joyce enjoyed a very structured life. He liked to write during the day and if he was dining out in the evening he limited himself to two or three restaurants, depending which was in favour at the time: the Trianons near Montparnasse station, the Café Francis by the Seine or Fouquets on the Champs-Elysées. He never went to any of the popular cafés of Montparnasse such as the Rotonde or the Dome (where Power occasionally drank; both were just a few paces from his apartment). Power, who wanted to live a more unconventional existence, found this frustrating. But if he took Joyce somewhere outside his routine, he noticed the writer became ill tempered. Once he wanted to go to the Deux Magots, which some American journalists, including Hemingway and Djuna Barnes, frequented. But Joyce refused to go there and they settled instead on a small café just a three-minute walk from the places where his friends met.

Power saw a different side to the man when at home, especially at one of his own parties when he was relaxed and happy. His guests were usually the same and included Beach and Adrienne Monnier, the composer George Antheil who lived above Shakespeare and Company, the Irish-American writer Robert McAlmon and the American artist Myron Nutting and his wife Helen. Around midnight he would sit down at his piano and run his fingers over the keys, breaking into an Irish ballad or two such as *The Brown and the Yellow Ale*, his favourite, about a man who lends his wife to a stranger.

It was clear to anyone who met them together that Joyce and Nora were very close. Power felt there was a perfect understanding between them. While there were those who were shocked to hear Nora tease her husband in public, Irish friends saw it as a measure of their closeness. Joyce enjoyed being teased - and didn't even seem to mind being chastised - by his wife.

Yet Nora had no interest in her husband's work. When in Power's presence Joyce presented her with the 1000th copy of *Ulysses*, which he had inscribed, she weighed it in her hand and looked at Power. 'How much will you give me for this?' she asked. Power felt that, far from displaying ignorance, Nora was simply cutting her man down to size.[11]

Sometimes Power would accompany the family on Sunday drives (in a hired car with driver). If a storm broke out, Joyce would order the driver to turn around and take them home. On one occasion, Power asked why was he so afraid of thunder while his children did not seem to mind. 'Ah,' replied Joyce, 'they have no religion.'[12]

Looking back on his friendship, Power found Joyce at his best during this time. He gave the impression of being calm and settled, although his confidence was inclined to fluctuate with his temperament. Despite his undoubted achievement with *Ulysses*, he sometimes questioned the ultimate value of his talent. But Power felt that that was one of the most attractive and human of Joyce's qualities. If he was down one day, a few days later there would be a gleam in his eye and his confidence would have returned.

It bothered Power that he could not give the same total admiration to Joyce's work as he could give to the man himself. Nevertheless their friendship continued. When Power asked him why he treated him so kindly, Joyce replied: 'I'm always friends with a person for a purpose.'

The two often disagreed over other writers. When Power praised Synge for the way he captured the language of the west of Ireland, Joyce said such 'fabricated' language was as unreal as his characters.[13]

On the other hand, when Power said Ibsen was full of dreary ideas, Joyce told him the Norwegian had plumbed new psychological depths, which influenced a whole generation of writers.

Proust was the most important French author of the day, according to Joyce, chastising Power for criticising Proust's long sentences. 'You should have given him more patience, for he is the best of the modern French writers.'

Power was of the opinion that, outside of literature, Joyce professed an extraordinary ignorance and was amazed that the writer could be so indifferent to modern art, regarding it as inferior to literature. Joyce's passion for Italian opera did not extend to modern music; he attended a performance of Stravinsky's *Le Sacre du Printemps* and did not care for it. And whereas Nora enjoyed Richard Wagner, he thoroughly disliked the composer: 'Wagner stinks of sex,' he once said.[14]

But Ireland was their main topic of conversation. Joyce's imagination was centred in Dublin, yet he had no inclination to return there. He feared that if he did someone would shoot him. Power felt that Joyce would most likely not be recognised in his home city. Yet Joyce's fear was real. He had been told that a man called into a bookshop in Nassau Street and asked for a copy of *Ulysses*. When told they had none, the man remarked that the author had better not set foot in this country again. Although Power argued that it was probably only some political or religious eccentric, Joyce replied it was just such an eccentric who would do these things.

Joyce told him that he wrote about Dublin because it was the focal point of Ireland at the time and a writer's purpose was to describe the life of his day.

Joyce's affection for the city, however, was confined to his writings. Power felt that Joyce disliked the provincial nature of the city where everything one said was echoed back, distorted. He told Power he was in Paris to escape from the soul-destroying political atmosphere in Ireland.

When *Work in Progress* began to appear in *transition* and in other publications, Power took an immediate dislike to it – and said as much to its author. Joyce did not seem to hold this judgment against him, although their relationship cooled considerably during the early 1930s. Power put this down to the passing of time. He had been away for several years, having returned to Waterford to look after the family estate, which he had inherited.

When he got back to Paris, he contacted Joyce who had moved into a flat at rue Galilée, near the Étoile. Joyce invited him to Fouquets, the most expensive restaurant on the Champs-Elysées and his then favourite. Power felt that Joyce had been taken over by Eugene and Maria Jolas, publishers of *transition*, and that the atmosphere that surrounded him was artificial.

It was to be their last meeting.

Power met Nora again in Paris several years after Joyce's death. They dined at the Café Francis but it only brought back memories for her. Power noticed how time had changed her: a heavier woman now, stiff from arthritis, she had at last become a believer in her husband's genius.

---

[1]Power: *Conversations with James Joyce* 36.

[2] Power: *From an Old Waterford House* 13.

[3] Ossip Zadkine (1890-1967) had been a stretcher bearer in north-east France during the war. His images of the wounded, especially the crippled, became a strong symbol of the period.

[4] Jo Davidson (1883-1952). Renowned for his warm personality, he later painted Joyce's portrait and arranged for *Exiles* to be staged in New York.

[5] Among others who studied at the academy were Mary Swanzy and Eileen Gray.

[6] Amedeo Modigliani (1884-1920) was an Italian Jew renowned for his images of women with long necks. When he died his mistress killed herself and her unborn child.

[7] Power: *Conversations with James Joyce* 38.

[8] Joyce took after his father in moving home often, but as Power observed, that was not unusual in Paris. 'We all did,' he said, referring to the expatriate community in general. 'People were coming and going, leaving and returning after a few months and in the meantime flats were re-let or sub-let.'

[9]A few months later, Ernest Hemingway moved into Number 74, a hundred metres up the street on the other side.

[10] Power: *Conversations with James Joyce* 39.

[11] Power in interviews with Ellmann in 1953 and with Maddox in 1984.

[12] Joyce was highly superstitious. He wrote Harriet Weaver that 1921 might cause him problems since its digits added up to 13.

[13] Joyce had met Synge in Paris during his visit in 1903. Synge had brought the transcript of *Riders to the Sea* to Joyce's hotel room. Joyce found him very difficult. 'In the end I had to give up seeing him' he told Power (*Conversations with James Joyce* 42).

[14] Ellmann: 382 and 460. Maddox: *Nora* 197

A Little Circle Of Kindred Minds

Chapter Three
The Importance Of Being Irish

Once Joyce knew *Ulysses* was going to be published an enormous weight seemed to lift from him. When his friend Constantine Curran went to Paris to see him in the autumn of 1921, he was pleasantly surprised to see the 'elegant figure, which alighted from a taxi.'[1] Old friends since their university days in Dublin, the two had kept in touch by letter and Curran was well aware of the difficulties Joyce was having with his eyes and the strain he had been under in Trieste.

Curran was delighted to see how well Joyce carried himself and he was impressed by the debonair way he used his cane. It seemed to distract attention from his eyes, which were covered by thick lenses.

As they talked over a plate of oysters, Curran observed Joyce's physical changes - the small moustache and beard - and his mannerisms. The once arrogant student was now a 39-year-old man and 'there was no trace left in his speech of his former abrupt silences, no needless reticence, but a quiet gravity and some courteous reserve.' It was also clear to Curran that the man who used to borrow frequently from him in Dublin was now free from financial worries thanks to Harriet Weaver's generous support.

Curran was eager to discuss literature but he soon learned that Joyce was more interested in gossip about Dublin. Curran was quizzed about Dubliners they knew and about the city's streets and the precise location of its shops, houses and their occupants. Joyce listened carefully to the answers as though storing them away for future use.

During subsequent visits to Paris, Curran and his wife met the Joyces as they moved from one apartment to another. They found him 'simple and unaffected.' He could become high-spirited but never bawdy. And even when in the 1930s he was concerned about Lucia's health or worried about the likelihood of war he never lost his sense of humour.

Curran recalled dining out with the Joyces and Eugene Jolas one evening at Fouquet's, then a fashionable restaurant frequented by famous actors. On the way Joyce, perhaps conveniently, said he had to go back for a book, sending the women on. A few Pernods later the men were ushered into the restaurant by the maitre d' and his staff who fussed over their hats and canes and guided them to Joyce's usual table. Nora was busy pointing out celebrities to Curran's wife, among them Marlene Dietrich. The pleasant conversation that followed suggested the Pernods were forgiven.

Curran, like all Joyce's friends, was 'useful' to him. Whenever he was in Dublin Joyce persuaded him to send over such items as theatre programmes, pantomime librettos, music-hall songs and newspaper cuttings of various kinds – much of which eventually appeared in various guises in *Finnegans Wake*.

Joyce asked him to keep an eye on his father, John Stanislaus Joyce, especially in his later years when his condition was deteriorating. Frank O'Connor, who did not visit Joyce until 1929, was given a similar request. Like Curran, O'Connor was keen to talk to Joyce about the literary life, since he was a young librarian who had just started writing. But he was exasperated when all he got was questions about Dublin's streets and shops.[2] When he asked Joyce about a picture in the hallway Joyce told him it was Cork. O'Connor remarked that he knew very well what his

native city looked like but he was curious about the frame.
To which Joyce replied it was cork.

Austin Clarke got similar treatment when, in the winter of
1923, he used to meet Joyce promptly at 6pm outside the
church of St Sulpice. The two would adjourn to a quiet café
where, after a long silence, Joyce would ask: 'Is Mulvaney's
shop still there at the corner?' – the first of many
questions.

When Kenneth Reddin arrived at Joyce's apartment in
Square Robiac he found it full of Irish newspapers, including
provincial ones. He was impressed that Joyce was able to
recall the smart remarks by witnesses at Kilmainham
District Court over which Reddin presided.

At dinner at the Trianons Joyce challenged him and the
artist Patrick Tuohy to name the shops from Amiens
Street station (now Connolly station) to Nelson's Pillar,
first on one side then back on the other. 'Mostly he was
three or four shops in front of us,' said Reddin. 'When
Tuohy and I left a gap, he filled it. When he named a new
proprietor, he named, and remembered the passing of, the
old.'[3]

Old friends and acquaintances that spent any time with
Joyce soon got to know the importance he placed on his
family and on special occasions such as his birthday. He
was determined that *Ulysses* would be published on his
fortieth birthday – 2 February, 1922 - and spent the weeks
beforehand busily correcting proofs (which amounted to
rewriting entire sections) and returning them to the
printers at Dijon.

His work was interrupted, one day towards the end of
January, by another visitor from Ireland. He was Desmond
FitzGerald, Minister of Information in the government of
the new Irish Free State[4] and he told Joyce that he was
about to propose that the government nominate the writer

for the Nobel Prize. Joyce was flattered by the visit - but he was level-headed in his reaction which he wisely kept to himself but which he revealed to his brother Stanislaus and to McAlmon some weeks later: that such a move would not gain him the prize and would probably lose FitzGerald his portfolio.[5]

FitzGerald asked Joyce if he intended to return to Ireland. Not for the present, replied Joyce.

It was an understatement by the man who was anxiously awaiting the birth of his new novel. Even if Joyce had the time to go to Ireland, he had little inclination to do so. He had not been home since 1912. Then, he had lost his fight to have *Dubliners* published by Maunsel & Company who destroyed the sheets. Furious, on the train home he wrote a broadside against his would-be publishers, which was also an invective against his own country.

Ten years on, Joyce felt that he could be the one to have quicklime thrown at him if he returned. He had little time for Irish politics. He supported the principles of Sinn Féin but he detested violence and satirised its extremist wing in *Ulysses* through the character of the Citizen. Now that the country had finally set up its own government he was pleased - at least momentarily - that the new beginning for Ireland coincided with the publication of *Ulysses*, which gave his country a new conscience.[6]

There is no record of FitzGerald having brought up the matter of the Nobel nomination with his government colleagues on his return. But then, he held his ministerial post outside the cabinet.[7] Equally, there is no evidence to suggest Joyce was in any way disappointed that the issue was not pursued.

Their conversation in Paris that January can only be guessed at but is likely to have been an animated and amiable one. Not only was Joyce keen to talk to someone from Ireland but the blue-eyed and curly-haired man facing him was of considerable intellectual stature. Desmond FitzGerald had been educated in France and had a deep interest in literature and philosophy.[8] He had been among the Imagist group of poets and it was he (along with Florence Farr) who had introduced Pound to Imagism while Pound was in London in 1909.[9] As the two men talked in Paris there can be little doubt that Pound would have featured prominently in their conversation.

The literary connection would have been very important to Joyce, for he loved coincidences and enjoyed pointing them out to friends, especially if they related to something he had written.

Around the same time, he delighted in telling those around him that he had named the Duke of Tetuan in *Ulysses* and that on that very day the Duke was in Paris attending an Irish convention.

In fact, Desmond FitzGerald was in Paris for the same meeting, his visit to Joyce being on the sidelines of what was billed as an Irish Race Congress. Joyce, in his enthusiasm for keeping in touch with Irish affairs, might have read of the Congress or been told about it by Pound who planned to attend the meeting with his old friend Yeats.

If he took time off to go for a stroll to clear his head on the afternoon of Sunday 22 January, Joyce might have witnessed a bizarre spectacle: a fleet of motor cars bearing flags of the Irish Free State driving through the streets of Paris. If his sight was not troubling him too much, he might have glimpsed within those cars the figures of Eamon de Valera, Sean T O'Ceallaigh and Douglas Hyde (all of whom were destined to hold the post of President of Ireland) among other prominent politicians. And if, in some magical way, he could have followed the convoy, he might have caught up with it at the Irish College on rue des

Irlandais in time to hear de Valera address the Irish students there and tell them that he hoped they would come back to Ireland good republicans.[10]

The motor tour of Paris took place on the eve of the Irish Race Congress[11] - what was to become a brief but controversial moment in Irish political history. The convention was conceived a year earlier by Irish republicans in South Africa as a purely political gathering. But as the idea developed, economics and culture were added to the agenda so that it was ultimately planned as a celebration of the Irish at home and abroad.

The timing, however, was unfortunate. Just weeks previously the approval by the Dáil of the Anglo-Irish Treaty had resulted in a bitter split in Sinn Féin.[12] Thus, the delegates who arrived from Ireland were divided into pro- and anti-Treaty factions; and although many of them travelled to Paris on the same boat and train, neither group spoke to the other.

Arthur Griffith, as leader of the Provisional Government, had appointed Eoin MacNeill, Michael Hayes, Larry O'Neill (Lord Mayor of Dublin), Hyde, Maud Gonne[13] and Diarmuid Coffey to attend. De Valera, who only two weeks before had walked dramatically out of the Dáil with his anti-Treaty supporters, insisted on leading his own group: Countess Markievicz, Mary MacSwiney (whose brother Terence had died on hunger strike in 1920), Donal O'Callaghan and Harry Boland.

The strangest travel arrangements of all were those made by Eamon de Valera. He dressed as a priest, taking on the guise of Father Patrick Walsh whom he knew from the Holy Ghost College in Rockwell where he had been educated. Sean MacBride, son of Maud Gonne, who helped finalise the arrangements for the Congress, travelled with de Valera via Rosslare and Fishguard. Stopping off in London, de Valera had his 'priestly' photograph taken for insertion into his forged passport. He also wanted to buy a new type of fountain pen and went to a special shop in the Strand. Trying out the nib, he proceeded to sign his name 'Eamon de Valera.' As soon as he had written it he received a strong kick from MacBride, who quickly stuffed the piece of paper into his pocket.[14]

Why de Valera went to such extraordinary lengths to disguise himself is not clear. His biographer Tim Pat Coogan suggests it was 'symptomatic of the atmosphere of intrigue and unreality in which he increasingly operated during those tragic days.'[15]

Seventeen countries from all five continents were represented at the Congress. There were delegations from countries as far apart as Argentina, South Africa, Australia, New Zealand, Java, the United States, Britain (the largest group) and other European countries. An attempt to make a head-count revealed that there could be as many as 50,000 of Irish descent in Argentina. Chile also had many of Irish extraction. Peru, however, had 'only one doubtful Irishman.'[16]

Identical reports in the *Freeman's Journal* and the *Irish Independent* suggested that 30,000,000 people of Irish blood the world over were entitled to attend. It would be the greatest hosting of the Irish race, they declared, since King Brian Boru brought the clans together in the eleventh century. In the event, about 250 people attended each session of the Paris Congress.

At the outset, the Irish delegates made their way to the Grand Hotel, where the Irish representative, O'Ceallaigh, was based. O'Ceallaigh had first come to Paris in 1919 and from there controlled a network of Irish envoys throughout Europe. For the next three years Paris became the diplomatic and propaganda centre for Sinn Féin.[17]

The escape of de Valera from Lincoln prison in February

1919 had generated press interest in Paris about the Irish situation for the first time and French newspaper reporters sought out O'Ceallaigh to learn more. This was just the opportunity he was seeking to develop relations with them. As his work expanded George Gavan Duffy, a fluent French speaker, joined O'Ceallaigh's office.[18]

Prior to the Treaty, the French authorities felt uncomfortable about the activities of the Irish office. They believed that its propaganda urging recognition of Ireland as a sovereign state was damaging Franco-British relations.

O'Ceallaigh and Duffy were the Irish delegates to the 1919-20 Paris Peace Conference. The chief American delegate, President Woodrow Wilson, despite pressure from the US Senate and from the Irish Race Convention held in Philadelphia[19] in 1919, refused to meet them. The conference chairman, the French Prime Minister Georges Clemenceau, considered that there was no way the Irish claim could come before the conference. If it did it would have led to Irish membership of the League of Nations (which is effectively what the Peace Conference became) and that would have been unthinkable in the context of French relations with Britain. A letter to Clemenceau by O'Ceallaigh demanding recognition was never answered.

Duffy went about his task with enthusiasm, writing articles for the French press and publishing pamphlets on Irish sovereignty. As a result he was expelled from Paris (by the French on the urging of Britain). Thirty years later (1948) the French government redressed this by appointing him an Officer of the Legion of Honour.[20]

The French authorities were well aware of the political situation in Ireland and of the tensions that were growing within Sinn Féin after the Treaty debate. The French Consul-General in Dublin, Alfred Blanche, kept the Ministry of Foreign Affairs in Paris fully informed. Meanwhile the Foreign Ministry liaised with the Interior

Ministry in connection with the movement of those travelling to the Congrès Mondial de race Irlandaise. A telegram from Alfred Blanche to the Foreign Ministry on the 18 January, 1922 read:

> *I have just been informed by a reliable source that M. John McNeill [sic], member of the new government, accompanied by the well-known professor Dr Douglas Hyde, leave this evening for Paris, via Calais, to attend the Congress.*[21]

The French Foreign Ministry urged the Interior Ministry to keep a discreet surveillance on the Congress to ensure that it would not degenerate into anti-British propaganda. As a result the Interior Ministry was able to inform the Foreign Ministry of many details. Here are just some points it made in a note[22] dated 20 January:

- The Congress organisers had hired five powerful limousines for the Irish delegation.

- The previous day a Mr Kelly [one of the organisers] arrived at his office at the Grand Hotel at 9.40am and left again at 11.30am in the company of Sean T O'Ceallaigh and two secretaries. The two men got into one of the limousines, the secretaries got into another, while a third followed without passengers. Because the cars were so powerful it was not possible to have them followed.

- Mr Kelly returned to the hotel at 2.55pm accompanied by a Miss O'Brien [another of the organisers] whose room number was 961. Mr O'Ceallaigh returned at 3pm.

- Mr Kelly paid a visit to Miss Hughes who, feeling unwell, did not leave her room for the whole day.

- The Duke of Tetuan was staying in Room 204 at a daily rate of 275 francs. Douglas Hyde was in Room 771 at a rate of 60 francs.

The Treaty and its divisive debate in the Dáil changed what had heretofore been a united Irish diplomatic/propaganda front.[23] People were choosing sides and when the various Irish delegates arrived at the Grand Hotel, O'Ceallaigh refused to receive the Free State group (he was sacked two months later).

The rancour, however, went over the heads of many of those present, including the 58-year-old Duke of Tetuan who was chosen to be Honorary President of the Congress despite his poor English.

The Duke was a Spanish nobleman who was descended from the O'Donnells of Co Donegal and held the title of The O'Donnell. The chiefs of the O'Donnell and other clans had fled Ireland at the beginning of the 17th century (in what became known as the Flight of the Earls) and spread throughout the world. Many of them held on tenaciously to their Irish identity and formed Irish brigades that for decades fought in other nations' wars.

While the Duke was undisputedly of Irish descent his Irish blood had become considerably diluted. His lineage, however, could not have been more impressive.

He was born Juan, son of Lieutenant Carlos O'Donnell who had held the ranks of Chamberlain, Minister of State and Ambassador. Carlos's uncle, Leopoldo (1809-67), had been Prime Minister of Spain in 1858. It was Leopoldo who, following a successful military campaign in Morocco was created Duke of Tetuan (a Moroccan town) in 1860.[24]

Such, briefly, is the esteemed background of The O'Donnell, Duke of Tetuan, who smilingly greeted Irishmen and women of sharply different political hues as they arrived for what was to be a celebration of Irishness. Despite the acrimony, the various Irish delegates behaved in a reasonably civil manner towards one another. Although ideologically opposed through the Treaty debates, some - like Maud Gonne and Constance Markievicz - still managed to maintain their personal friendships.

This behaviour is reflected in the official report drawn up for the Free State Government. It describes the initial meeting between the Duke, O'Ceallaigh and de Valera: O'Ceallaigh formally welcomed the Duke, who made some remarks in Spanish, which were translated into English.

O'Ceallaigh then introduced de Valera in Irish and Dev replied to the Duke in Irish 'in a speech in which no exception could be taken, and stated that he knew that he was expressing the view of the present President of the Republic, Arthur Griffith.'[25]

The Congress, known in Irish as Aonac na nGaedhal, took place at the Salles des Fetes in the Hotel Continental (where George Moore often stayed) near the Tuileries Gardens.

The opening session was a typically Irish mixture of religion, literature and politics. The Duke read out a telegram of condolence, which would be sent to the Vatican via the Papal Nuncio in Paris on the death of Pope Benedict the Fifteenth. This was followed by a minute's silence.

There were addresses by Hyde and the Yeats brothers. WB Yeats talked about Anglo-Irish literature and described how Irish writers were writing in an English 'scented with the Irish dialect' (*parfumé d'idiomes irlandais* according to the French translation of his lecture). Jack Yeats and Hyde spoke about Irish art, language and literature.

There was potential, at least, for serious debate at several intellectual levels. Many of the politicians present were also writers - among them Hyde and FitzGerald. Griffith, President of Dáil Éireann, was not at the Congress but his economic theories had attracted the interest of Pound who was.[26]

Instead there was an atmosphere of divisiveness, and it was not confined to the Irish. A French delegate, who called for a publicity campaign to rid Ireland of its image as an uncultured nation of whiskey drinkers, said he believed the real President of the Irish Republic was de Valera and not Griffith.

As a celebration of Irishness, the conference proved a disappointment not only because of political differences but also due to the language barrier (there was neither amplification nor simultaneous translation). The Duke of Tetuan - seated on a red-draped throne - often fell asleep during the proceedings for, as Maud Gonne later suggested, he knew nothing of Ireland except its horses. He awoke only when a pretty woman rose to say something. Yeats understood only English. He was accompanied by Pound who prepared a speech for one of the delegates in poor French. Those French who were present were uncertain which language they were being addressed in, thinking it might be a Spanish dialect of Tetuan.[27]

But as the week went on, tension between pro- and anti-Treaty delegates increased and political rancour dominated most of the sessions. The majority of the Irish delegates were opposed to the Treaty. When FitzGerald arrived (as he put it, 'to the obvious discomfiture of Mr Boland and others'), he found that responsibility for publicity had been taken over by the anti-Treaty side, which was 'quite unscrupulous in misrepresenting Irish affairs.' Boland bluntly told him he would not tolerate the Minister's interference. The feedback FitzGerald was getting from French and American journalists was that the 'campaign of advertisement for Mr de Valera was most undignified.' He felt the best thing he could do was to discourage publicity completely.[28]

De Valera pulled the biggest political stroke of the week. After much arguing over the setting up of a world organisation - to be known as Fine Ghaedheal - and whether or not it should take into account the 'minority party,' de Valera threatened that if the Congress did not form such an organisation he would go out and form one for himself.

Despite his threat to leave the meeting, Congress did not do so. Later in the week, however, de Valera himself was in the chair and the press excluded. The minutes of the meeting read: 'Many of the delegates who had voted in the majority in [sic] Wednesday now seemed to be absent. The de Valera party had, therefore, a majority.' Dev was elected unanimously President of the Congress, which it was agreed would meet again in Dublin in three years time.

During the closed session, according to a French report, Dev tried to get those present to try to examine how the divisions among the different elements in Sinn Féin could be resolved.

The media, however, took their exclusion from that session badly. Reporters from Irish, French and English newspapers expressed unhappiness at the way de Valera conducted the debates since, they claimed, he represented only one side of Irish opinion.

Once the Congress was over, de Valera visited the Cathedral of Notre Dame where, slipping behind a confessional, he once more put on his priestly garb and set off for London via Antwerp.[29] He was back in Dublin on 3 February.

Given the political turmoil that was to follow, resulting in a bloody civil war, it is no surprise that the Congress never did meet again.

---

[1] Curran: *James Joyce Remembered* 84.

[2] James Matthews: *Voice. A Life of Frank O'Connor* 61.

[3] Reddin: *Recollections of Joyce*, Envoy magazine, Dublin, April 1951.

[4] He was also a poet, philosopher, journalist and father of the former taoiseach, Dr Garret FitzGerald.

[5] Letters to Stanislaus Joyce and McAlmon in February and March 1922 (Ellmann ed., *Letters of James Joyce Vol. 3*, 60, 61).

[6] Ellmann: 535. 'Ireland was achieving emancipation just as Joyce's own lifetime work was achieving culmination.'

[7] Letter to me from Dr Garret FitzGerald. The following August FitzGerald was made Minister for External Affairs.

[8] Padraic Colum described FitzGerald as 'courageous, faithful and efficient.' (Colum: *Arthur Griffith*)

[9] FitzGerald and Pound became friends, but they did not always agree. In 1928, Pound attacked FitzGerald's Censorship Bill as 'a worse piece of garbage than the US thing it is modelled on...'

[10] Papers of Desmond FitzGerald, UCD.

[11] It was not the first international Irish Race convention. 2,300 people attended one in New York in March 1916 at which a 'victory fund' for Ireland was established. Over 5,000 delegates attended one in Philadelphia in February 1919.

[12] On Monday 16 January the Provisional Government of the Irish Free State was set up with Arthur Griffith at its head.

[13] Griffith had introduced Maud Gonne to John McBride, but advised her not to marry him. 'You are so unconventional – a law unto yourself; John is full of conventions.' (Gonne: *A Servant of the Queen*).

[14] Sean MacBride : *Memoirs* 61.

[15] Coogan: *De Valera* 305.

[16] Kennedy/Skelly: *Irish Foreign Policy.*

[17] Keogh: *Ireland and Europe 1919-1948.*

[18] Duffy became Minister for Foreign Affairs in January 1922. He resigned at the outbreak of the Civil War and was replaced by Desmond FitzGerald. (Mitchell: *Revolutionary Government in Ireland* 38).

[19] The Philadelphia Race Convention had appointed a committee to meet with President Wilson and dispatched a delegation to the Paris Peace Conference. That convention was organised by the Friends of Irish Freedom, a front organisation for Clan na Gael (the American equivalent of the Irish Republican Brotherhood).

[20] Mary Kotsonouris article in *History Ireland,* Winter 2000.

[21] NLI correspondence, *Ministère des Affaires Étrangères, Archives*

Diplomatiques, Europe 1918-'29: *Irlande, p7398.*

[22] Idem.

[23] According to the historian Dermot Keogh: 'It is impossible to separate the functions of diplomacy and propaganda in the Dáil Éireann period' (*Ireland and Europe 1919-1948*).

[24] A descendant of Juan - Leopoldo, Duke of Tetuan - was honoured by the National University of Ireland in 1956.

[25] Desmond FitzGerald papers, UCD.

[26] Pound, who met Griffith in Paris, wrote later: 'One of the most illuminating hours of my life was spent in conversation with Griffith, the founder of Sinn Féin. We were in his room to avoid the detectives who infested the hotel. It was the time of the armistice when the Irish delegates had been invited to London... Griffith said: 'You can't move 'em with a cold thing like economics.' (Quoted in *A Companion to the Cantos of Ezra Pound* by Carroll Franklin Terrell).

[27] Mary Colum: *Life and the Dream* 265.

[28] FitzGerald papers, UCD.

[29] Longford/O'Neill: *Eamon de Valera* 183.

A Little Circle Of Kindred Minds

Chapter Four
Geniuses Together

Around the same time that Arthur Power was becoming acquainted with the Joyces in the spring of 1921, another young man knocked on the door of the apartment at boulevard Raspail. Small, lean 25-year-old Robert McAlmon was an Irish-American writer who had just married the daughter of a multi-millionaire. Over the following ten years he would spend much of his time in the bars of Montparnasse, gaining a reputation as a big spender, heavy drinker, storyteller and serious writer – usually in that order. Now all but forgotten, McAlmon was once described by Pound as a better writer than Hemingway. Like Hemingway, McAlmon became a close friend of Joyce, helping him with his typing. He also provided him with the princely allowance of $150 a month (about €1,000 today) until the publication of *Ulysses* almost a year later.

McAlmon's father was a Protestant from Co Armagh who had emigrated to Canada where he married a Scottish Canadian. He then moved to the US where he became a Presbyterian minister (Sylvia Beach's father was a minister of the same religion). Young Robert was born in the small town of Clifton in Kansas, the last of ten children. He grew up feeling unwanted and one of his sisters later remarked that, even as a little boy, he believed that everyone was out to get him.

McAlmon became a drifter, holding a variety of jobs while he wrote poetry. When he moved to Greenwich Village in New York, he earned a dollar an hour posing nude for drawing classes. In 1920 he met the American writer William Carlos Williams who had started a small literary magazine called *Contact*. Williams was amazed at the hardness of expression in McAlmon's eyes and the coldness of his manner. He noticed that, to get attention, he often told untrue but believable stories about others.

Yet McAlmon's own story, of his marriage and subsequent fortune, was what most people talked about behind his back.

Williams introduced him to the writer Hilda Doolittle[1] (former wife of the poet Richard Aldington) who was accompanied by a small, dark, English girl named Annie Winifred Ellerman who wrote under the pseudonym of Bryher (after one of the Isles of Scilly). McAlmon was attracted to Bryher, the daughter of the English shipping magnate John Ellerman who, when he died in 1933, was reportedly the richest Englishman who had ever lived. Bryher, however, was in love with Hilda – an Imagist poet known by her initials HD - and wanted to live with her. Knowing that Daddy would not approve (and not wishing to jeopardise her inheritance) she entered into an agreement with McAlmon to get married. With the 'respectability' that would bring, Bryher could then break away from her possessive father and go to live in Europe with HD. It was a business agreement whereby McAlmon – who boasted that he was bisexual - would benefit from part of a substantial allowance that Bryher received from her father. The marriage took place six months later in February 1921. Bryher later explained how she came to marry McAlmon:

> *He wanted to go to Paris to meet Joyce but*
> *lacked the passage money. I put the problem*
> *before him and suggested that if we married my*
> *family would leave me alone. I would give him*
> *part of my allowance, he would join me for*

occasional visits to my parents, otherwise we
would lead strictly separate lives.[2]

McAlmon called the marriage 'legal only, unromantic and strictly an agreement,'[3] although it has been suggested there was at least some emotional involvement on his part. But the regular income that ensued gave McAlmon the freedom to concentrate on his writing (and drinking). When, six years later, the couple got divorced and McAlmon received a hefty settlement, his American friends gave him the nickname 'McAlimony.'

Bryher acknowledged the advantages that such a marriage had for each of them:

> *He introduced me to my lifelong friend Sylvia*
> *Beach, to Joyce, Hemingway, Gertrude Stein,*
> *Berenice Abbott, Man Ray, and many others...*
> *He received, in his turn, the freedom of Paris in*
> *the twenties.*[4]

On their way to France, the couple spent some time in London where they stayed in the Ellerman mansion. McAlmon made contact with the *Egoist* literary magazine, which had published some of his poems (the magazine had also published Joyce's *Portrait of the Artist as a Young Man*). He also met TS Eliot who urged him to get to know French writers and writing and to model himself on Joyce who was 'likely to go on producing first rate work until he dies.'[5]

Also at the *Egoist* he met the feminist Harriet Shaw Weaver, Joyce's principal benefactress (although McAlmon would not have known this) who agreed to publish a collection of his poems.

The *Egoist* had published some sections of *Ulysses*, but the book was serialised monthly in the American journal the *Little Review*. In late 1920, the New York Society for the Prevention of Vice brought an action for obscenity against the editors of the magazine, the feminists Margaret Anderson and Jane Heap. Joyce and the tireless Ezra Pound got the Irish-American lawyer John Quinn to defend the action.

The case came before a New York court on 14 February, 1921 (the day McAlmon and Bryher were married) and ended while they were crossing the Atlantic. When he arrived at the office of the *Egoist*, Weaver told McAlmon the *Nausicaa* episode had been declared obscene and that Anderson and Heap had been found guilty and fined $50 each.[6] Worse, they were prohibited from publishing any more of the book. Effectively *Ulysses* was banned in the United States. In Britain no printer was prepared to take a risk. No publisher would now touch Joyce's book.

Whether or not she knew that McAlmon was hoping to establish a publishing company when he got to Paris, Weaver gave him a letter of introduction to Joyce.

As soon as the couple arrived in Paris, their first stop was at Shakespeare and Company where they learned of Sylvia Beach's plan to publish Joyce's book. Sylvia fell in love with what she called McAlmon's 'Irish sea-blue eyes.' Bryher arranged to use the bookshop as a forwarding address (so her father would not suspect she was living in Switzerland with HD). McAlmon, too, used Shakespeare and Company as a post office. He called to the bookshop at least once a day and he and Sylvia became good friends - although Sylvia, a teetotaller, frowned upon his heavy drinking.

As he made his way to Joyce's flat on boulevard Raspail, McAlmon must have wondered what sort of person he would meet. He had not thought much of the character of Stephen Dedalus in *A Portrait of the Artist*, whom he felt was 'precious.' But he had read the passages of *Ulysses* that had been appearing in the *Little Review*, and he had enjoyed the short stories in *Dubliners*, which led him to believe that Joyce would at least be approachable.[7]

At the door of the apartment, McAlmon was greeted by Nora, whom he thought very pretty, dignified and reassuring. He knew Joyce's eyesight was weak, but he thought he had used it well in choosing a wife. After a while, Joyce emerged, having been resting in bed. The two men hit it off almost immediately. Neither knew many people in Paris and both enjoyed company, so Joyce invited McAlmon to dine out with him that evening. They became firm friends and met for a drink almost every night.

Joyce admired McAlmon's directness and frankness. But in all their discussions, McAlmon was too polite to tell him of his disdain for Stephen Dedalus. He had no sympathy either for Joyce's obsession with the Catholic Church and was uninterested in hearing about Thomas Aquinas and the Jesuits. Although his own father had been a Presbyterian minister, he himself had never had a religious crisis growing up and could not understand anyone else having one. He remained agnostic.

Despite the huge differences between them at many levels, they enjoyed each other's company. McAlmon was proud of his Irish roots and that certainly attracted him to Joyce. Yet it was McAlmon's American side that Joyce liked about him, later working many of his American sayings and slang expressions into his *Work in Progress*. Although McAlmon had a vicious tongue that often got him into trouble, such was his respect for Joyce that he kept it under control in the other's company. In the early months of their friendship, Joyce was indebted to McAlmon for regular payments into his bank account and he would have been unwise to bite the hand that fed him.[8] In any case, McAlmon might come in handy; he was after all a publisher and Joyce knew he could always call upon him to perform a favour.

For his part, McAlmon looked up to Joyce as a successful writer, even though he did not like much of what he wrote. He also had a certain empathy with the man whom he described as 'an alert observant Irishman, disturbed about life. I believe I understood him better than most people because of the Irish in me.'[9]

It may have been the Irish in him that led him to interpret Nora's criticisms of her husband and his writing as something positive for Joyce. 'Had it not been for her keeping him down to earth, Joyce would have remained the word-prettifying bard, the martyred sensibility, Stephen Dedalus,' he wrote.[10]

Over a few drinks together, Joyce would sometimes become emotional as he talked about his love affair with words. One night, telling McAlmon about his ancestry, Joyce wept as he described how his father and his grandfather had parented large families of between 12 and 18 children and how he himself was still young enough to have more. McAlmon (on whose mind procreation must have been the last thing) suggested that to produce many children one ought to have the money to care for them. But Joyce would not listen.[11]

Years later, in a poem, *The Revolving Mirror*, McAlmon satirised Joyce's drunken fears and his Irish colloquialism:

> *That his father,*
>
> *and his father's father*
>
> *and fathers before them*
>
> *were parents of families*

twelve to seventeen in number.

But his economic circumstances –

Neverthless:

'I'm a young man yet,

and my wife is strong.

I'll make me a few more

before it's ended by the grace of God.[12]

Joyce was not the only writer McAlmon satirised. In another poem he lampooned Eliot and Pound's obsession with European history. While Eliot appeared not to hold a grudge, Pound was less forgiving. When McAlmon met Pound for lunch in order to mend fences he found him 'very instructorial indeed.'[13] The two avoided each other for years. Eventually Joyce and the English painter and writer Wyndham Lewis mediated and got them to be more civil towards each other.

Like Power, McAlmon became a close friend of Joyce who was not slow to find a 'use' for the other writer. One evening, over a few drinks, Joyce suggested McAlmon might help him by typing 50 or so pages of the *Penelope* chapter. No one else was available after the husband of the typist of *Circe* had burned about 40 pages he considered obscene. McAlmon, who was a faster typist than he was accurate, readily agreed.

The following day, Joyce gave him the manuscript.

McAlmon was shocked by what he saw. The handwriting was minute and difficult to decipher. Joyce had given him four notebooks and throughout the script were marks in red, yellow, blue, purple and green referring to phrases to be inserted from each of them.

McAlmon began typing painstakingly, carefully placing the appropriate insertions where they were required. After a while he became less meticulous, putting the additional words wherever he happened to be typing.

After publication he was surprised to notice that Joyce had not changed them back. When he asked Joyce had he not noticed he was told that he had, but that he agreed with McAlmon. (Joyce admitted later that he had in fact retained very few of McAlmon's 'changes.').[14]

McAlmon knew Joyce was manipulating him and he resented it. His ego was such that he preferred to be the centre of attention rather than be seen as a kind of editorial assistant to a great writer.

He was not around on the publication day of *Ulysses*, even though Joyce had sent him a telegram advising him of the date and thanking him for his 'kind help during the past year.' McAlmon had instead set off for the Riviera. A few days later, Joyce sent him a copy of his new book. McAlmon invited Joyce to join him but Joyce was intent on getting more copies from the printers. Declining the invitation, Joyce asked McAlmon to send him 'a nice necktie.' The spendthrift bought several ties as well as a ring for Joyce, who reacted with the characteristic sarcasm he seemed to reserve for McAlmon: 'I thought you always travelled with a trunk full of them and threw out a few dozen a week, but evidently I was misled by a rumour.'[15]

Despite his thirst for socialising, McAlmon found the time to complete a set of short stories, which he showed to Joyce. Joyce suggested he call the collection *A Hasty Bunch* since he found McAlmon's use of language 'racy' (he may also have thought they had been written in a hurry). He told McAlmon the stories reminded him 'in a way of *Dubliners* — not in treatment or the characters — rather in mental predisposition.'[16]

Joyce knew McAlmon was having difficulties in getting his book published (one English printer regarded it as obscene) and asked him would he get Shakespeare and Company to publish it or would he do so himself. It was the suggestion of self-publishing that led McAlmon to bring out the book under his own *Contact* publishing company, printed in Dijon by Maurice Darantière, printer of *Ulysses*. In fact, McAlmon's collection was published a month or so before *Ulysses*, at the end of 1921 or in January 1922. It was well received, even by Pound who had once, behind his back, called him 'another young one wanting me to make a poet out of him with nothing to work on.'[17]

Having already helped with drawing up American names for the *Ulysses* subscriber list, McAlmon became useful to Joyce again soon after the book's appearance. When reviews of his work came in much too slowly for Joyce's patience, he began to lean on friends and acquaintances to review the novel and McAlmon was among the first to be called upon. Joyce established a pattern: first sending a copy, and then asking their opinion before suggesting they write a review. But Joyce did not leave it at that. He then suggested phrases they might use and even where the review should be sent.[18] McAlmon bashed out a glowing review without bothering to finish reading the book. He then sent it to Joyce who made a small correction and urged McAlmon to use his influence with his father-in-law (Sir John Ellerman was a shareholder with *The Times*) but the article never appeared. McAlmon had found the novel hard going and when he confessed to Joyce that he intended to throw his copy out the window, Joyce asked him to refrain from doing so and to 'write again when recovered from Bloomitis.'[19]

Joyce succumbed to McAlmon's charm and sociability to

the extent that he stayed out all night at least once a week. Over drinks the two discussed a variety of topics including necrophilia, mysticism and writers such as Moore, Shaw, Pound and Eliot. Although not a naïve person, McAlmon regarded Joyce's infatuation with words as something all writers go through before they mature. Yet he admired Joyce's erudition and great memory and felt that the older man's writing 'could be dull, inanimate and pretentious if it were not that Joyce is full of sentiment, sentimentality and Irish twilight, even when he is most cruelly ironic.'[20] McAlmon felt Joyce's genius was provincial and told him the short stories of *Dubliners* were more likely to stand the passage of time than his novels.

Sometimes, as the evening progressed, Joyce would begin to recite Dante in Italian. A misty look would enter his eyes, suggesting to McAlmon that he would not be going home until the early hours of the morning.[21]

One such bender took place not long after the publication of *Ulysses*, during a period when Joyce's eyes were not troubling him. He had recovered well following an operation and his old friend from his Zurich days, Frank Budgen,[22] had arrived in Paris. The two went to the Gypsy Bar - off the boulevard St Michel - where they were joined by McAlmon, the American writer Djuna Barnes and the English-born poet and artist Mina Loy. Much drink was consumed. While the women tolerated McAlmon, they did not have much time for Budgen who suddenly left with what McAlmon described as 'a drunken man's feeling of having been cut down and thought inferior.'

Joyce, thinking Budgen must have thought him bigheaded following the success of *Ulysses*, went into a drink-induced melancholy from which the women tried, unsuccessfully, to bestir him. Eventually they too left in a huff. Joyce and McAlmon continued drinking until the patron asked them to leave. It was 5am.

But the night was young and the two went on to a small bistro on the boulevard St Germain. McAlmon takes up the story:

> *We bought cigars and we drank. As we decided to drink through the list of French drinks, Joyce began dropping his cigars. At first I leaned to pick them up and return them to him. When I could no longer lean without falling on my face I took to lighting the cigars and handing them to him. He almost immediately dropped them, and I lighted cigar after cigar until they were all gone, and then we took to cigarettes. At ten in the morning we sat alone in the small bistro, the floor covered with some twenty cigars, innumerable cigarettes, and the table with the forty glasses, which had held our various drinks.*[23]

The patron, who could hardly believe his eyes, helped McAlmon get Joyce into a taxi, which took the pair to Joyce's apartment. McAlmon carried Joyce up the stairs and into his room. Nora's impatience with her husband was hardly surprising:

'Jim, you've been doin' this for 20 years, and I'm tellin' you it's the end. Do you understand? You've been bringin' your drunken companions to me too long, and now you've started McAlmon in the same way.'

As he let Joyce fall from his arms onto the bed, McAlmon used his considerable charm to ease the tension, telling Nora that her husband had received a big disappointment in having been deserted by Budgen.

'I always told him that man would do him no good,' was her response.

McAlmon returned to his hotel. He was not long asleep - at three in the afternoon – when a telegram arrived. It was from Joyce asking him to come around for tea at half past four and on no account to let him down.

Later, facing Joyce, with Nora only feet away, he was surprised to be asked: 'McAlmon, what have you been hearing today about the apartment the man said we were to have?'

Recognising a cover-up story that Joyce must have told Nora (for she was keen to move into a new apartment), McAlmon sprang to the rescue.

'Oh, he's seeing about it now. I'm to meet him at six o'clock.'

The response seemed to placate Nora and took some pressure off Joyce.

Some of the stories of an inebriated Joyce being helped into a taxi and carried upstairs to his apartment may have been exaggerated, for as he became better known stories about him were legion and journalists even wrote about his daily swim in the Seine or the number of mirrors in his apartment. Certainly, McAlmon was the type of person who would ensure that his tales lost nothing in the telling. But there is enough evidence to confirm such incidents did indeed take place from time to time.

Yet sometimes Joyce was capable of playing a practical joke on the 'good Samaritan' who brought him home. One of McAlmon's friends, William Bird,[24] had spent an evening in the company of Joyce and Nora indulging in Joyce's penchant for 'natural champagne' when the

Irishman insisted they go on to Fouquets - despite appeals by Nora to go straight home. At about five in the morning, Bird got Joyce and Nora into a taxi, but when they arrived at Joyce's apartment block they discovered the lift was out of order. On getting out of the taxi, Joyce flopped and Bird had no alternative but to carry him up the five flights of stairs to his flat.

Once there, however, Joyce stood up and was well able to unlock the door and enter his flat. He then locked himself in the bathroom and refused to come out. As they tried to cajole him into unlocking the door, Nora turned to Bird: 'Mr Bird, what are you to do with such a man? And to think I have put up with him like this for all these years. What a damn fool his admirers would think me if they knew it all! He may be a genius to them, but look at him, what is he to me?'[25]

Joyce and McAlmon often exchanged views on literature and asked each other's opinion of what they were writing. Some years later, when Joyce was in despair over the negative reactions he was getting to his *Work in Progress* from Pound and Miss Weaver among others, he went to McAlmon for advice. 'Do you think I may be on the wrong track with my Work in Progress? Miss Weaver says she finds me a madman. Tell me frankly, McAlmon. No man can say for himself.' To which McAlmon reassured him that he was not mad: 'Just touched enough for genius in the James Jesus Joyce manner.' Nevertheless Joyce enjoyed the other's company and often ended the evening with: 'You'll be around tomorrow, McAlmon?'

In the autumn of 1923, McAlmon decided to spend the winter in Scandinavia rather than the south of France. By a coincidence, he found himself in the same hotel in Stockholm as William Butler Yeats who was there to receive the Nobel Prize. McAlmon learned of Yeats's presence only on the day the Irish poet was due to return to Dublin. He phoned Yeats's room and, using their common friendship with Pound as a lever, got himself invited for a cup of coffee. McAlmon found Yeats 'entirely likeable, amiable and sympathetic' but also 'too Irish twilighty and sweetly mystic' for his taste. The only words he could remember of Yeats's conversation were 'truth and beauty, and art.'[26] For his part, Yeats found it difficult to understand this young American poet. McAlmon came up with an excuse about having another appointment and left as quickly as he could. Perhaps, like Joyce, he had met Yeats too late.

Around this time another American expatriate from the Midwest arrived in Paris and she would come to be associated closely with McAlmon. Kay Boyle went on to write novels and to campaign on human rights issues but she is probably best known today for contributing important additional chapters to McAlmon's memoirs *Being Geniuses Together* which is regarded as one of the fullest and most candid accounts of expatriate Paris.

She wanted to meet Joyce or George Moore but she was too timid to enter Shakespeare and Company so she waited outside in vain. She was introduced to McAlmon in a Montparnasse café but it was Eugene Jolas, publisher of *transition*, who introduced her to Joyce.

She never got as close to Joyce as McAlmon but she took a keen interest in Lucia. Once Boyle and McAlmon were having dinner with the Joyces at the Trianons when the talk was almost entirely about Lucia, the turn in her left eye and her dancing career. McAlmon suggested that the squint might disappear as her dancing released Lucia's inner tensions. Joyce, who would grasp at any hope for his daughter, mentioned that she would be going to Salzburg to study dance with Elizabeth Duncan as her famous sister Isadora was no longer holding classes.

'She's no longer holding her liquor,' said a probably inebriated McAlmon.

Nora sighed. 'Ah, the poor soul.'[27]

Kay Boyle had an Irish grandfather and a mother who
was a political and social activist and this combination
heavily influenced her interest in Ireland and her concern
for human rights internationally. Her deep yearning for
Ireland and its literature was exceptional, even when
compared with other writers of Irish descent such as
McAlmon and F Scott Fitzgerald. In Paris she picked up a
cheap edition of George Moore's *The Lake* and when she
finished reading it felt 'there is only Ireland speaking to
me now.'[28]

Always a rebel at heart, she had been an enthusiastic
supporter of the War of Independence and carried with
her a copy of a letter by Terence MacSwiney to Cathal
Brugha written while on hunger strike in Brixton Prison
in 1920. As a teenager she wanted to go to Ireland to
fight for the rebels but had to settle for a secretarial job
at *Brooms* magazine in New York where she worked
closely with Lola Ridge, an Australian poet born in
Dublin, who introduced her to McAlmon's poetry. She
met many writers at *Brooms* (it was at a *Brooms* literary
party that McAlmon had met William Carlos Williams).

When Williams arrived in Paris, McAlmon threw a party
at the Trianons restaurant to introduce him to 'the
crowd.' Among those invited were the Joyces, the Fords,
the Vails (Laurence and his then wife Peggy
Guggenheim), the Antheils, Sylvia Beach and Adrienne
Monnier, Man Ray, Louis Aragon and Marcel Duchamp.
The evening started tense when McAlmon sang 'Bollicky
Bill' (Williams wondering aloud if it was a reference to
himself), but the atmosphere improved when Joyce sang
a few ballads. The French left early and the main group
went on to the Dingo where they drank until 3am.

In early 1924 McAlmon, who was with Williams in
Villefranche, asked Joyce to join them. Joyce declined,

citing financial problems. The New York lawyer John Quinn had sold the manuscript of *Ulysses* for a mere $1,975, which he offered to share with the author but Joyce was not prepared to accept such a low sum. However, Joyce availed of the opportunity to ask McAlmon for another loan which he would repay in March. McAlmon promptly sent him a cheque for £20, on receipt of which Joyce asked him for the same amount again – to which request McAlmon responded with yet another sum.

McAlmon and Williams were approached by the owner of their *pension* in Villefranche with an unusual request. He was impotent as a result of a war wound, he said, and since he and his wife desperately wanted a baby would either of the two virile young men oblige? When Williams, a married man, declined on moral grounds, the issue became a test of McAlmon's sexuality. Grudgingly agreeing to the proposition, he told the proprietor he would leave his bedroom door unlocked if his wife 'wished to crawl in with me.' In the event, McAlmon slept undisturbed.[29]

Returning to Paris, McAlmon resumed the social round of bars and parties. Sylvia and Adrienne accompanied him to the Quatres Arts Ball – a sort of Trinity Ball for arts students at which nudity was the norm and open sex was sometimes to be expected. The evening ended with the two women carrying a naked McAlmon back to his hotel room.

McAlmon was attractive to both men and women, just as he claimed to be attracted to either sex. According to Sylvia Beach, he was never lost in a crowd and 'dominated whatever group he was in.'[30] TS Eliot called him a man 'of promising general intelligence and very amiable personality.'[31]

However, a combination of heavy drinking and a wicked

tongue often got him into trouble. Even in the company of Joyce, McAlmon had a tendency to put his foot in it. On one occasion, he proposed a toast 'to sin.' When Joyce refused, McAlmon changed the toast 'to crime and Christianity,' but Joyce would not drink to that either. Despite the silence that followed, the evening's conviviality was restored following a generous quantity of white wine and coffee at the Dingo.[32]

While drink had a gentle inebriating effect on Joyce, easing him into nostalgia, sentimentality and song, in the case of McAlmon it sometimes led to barroom brawls, although not necessarily of his own making. As someone who spent much of his time on a stool in any of the numerous bars or cafés in Montparnasse, it is no surprise that one of his closest friends was a barman. Liverpool-born Jimmy Charters, who served in some of the most famous bars in Montparnasse, became something of a celebrity among the expatriate community.

Sometimes Charters and McAlmon would go on a bar crawl, perhaps ending at Le Boeuf sur le Toit (run by Jean Cocteau) or at Bricktop's in Montmartre. Bricktop's was run by Ada Smith, a black woman from West Virginia with, it was said, Irish blood. Her nightclub attracted a wide range of performers and clientele, from the exotic dancer Josephine Baker and musician Duke Ellington to Hemingway and Fitzgerald and even the Duke and Duchess of Windsor. Both McAlmon and Charters spent a night in jail after they were thrown out of Bricktop's for starting a brawl.

Despite his low stature, McAlmon was well able to fight. But sometimes he used his considerable charm to get him out of trouble. When a tough-looking American gave a party in one of the bars, he celebrated by singing popular songs in a loud voice. McAlmon, propped up at the bar with several Pernods inside him, felt he could do better and started singing operatic arias. When he would not stop, the furious party-thrower advanced towards McAlmon, gritting his teeth, fists closed tightly. The bar's customers, fearful of a fight, watched in horror, only to see McAlmon smile broadly at his opponent. Slowly the man's fists unclenched and the two ended up drinking together.

Sometimes Laurence Vail and McAlmon would end an evening's drinking by throwing their beer glasses at the mirrors of an all-night bistro in Montmartre. They would then happily pay for their destruction before letting themselves be thrown out.

Countless similar instances have been recorded giving the impression that daily life in 1920s Montparnasse was little more than a series of pub-crawls and fights. But extreme misbehaviour has been denied by several writers. 'There is a great deal of tosh about this,' wrote Ford Madox Ford as early as 1927, 'and the last gentleman who leeringly interrogated me as to the habits of American-Parisian expatriates was considerably drunker than I have ever seen any of his compatriots across the water.'[33] Jimmy Charters, from his perspective behind the bar, saw the serious side among his clientele. Montparnasse, he recalled, became the home of those with new ideas that 'were developed, not only in the attics or studios, but also in the companionship and stimulation of the cafés and bars.'[34]

In between drinking sessions, McAlmon found the time to publish the *Contact Collection of Contemporary Writers* (1925), which included five pages of the *Shaun* section of *Finnegans Wake*. The edition also featured work by Hemingway (*Soldier's Home* from *Three Stories and Ten Poems*), Djuna Barnes, Bryher, Ford Madox Ford, Pound and Stein.

Howsoever others regarded him; there is no doubting that McAlmon was one of the most prolific of the young

American writers in Paris. Between 1921 and 1925 he produced a book of poems, three volumes of short stories and two novels. *The New Review* described him as 'perhaps the most significant of the young American short-story writers.'[35] His misfortune was to be constantly compared with Hemingway - and there was no comparison.

McAlmon met Hemingway and his wife Hadley when he visited Pound's home in Rapallo in February 1923. Both men came from the Midwest, with middle-class backgrounds, and both boasted of their toughness. When Hemingway told him that Hadley had lost a suitcase containing most of his writing at the Gare de Lyon, McAlmon promised to publish his *Three Stories and Ten Poems*.

That May he met Gertrude Stein and agreed to publish *The Making of Americans*. The enormous tome was slow to move off the shelves so McAlmon asked Stein to contribute towards the printing bill of about $3,000 or he would pulp the book. She never did pay and he never carried out his threat.

Sometimes the French critic and writer, Valery Larbaud, would join Joyce and McAlmon for a meal. Afterwards, they would go on to the Gypsy Bar where they might be joined by Wyndham Lewis, who had come to Paris with TS Eliot shortly after Joyce's arrival. The patron of the Gypsy was pleased to see them for he knew they would stay drinking until four or five in the morning. The poules or local prostitutes got to know them too, and as a jazz orchestra played badly, McAlmon would dance with the prostitutes, Lewis would recite Verlaine and Joyce declaimed long passages of Dante in sonorous Italian 'as though saying mass.'[36]

Tension was developing between Joyce and Lewis, however. Lewis never liked *Dubliners* and regarded Joyce as a little too Irish for his taste. Things reached breaking point when the Englishman mischievously informed Harriet Weaver (his own publisher) that Joyce was terrific company, drinking until dawn and picking up everyone else's bill.

It was the last thing Weaver needed to be told and she wrote Joyce of her fears. He responded by enlisting the support of McAlmon to assure her that he drank only in moderation and that he never failed to 'hold his drink properly and as a gentleman.'[37] Joyce then wrote her a long, rambling but clever letter in which he named numerous other ridiculous and imaginary vices of which he had been accused, thus distracting her from the vice that worried her the most.

Weaver came from a very strict Quaker background and had a pathological fear of people who drank. When, during a visit to the Ellermans in London, McAlmon defended Joyce to her face, she admitted that she had never faced life with the courage to accept things as they were. But she was content to be reassured about Joyce and she looked forward to meeting him soon in Paris, hoping to be spared seeing him intoxicated.

Despite her worries, Weaver continued to finance Joyce to the extent that by 1923, when he started on *Finnegans Wake*, she had given him a total of £21,000 since the beginning of her patronage six years earlier – more than €1m in today's terms. Joyce, in a letter thanking her for her munificence, told her 'how impossible the task would be but for your generosity.'[38] Weaver's financial sponsorship would continue for many more years.

Her concern, however, grew as she was hearing more and more about this extraordinary book he was writing which, he had told her, would be a history of the world. In 1927, she expressed her anxiety brutally by telling him: 'It seems to me you are wasting your genius.'[39] But in an attempt to mend fences, she crossed over to Paris in early 1928, when Joyce succeeded in assuaging her feelings.

She was there on 2 February, Joyce's 46th birthday, and was invited to join in the celebrations in Joyce's apartment at Square Robiac. She sat on the sofa beside McAlmon, she still and quiet, he gradually becoming louder as he mixed champagne and whiskey. Adrienne Monnier sat nearby, trying to keep the conversation going. Arthur Power was there too, drinking little as usual, dressed impeccably with a silk tie with violet and red checks and a matching silk handkerchief peeping from his top pocket. So was George Antheil, the American modernist composer whom Joyce had befriended.

As Antheil played the piano, Joyce and McAlmon danced quietly – Joyce improvising to the rhythm of the music. McAlmon sang a ballad on the sinking of the Titanic (telling those assembled he would leave out the bawdy verses). Joyce sang three songs, among them *The Brown and the Yellow Ale*. Only Weaver, a quiet, reserved woman, did not enter into the spirit of the occasion. Joyce felt reassured, however, that she would continue her patronage.[40]

Lewis continued to cause problems for Joyce with an attack on his writing. In his *Time and Western Man*, published the previous September, Lewis called Joyce 'the poet of the shabby-genteel, impoverished intellectualism of Dublin. His world is the small, middle-class one.'

Afterwards Joyce often referred to the description sarcastically, telling Power and McAlmon: 'I'm only a simple middle-class man.' It was little consolation to Joyce that Lewis also attacked Stein and Pound as well as McAlmon, whom he called a 'natural illiterate.' When

Lewis later tried to make amends in a letter to Joyce, signing himself 'an everdevoted friend,' Joyce took the opportunity to write into *Finnegans Wake* 'an everdevoted fiend.'[41]

A man of strong political views, Lewis insisted that *transition*, the best-known and most enduring of the literary magazines, was part of a Communist-Surrealist conspiracy headed by Joyce and Stein.

Although he regarded himself as an equal of Joyce, rather than an acolyte, McAlmon became one of his twelve 'apostles' when Joyce asked him to write a piece for *transition* defending his *Work in Progress*. McAlmon was in the best of company; among the others were Samuel Beckett, Stuart Gilbert, Thomas MacGreevy and William Carlos Williams.

Mr. Joyce Directs an Irish Prose Ballet was the title of McAlmon's contribution. It attacked those critics who claimed Joyce's work was unintelligible.

McAlmon was among those invited to readings by Joyce of extracts from his *Work in Progress*, but he became irritated by the sycophants who all but genuflected before the great man. Joyce, who also despised hypocrisy, sympathised. And when McAlmon arrived for one such reading, Joyce took him aside, gave him a glass and told him where to find the whiskey. Joyce, McAlmon thought, probably felt he was about to be put to a severe test.

As the reading of *Anna Livia* progressed, McAlmon enjoyed Joyce's melodious tenor voice but little else. He did not care that the passage contained the word 'peace' in 29 languages and the names of hundreds of rivers. And as he looked around the room to see how the others were reacting – among them Hemingway, Sylvia Beach, Bill and Sally Bird and the Colums – they looked 'grave as owls.' Mary Colum, he observed, was the only one who occasionally smiled.

In March 1931, Monnier decided to hold a reading of the French version of *Anna Livia,* which she had helped to translate. McAlmon had taken a few drinks before he arrived – perhaps anticipating the ordeal to come. Two hundred people crowded into two rooms at Monnier's bookshop, La Maison des Amis des Livres. As she was reading aloud in one room, McAlmon in the other observed 'the ghouls, the frustrated old maids of various sexes, the dandruffy young men and the badly dressed women who clutter up literary gatherings.'[42] To illustrate to a friend how he felt about the 'worshipful' faces around the room, he lifted his hands momentarily and joined them in a gesture of prayer. Suddenly an elderly man ran across the room and slapped him in the face.

The next day McAlmon heard that the person who struck him was none other than Édouard Dujardin who had thought McAlmon was raising his hands in mock horror at the sight of his wife's thick ankles. McAlmon clarified the matter to Joyce and Beach who must have passed on the explanation, for Dujardin subsequently - through Joyce – apologised.

As more Americans came to Paris, McAlmon was never short of an old acquaintance from Greenwich Village with whom to socialise. Sometimes he would bring them to see Joyce, although he was usually respectful of Joyce's desire for privacy. When Canadian writer Morley Callaghan and his wife arrived in Paris, McAlmon suggested they call on the Joyces. Callaghan hesitated, having been warned by Hemingway (with whom he had worked at the Toronto Star) that Joyce hated strangers, McAlmon insisted: 'Oh nuts. Don't you want to see Jimmy? You'll like him. You'll like Nora too.'

Eventually the three met the Joyces at the Trianons and

Callaghan fitted in well. But he was surprised when, after McAlmon had gone to the toilet, Joyce asked him what he thought of McAlmon's work. Following a tactful answer, Joyce gave his own opinion: 'He has a talent... a real talent; but it is a disorganised talent.' The conversation stopped abruptly when McAlmon returned to the table, his face washed, his hair combed. Later, Callaghan observed how McAlmon would make himself vomit if he thought he was getting too drunk in company he respected.[43]

In fact McAlmon was at his most convivial in such company. Callaghan recalled that 'the rich pleasure he [McAlmon] got out of his boyhood recollections was so pure that neither the Joyces nor my wife nor I could bear to interrupt.'[44]

McAlmon liked to socialise with everyone, whether English speaking or French (although his French was far from perfect, he enjoyed Valery Larbaud's 'quick and responsive' intelligence). By the summer of 1929, however, many of McAlmon's drinking companions had gone home and he did too. The cafés of Montparnasse had lost much of their expatriate clientele and when Wall Street 'crashed' in October the money they were living on (often in the form of remittances from home) dried up. McAlmon seemed to escape the worst of the economic downturn. After a sojourn of less than two years in New York he was back in Paris, barhopping with Nancy Cunard, Kay Boyle and Peggy Guggenheim and, of course, dining with the Joyces.

On St Patrick's Day, 1931, he and Joyce were invited to a party at the Trianons given by Beach and Monnier. When Joyce asked McAlmon to make an after-dinner speech, he agreed reluctantly as he had imbibed a considerable amount of alcohol. 'This is the day that St Patrick drove a lot of snakes out of Ireland,' he declared. 'But one gathers there are many things left in that island that he might better have driven out.'

Despite the cryptic remarks, the party continued with Joyce singing Irish ballads such as *Love's own Sweet Song*. Joyce and Nora took a taxi home, but McAlmon, Lucia Joyce, Giorgio and his wife Helen went on to a few bars in Montmartre.[45]

With fewer distractions from fellow ex-pats, McAlmon got down to writing poetry and his memoirs. He started *Being Geniuses Together* in Barcelona in 1933, finishing it in Strasbourg the following year. Returning to Paris, one of the first persons he told about the book was Joyce.

Joyce asked him to read the manuscript to him. His depiction of Joyce was not as complimentary as the latter would have wished, associating him less with other writers and more with the socialites and drinkers with whom McAlmon had come into contact over the preceding years. Joyce told Weaver the book made him feel 'actionable.' When McAlmon heard that Joyce had referred to his book as 'the office boy's revenge,' he too was unhappy. According to Ellmann, McAlmon was only trying to be candid in his memoirs, not malicious.

Fortunately, the episode did not end their friendship (which had been losing much of its warmth anyway). When McAlmon went to London seeking a publisher, Joyce wrote to advise him about pitfalls in dealing with literary agents.

With the Depression in the United States, Fascism in Europe and a generally unsettled world, it was four years before McAlmon's memoirs were published. Reviews were poor and some readers, including Joyce, regarded the book as vengeful. McAlmon's biographer, Sanford J Smoller, however, concluded the memoirs were more honest than *A Moveable Feast* in which Hemingway wrote of events of the same period as he wished they had happened. McAlmon was a sincere man, Smoller wrote, who was 'grievously maligned, exploited and betrayed.'[46]

It was not until the 1960s, when Kay Boyle revised parts of the book and added her own memories, that the book became recognised as an important document of the period.

In the 1950s, as McAlmon's health deteriorated, he learned that Hemingway (whom he had been the first to publish) had been awarded the Nobel Prize. As Smoller put it: 'McAlmon could remember a time when he was a somebody and Hemingway a relative nobody; and now, while he was dying, unpublished and all but forgotten, Hemingway was the toast of the literary world.'[47]

McAlmon died of pneumonia in California on the 2 February, 1956.

That he died on the anniversary of Joyce's birth seems only to magnify the differences between the two writers. For who would remember McAlmon's birthday or what he had written? Although his work is rarely read today, McAlmon's role in modern literature should not be underestimated. Besides his own work, he provided a launching pad for Joyce, Hemingway, Stein and many others at a time when they needed it.

His biographer compared him to Beach in his ability to bring together disparate creative people: 'He served as a conduit through which people and ideas separated by time and distance flowed and often merged.'[48]

But today the man is best remembered for his book *Being Geniuses Together*[49] and what has been written about him in the Paris memoirs of others. His friend William Carlos Williams often said McAlmon had 'a genius for life.' To which McAlmon himself responded in *Being Geniuses Together*:

He may be right about me. If absolute despair, a
capacity for reckless abandon and drink, long
and heavy spells of ennui which require bottles of
strong drink to cure, and a gregarious but not
altogether loving nature is 'a genius for life',
then I have it.[50]

---

[1]Doolittle was the first of the Imagist poets whose ranks would include Desmond FitzGerald. Ezra Pound, Doolittle's ex-fiancé, declared her poetry *imagiste* over coffee in London in 1912.

[2] Bryher: *The Heart to Artemis*, 201, quoted in Smoller: *Adrift Among Geniuses* 37.

[3] McAlmon to William Carlos Williams, 1921.

[4] Bryher: *The Heart to Artemis* 201, quoted in Smoller 39.

[5] Eliot to McAlmon, 2 May 1921.

[6] They escaped prison but Joyce was disappointed with Quinn's defense.

[7] Smoller: *Adrift Among Geniuses* 59.

[8]Joyce was not the only recipient of McAlmon's largesse. He financed the American modernist composer George Antheil and partly financed Hemingway's first trip to Spain. McAlmon once remarked: 'Owning things ties one.'

[9] McAlmon to Williams 1921.

[10] McAlmon: *Geniuses* 167.

[11] Idem 24-27.

[12] McAlmon: *A Portrait of a Generation*, 1926.

[13] McAlmon: *Geniuses* 29.

[14] Ellmann 514.

[15] Joyce to McAlmon, March 1922 (Ellmann ed., *Letters of James Joyce Vol. 3,* 60).

[16] Joyce to McAlmon, 10 October, 1921.

[17] McAlmon: *Geniuses* 29.

[18] Joyce to McAlmon, 17 March, 1922, (Ellmann ed., *Letters of James Joyce Vol. 3, 60*).

[19] Idem.

[20] McAlmon: *Geniuses* 278.

[21] McAlmon: *Geniuses* 27.

[22] Budgen was a diplomat/painter whom Joyce had befriended in Zurich during the war. The two met almost daily and discussed in detail Joyce's work, resulting in Budgen's book *James Joyce and the Making of Ulysses.*

[23] McAlmon: *Geniuses* 117-118.

[24] Bill Bird was an American journalist who set up the *Three Mountains Press* in a cellar in Quai d'Anjou which also housed McAlmon's *Contact Editions* and Ford Madox Ford's *Transatlantic Review.*

[25] McAlmon: *Geniuses* 277.

[26] Idem. 227.

[27] Kay Boyle: *Being Geniuses* Together 296.

[28] Kay Boyle: *Being Geniuses Together* 109.

[29] Williams: Autobiography 203-205.

[30] Beach: *Shakespeare and Company* 25.

[31] Eliot to John Quinn, 9 May, 1921.

[32] Ellmann 565.

[33] Ford Madox Ford: *Some American Expatriates, New York Essays*, Rudge, NY, 1927

[34] Jimmy Charters: *This Must be the Place* 37.

[35] *New Review 1*, Number 4, 1931.

[36] McAlmon: *Geniuses* 28.

[37] McAlmon to Weaver (Lidderdale and Nicholson: *Dear Miss Weaver* 188).

[38] Unpublished part of letter, July 1923, quoted by Ellmann 556.

[39] Weaver to Joyce, 4 February, 1927.

[40] *The Diary of Helen Nutting*, quoted in Ellmann 599.

[41] Ellmann 595

[42] McAlmon: *Geniuses* 279.

[43] Morley Callaghan: *That Summer in Paris* 140-141.

[44] Idem.

[45] McAlmon: *Geniuses 306..*

[46] Smoller: *Adrift Among Geniuses* 8.

[47] Idem. 319.

[48] Idem. 54.

[49] His Paris memoirs overshadow McAlmon's other works such as *Distinguished Air: Grim Fairy Tales* (Contact Editions, Paris, 1925) which was hailed by Joyce, Pound and others as his most important book. Joyce arranged for it to be translated into French.

[50] McAlmon: *Geniuses* 169.

Chapter Five
The Making Of Americans

It was not just those who came from Ireland or with Irish connections who were drawn to Joyce. Many a true-bred American was eager to meet him too and among the first to do so was a young enthusiastic journalist from Chicago named Ernest Hemingway.

Hemingway arrived in Paris in December 1921. Over the following years he would transform himself from a newspaper reporter into a first-class novelist; and like McAlmon, whom he liked and hated in equal measures, he would become a part of Joyce's circle of helpers and friends.

Hemingway had caught a glimpse of Paris when he was 18 and on his way to serve in the Red Cross in Italy. He liked what he saw and wrote home: 'If the war ever ends I intend to bum all through this country.' Seriously injured by mortar fire, he spent months recuperating before returning to journalism, writing for the *Toronto Weekly Star*.[1] Two years later the newspaper assigned him to cover political and sporting events in Europe. Just before he set sail – with his bride Hadley Richardson - his friend and mentor Sherwood Anderson, who had just returned from Paris, told him the city was the ideal place to start a writing career. Anderson had met many literary figures in Paris and gave the young reporter letters of introduction to some of them: Ezra Pound, Gertrude Stein, Sylvia Beach, James Joyce and two journalists, Lincoln Steffens and Lewis Galantière.

The first of these Hemingway made contact with was

Galantière, a writer and translator, who invited the couple to join him for a meal at Michaud's, a fashionable restaurant off the rue Jacob where Joyce dined regularly. Hemingway was relieved when Galantière paid the bill. Although he had an income from Hadley's trust fund (giving them $3,000 a year), Hemingway regarded himself as poor and booked into a cheap hotel before moving into a cramped apartment at 74 rue du Cardinal Lemoine.[2] Only occasionally would he and Hadley go to Michaud's. Once, they stood outside the crowded restaurant, cautiously reading the menu.

> We were hungry again from walking and Michaud's was an exciting and expensive restaurant for us. It was where Joyce ate with his family then, he and his wife against the wall, Joyce peering at the menu through his thick glasses, holding the menu up in one hand; Nora by him, a hearty but delicate eater; Georgio thin, foppish, sleek-headed from the back; Lucia with heavy curly hair, a girl not quite yet grown; all of them talking Italian.[3]

One of his first letters to Anderson was to say that, while the talk in Paris was that Joyce and his family were starving, 'you can find the whole celtic crew of them every night in Michaud's.' He did not know that Harriet Weaver and Robert McAlmon were keeping Joyce in a style to which he was becoming very accustomed.

Hemingway's next port of call was Shakespeare and Company where he was charmed by the lively, petite Sylvia Beach with her brown eyes and boyishly bobbed hair. He was especially taken by her pretty legs. 'No one that I ever knew was nicer to me,' he wrote later. Hadley, her hair worn short, also endeared herself to Beach who found her 'an attractive boyish-looking girl.'[4]

Hemingway joined the lending library and as he and Beach talked about her books she told him she would soon be publishing *Ulysses.*

'When does Joyce come in?' inquired Hemingway.

'If he does come in it's usually very late in the afternoon,' she replied.

And so it was at Shakespeare and Company that Hemingway met Joyce, as well as many other French and American writers, among them Ezra Pound who was to have a formative influence on his writing.

With just weeks to the planned publication date of *Ulysses*, Beach was busy collecting subscriptions and Hemingway spent much of his time helping her. She had prepared a prospectus which contained Valery Larbaud's commendation: 'With *Ulysses*, Ireland makes a sensational return into the best European literature.'

Hemingway and McAlmon were among the first Americans to subscribe. Winston Churchill was one of the first of the British to do so. Pound brought in Yeats. But George Bernard Shaw refused. In a vicious but somewhat droll letter to Beach he wrote of the book's 'foul mouthed, foul minded derision and obscenity' and ended:

> *I must add, as the prospectus implies an invitation to purchase, that I am an elderly Irish gentleman, and that if you imagine that any Irishman, much less an elderly one, would pay 150 francs for a book, you little know my countrymen.* [5]

Shaw had a point about the price: at 150 francs, the cheapest edition of *Ulysses* cost $11.50 – well over $100 today. Signed copies sold at 350 francs.

Nevertheless, demand for Joyce's book grew rapidly, and not only among the literati. By June 1922 it was on sale at Brentano's English language bookshop on Avenue de l'Opéra. Many American tourists wished to bring a copy home with them since the book was banned in the United States.

At Shakespeare and Company, the bill from the printers in Dijon was mounting up. It was then that Hemingway, always keen on a new adventure, came up with an ingenious way of increasing the book's distribution. He would arrange to have copies smuggled into the United States.

The plan was born out of Hemingway's knowledge of the Canadian-American border along the Great Lakes and his acquaintance with a journalist he had known in Chicago with the endearing name of Barney Braverman. Braverman was now working for an advertising agency in Windsor, Ontario and commuted by ferry from his apartment in Detroit. Hemingway was aware of methods employed by bootleggers to illegally import Canadian whiskey into the US. He came up with a plan. Barney would rent a room in Windsor and Beach would mail copies of *Ulysses* to this Canadian address. Braverman would bring them with him to Detroit from where they would be posted on to American subscribers (among them Sherwood Anderson).

It was a slow process. Beach sent 40 books but, before Braverman brought them anywhere, customs duty had to be paid. In Canada, foreign printed matter was levied with a charge of 25 per cent and he faced a bill of $300. Asking to see the customs inspector, Braverman persuaded him the books were cheap novels worth no more than 50 cents each. As a result his customs bill was reduced to $6.50.

Then they had to be taken to Detroit by ferry.

Braverman decided to test the water with one book first. On arrival in Detroit, the customs official asked him to open the copy he had wrapped. Fortunately, the man showed no sign of recognition and let the book through. Over the following weeks, Braverman repeated the process for the other 39 books.

In gratitude for all his help, Beach presented Hemingway with a copy of the book. He wrote to Anderson: 'Joyce has a most god-damn wonderful book' and he told Morley Callaghan that Joyce was 'the greatest writer in the world.'

His enthusiasm, however, may have been influenced by the fact that it was now fashionable, among the literary circle he was beginning to move in, to say you had read Joyce's book. And undoubtedly the young American saw much in the novel that he liked – especially, it seems, the *Penelope* episode. Many years later his copy of *Ulysses* - donated with his papers to the John F Kennedy library in Boston - revealed that only the 50 or so pages of the first half of the book had been cut, as well as those of Molly Bloom's soliloquy. Perhaps that had its own significance, for as his writing matured, Hemingway came to believe that a man must cultivate the feminine side of himself to be able to write both male and female.

Like McAlmon, he was critical of the characterisation of Stephen Dedalus. Dedalus was Joyce himself and therefore a weakness in the novel. As Hemingway saw it, 'the only writing that was any good was what you made up, what you imagined.'[6] By comparison he was highly enthusiastic about the Blooms, regarding Molly as 'the greatest in the world.' Later, in 1932, in a letter to John Dos Passos about writing, Hemingway advised him: '... Don't let yourself slip and get any perfect characters in – no Stephen Daedeluses [*sic*] – remember it was Bloom and Mrs Bloom saved Joyce – that is the only thing could ruin the bastard from being a great piece of literature.'[7]

While Hemingway could be critical of Joyce behind his back, the two never quarrelled (though Hemingway fell out with many other writers). They admired each other as writers,[8] while Joyce saw through the 'tough guy' image that Hemingway liked to portray in public:

> *He's a good writer, Hemingway. He writes as he is. We like him. He's a big, powerful peasant, as strong as a buffalo. A sportsman. And ready to live the life he writes about....But giants of his sort are truly modest; there is much more behind Hemingway's form than people know.*[9]

The two writers were poles apart in many respects, not least in their writing styles; while Joyce was putting everything into his latest work (*Finnegans Wake*) Hemingway was cutting his (*The Sun Also Rises*) down, leaving out adjectives and adverbs he deemed unnecessary.

Even in their manners and mannerisms, the two differed widely. It was the custom in France to call writers by their surname, such as 'Proust.' Joyce, however, insisted on being called 'Mr Joyce.' This seemed to provide a cultural difficulty for some of the more informal Americans and Hemingway is reported to have once called the writer 'Jim,' a name that only Nora was heard to use.[10] Such flippancy was not lost on Joyce. Arriving at Beach's bookshop, Joyce found Hemingway minding things.

'Sylvia is not here,' Hemingway told him.

'Oh... You mean Miss Beach,' said Joyce.

'And Myrsine is not here either,' said Hemingway, ignoring the reprimand.

'Oh… You mean Miss Moschos.'

Beginning to enjoy the encounter, Hemingway added:
'Helene is not here either.'

'Oh… You mean little Miss Moschos,' replied Joyce as
he left the shop.[11]

Hemingway revelled in the way he could be physically
protective of the frailer Joyce. In an interview with *Time*
magazine in the 1950s, he recalled – not without
considerable exaggeration - how helpful he could be when
the two were on a pub- or café-crawl:

> *We would go out to drink and Joyce would fall
> into a fight. He couldn't even see the man so
> he'd say: Deal with him, Hemingway! Deal with
> him!*[12]

As Joyce and Beach were chatting in her bookshop one
day, they discussed the relative physical abilities of
Hemingway and McAlmon. Both agreed that it was the
slighter-looking McAlmon who was the aggressive one
although Hemingway was better built. While Hemingway
liked to be regarded as a tough guy and McAlmon as a
sensitive type, the truth was the other way around.[13]

The person who drew out this sensitive nature of
Hemingway's more than anyone else was Gertrude Stein.
She became a surrogate mother to him, much as Pound
was his surrogate father. Where Pound advised him to use
no superfluous words and to distrust adjectives, Stein
taught him to write freely, letting the words pour out
without thinking too hard about them. The contradictory
advice he received from his surrogate parents seems not
to have caused the young writer much harm.

When Hemingway and his wife first visited the two-
storey apartment at 27 rue de Fleurus where Stein lived

with Alice B Toklas, the protocol was made clear: he would sit with Stein at one end of the room while Hadley would talk to Toklas at the other end. It was the same for any couple who came to their home.

Stein was fat and small. Hemingway estimated that each of her breasts weighed 5kg. She had 'lovely, thick alive immigrant hair' which she would cut shorter over the coming years until it looked like that of a Roman emperor. She had a 'strong German-Jewish face' and beautiful eyes.[14] Her voice commanded attention and she was intelligent, with a flair for words and for self-publicity. She wore loose, comfortable clothes.

Toklas was the more discreet partner, walking behind, carrying the bags. It was she who did the cooking and typed Stein's manuscripts. Toklas had a moustache under a large hooked nose and was a heavy smoker. She combed her hair forward to hide a cyst between her eyebrows.

The two had met in Paris in 1907 and never parted until Stein's death 39 years later. Toklas moved into the apartment in rue de Fleurus which Stein's brother Leo had recently vacated, its rooms decorated with the numerous paintings by Matisse, Cezanne and other French artists that the siblings had collected.

The women regarded themselves as a happily married couple, Toklas sometimes referring to Stein as her husband, Stein sometimes signing letters 'from Gertrude and Alice Stein.' When they visited Natalie Barney's promiscuous salon they stayed together rather than allow themselves be paired off.

Their relationship was carefully balanced. While to the outsider Stein was the dominant partner, it was Toklas who controlled things. Toklas was the diplomat who decided who Stein should see, protecting her from other people's wives, keeping silent so that Stein could converse authoritatively with her guest. Some thought of her as menacing and interfering. But they were devoted to each other and knew precisely each other's role.

The Hemingways' first visit to rue de Fleurus was so successful they invited Stein and Toklas to their apartment where Stein asked to see Hemingway's writings. She offered encouragement and criticism and her advice, coming from someone who had developed a unique modernist writing style, was to help him forge a style of his own.

'Gertrude Stein and me are just like brothers and we see a lot of her,' Hemingway reported back to Sherwood Anderson. And Stein wrote to Anderson: 'They are charming. He is a delightful fellow and I like his talk.'

Nevertheless, Stein was psychologically astute and was constantly weighing up those she met. Like Joyce, she could see through Hemingway.

Hemingway was given an open invitation to call to rue de Fleurus anytime after five in the evening. Stein showed him her work, gave him advice in her inimitable style ('a sentence is not emotional a paragraph is'[15]) and told him that she disliked revising and that she had not achieved the recognition she felt she deserved.

She was jealous of writers who had not praised her. What especially annoyed her was the rivalry threatened by the American poet Ezra Pound and the Irishman James Joyce, both of whom were living close by, the latter allegedly in poverty. Stein claimed that Joyce reminded her of an old woman she had known in San Francisco whose son had struck it rich in the Klondike but who went around wringing her hands exclaiming: 'My poor Joey, my poor Joey, he's got so much money!' Hemingway retold the story to Anderson, adding:

*The damned Irish, they have to moan about
something or other, but you never heard of an
Irishman starving.*[16]

A *Paris Tribune* reporter who visited Stein around this
time was given a brief lesson in American history:

'America made the 20th Century just as England made the
19th. We have given Europe everything. The natural line
of descent is the big four: Poe to Whitman to James to
myself. I am the last.'

'You are the last?' asked the reporter.

'Of course. My reputation is international and is
spreading all the time.'

'There is James Joyce,' said the interviewer.

Stein smiled.

'Joyce is *good*. He is a *good* writer. Let's not say
anything about that. But who started the whole thing?
My first book, *The Making of Americans*, was published
in 1905. That was long before the birth of *Ulysses*. But
Joyce has done something even if his influence is local.
John Synge, another Irish writer, has had his day. Have
some more tea.'[17]

Joyce and Stein encountered each other at a party held by
Eugene Jolas. It was the only occasion on which they
met.[18] As with Joyce's meeting with Proust, little was
said. According to Alice B Toklas, Joyce said: 'How
strange that we share the same *quartier* and have never
met.' To which Stein replied: 'Yes.'[19]

Many years later Maria Jolas recalled, in dialogue, how
Stein upbraided her husband Eugene for his commitment
to Joyce:

> *Miss Stein: Jolas, why do you continue to lay*
> *such emphasis in transition on the work of that*
> *fifth-rate politician, James Joyce? Haven't you*
> *understood yet that the leading English-language*
> *writer today is me, Gertrude Stein?*
>
> *Eugene Jolas: Miss Stein, you will excuse me, but*
> *I do not agree with you. (Jolas rises, walks to the*
> *door, picks up his hat.) Miss Stein, I bid you*
> *good morning. (Exit Jolas.)*[20]

When Hadley became pregnant, the Hemingways sailed
for Toronto where they wanted their baby to be born.
Ernest took with him several copies of *Ulysses.* 'Someday
someone will live here and be able to appreciate the
feeling with which I launched *Ulysses* on the States (not a
copy lost) from this city,' he wrote to Pound.[21]

The downside of the trip was that he had to knuckle
down to the daily grind and duties of a desk reporter on
the *Toronto Star.* The assignments bored him and he
could hardly wait to get back to cover the more exciting
post-war happenings in Europe. His enthusiasm for
literature continued, however, as was evident in a piece
he wrote on the award of the Nobel Prize to WB Yeats in
which he could not resist the opportunity to praise his
American mentor. Yeats, he said, 'has written, with the
exception of a few poems by Ezra Pound, the very finest
poetry of our time.' He would later claim that Yeats was
among his three favourite poets, the others being Pound
and Anonymous.

Hemingway took every opportunity to repay his debt of
gratitude to Stein, even asking her to be godmother to his
son, John. The godfather would be an old Irish friend
Ernest had met while recuperating from his war wounds in
Milan. Eric Dorman-Smith,[22] nicknamed Chink, was a
complex person. Born in his parents' large estate near

Cootehill in Co Cavan (where his best friend was the local doctor's son named John Charles McQuaid, later to become Archbishop of Dublin) and brought up a Catholic, Chink joined the British Army, was wounded twice in Normandy and Belgium and quickly rose through the ranks. The two kept up their friendship and when Chink was in Paris in the summer of 1923, Hemingway introduced him to Beach, Pound and Stein. Chink, however, dreaded the visits to rue de Fleurus, finding Stein too domineering, flaunting her lesbianism.[23]

The christening was at St Luke's Episcopal Chapel in rue de la Grande Chaumière where Giorgio Joyce sang in the choir. The Hemingways had decided their son would be brought up an Episcopalian, the religion of Ernest's mother. For a religious ceremony those officiating were a bizarre mixture. The parents were agnostic, the godfather Catholic and the godmother Jewish. Nineteen-year-old Giorgio Joyce, who played the organ, had never been baptised. At one point in the ceremony, Stein interrupted the Minister to ask her fellow-godparent loudly: 'Chink, what *is* the Apostles Creed?'

Around this time a new literary magazine began to come off the printing presses of Paris. The *Transatlantic Review* had been set up by the English novelist Ford Madox Ford.[24] Pound, as usual, was spending much of his time helping new writers and persuaded Ford to take on the young Hemingway as his assistant.

Ford had just set up the *Review* in the loft of Bill Bird's *Three Mountain Press* at 29 Quai d'Anjou on the Ile-St-Louis. The same printing press was used by McAlmon's *Contact Editions*, which published Joyce and Hemingway; and later by Nancy Cunard who set up *Hours Press, which* published Moore (*Peronnik the Fool*) and Beckett (*Whoroscope*).

The first issue of the *Review*, in January 1924, featured a short story by McAlmon and two of Pound's recent *cantos.* When Hemingway took over as Assistant Editor in time for the second issue, he pulled a fast one on Ford. He persuaded him to publish all of Stein's *The Making of Americans* in serial form – a major commitment since the book ran to some 900 pages.[25] He also urged Stein to extract as much money as possible for the privilege since the magazine was financed by the wealthy Irish-American John Quinn.[26]

In April, 1924, Ford published a literary supplement to the *Transatlantic Review* entitled 'Work in Progress.' It included Joyce's *Mamalujo* (four evangelists) segment of *Finnegans Wake* and was the first fragment of Joyce's new book to be published. Joyce was so taken by the term 'Work in Progress' that he used it as the title of his book until its publication in 1939. Joyce said later that Ford was the book's 'godfather' just as he became godfather to one of Ford's daughters in 1928.

Ford's friendship with Joyce is a plausible explanation for his decision to appoint a Dublin correspondent for the magazine (alongside 'Letters' from Paris and New York, though not from London).[27] He wrote to his daughter, Katherine, who lived in London: 'I really want a Dublin correspondent who will inform the world as to either the political or literary activities of Dublin.'[28] She recommended an Irish journalist named Geoffrey Coulter and her father agreed. Coulter was a staunch republican who had worked for IRA Intelligence and took the anti-Treaty side in the Civil War.[29]

Coulter wrote his Letter as *Litir o Eirinn.* One such contribution was nine pages long. A biographer of Ford suggested that was 'probably more than Ford's readers could stand, but it gave the Review a cosmopolitan style.'[30] Another issue of the magazine featured a short story by Coulter entitled *Decoy*, about guerrilla warfare in Ireland.

The *Transatlantic Review* folded with the premature death of John Quinn in August 1924.[31] It was soon replaced by *This Quarter*, which was co-owned and edited by Ernest Walsh, a Catholic Irish-American,[32] and Ethel Moorhead, a wealthy Scotswoman. It would become one of the most respected of the 'little magazines' but it would also infuriate Hemingway.

True to his adventurous spirit, Hemingway helped Walsh establish the magazine by successfully encouraging well-known writers to contribute. One of the secrets of its success was that it paid well. And one of the contributors Hemingway hustled for was Joyce, whom he persuaded to send Walsh the *Shem* chapter of *Finnegans Wake*.[33]

Like many who were reading extracts of Joyce's latest work as they appeared in magazines, Hemingway was perplexed. 'Joyce is swell,' he wrote to Walsh. 'I would always rather know what it is all about but I like Joyce straight, with orange juice, with Liffey water or what have you.'

That was mild compared with a diatribe against Joyce that Hemingway made behind his back. It can, perhaps, be explained only by Hemingway's obsessive enthusiasm for bullfighting. In a letter to Pound, Hemingway wrote:

> *'In all the other arts, the more measly and shitty the guy, ie Joyce, the greater the success in his art. There is absolutely no comparison in art between Joyce and Maera – Maera by a mile – and then look at the guys. One breeds Giorgios the other gets killed or breeds bulls... I wish to hell I was 16 and had art and valor.'*

Ernest Walsh was a thin, lanky young poet who was suffering from tuberculosis. Hemingway, who had met him in Pound's studio just after his arrival from New

York, described him as 'dark, intense, faultlessly Irish, poetic and clearly marked for death as a character is marked for death in a motion picture.'[34] He regarded Walsh as a con man who traded his consumption for sympathy and sexual favours.

Around this time Hemingway was living beside a sawmill at rue Notre-Dame-des-Champs near rue de Fleurus. If the sawmill was noisy or the baby was crying he would do his writing at the Closerie des Lilas where he was less likely to run into fellow Americans. And one of those he was keen to avoid was McAlmon. He was pleased when McAlmon's Contact Editions brought out *Three Stories and Ten Poems* – his first published work. But he got nothing from it except personal satisfaction and it made him angry to see his drunken publisher vomiting what should have been his royalties.

So when *This Quarter* proclaimed McAlmon as a writer superior to Mark Twain, Hemingway – an admirer of Twain – was furious. He wrote to Walsh: 'Well, you read Huckleberry Finn and if you really, honest to ourselves, believe McAlmon has ever written anything or everything together that deserves to be mentioned in the same room, house, city, continent or magazine, with Huckleberry Finn, I will stop writing because there will be no damn use to write if such a state of things can be.'

After the first four issues, the magazine announced a large award to the contributor whose work would be judged the best. Shortly afterwards, Walsh invited Hemingway to an expensive lunch. Over oysters and excellent wine, Walsh talked of writers they both knew.

'Ezra's a great, great poet,' said Walsh.

'Yes,' said Hemingway, 'and a fine man.'

'Joyce is great,' Walsh said.

'Great,' agreed Hemingway, 'and a good friend.

'I wish his eyes were better,' Walsh said.

'So does he.'

As the meal was drawing to a close, Walsh could hold himself back no longer. 'There's no use beating around the bush,' he said. 'You know you're going to get the award, don't you?'

'I don't think I deserve it, Ernest,' said Hemingway.

'It's strange we have the same name, isn't it?'

'Yes, Ernest,' Hemingway replied. 'It's a name we must both live up to.'

Much later, Hemingway came across Joyce walking along the boulevard St-Germain on his way back from a theatre matinée. Joyce asked him to join him and they sat over dry sherry in the Deux Magots. Joyce asked him if Walsh had promised him the award and Hemingway told him.

'I thought so,' said Joyce.

'Did he promise it to you?' Hemingway asked.

'Yes,' replied Joyce. 'Do you think he promised it to Pound?'

'I don't know.'

'Best not to ask him,' said Joyce.[35]

Walsh had dedicated the first issue of *This Quarter* to Pound. That gave Joyce the opportunity to publicly acknowledge the enormous assistance the American had given him: 'I owe a great deal to his friendly help, encouragement and generous interest in everything that I have written.' Hemingway's tribute was precise: 'There is only one living poet who ranks with Pound and that is William Butler Yeats.'[36]

Walsh continued to nurture Hemingway. In the same issue of *This Quarter* that featured Joyce's piece, Walsh reviewed Hemingway's short story collection *In Our Time*, just published: 'There are lines in Hemingway's stories that come at one reading them as if they had grown in the reader's heart out of an old memory or an old wish to remember.' Hemingway was flattered: 'I only hope I will be able to write the way you say I write,' he wrote Walsh.[37]

A charmer when praised, Hemingway could be vitriolic when damned, and hardly more so than when Walsh's review of *The Torrents of Spring* was highly critical of his satirising of Sherwood Anderson and Ford - both of whom had helped Hemingway's writing career.[38] The review would almost certainly have ended their friendship but Walsh died the same month. Even then, Hemingway could not hold himself back. 'I have known too many good guys die to be able to sweat much from the eyes about the death of a shit.'[39]

In fact Paris seemed to be full of 'an enormous number of shits,' as he told Pound. But he managed to escape them by taking trips to Switzerland (to ski) and to Spain (to watch bullfights).

A Lost Generation

Hemingway had wanted to see a bullfight ever since Stein had told him of her experiences at a *corrida* during the war. He wanted to write about violent death and, with the war over, the only place he could see death up close was in the bullring.

So when, in the late spring of 1923, McAlmon told him he would help finance such a trip, Hemingway needed no persuading. The two men – later to be joined by William Bird – went to *corridas* in Madrid, Seville and Granada. Hemingway saw bullfighting as an exciting ritual, a dance of death, and it marked the end of his apprenticeship as a writer. McAlmon, on the other hand, was appalled at the cruelty of the spectacle (he did, however, admire the way the matadors 'moved beautifully'). The two men argued a lot, their rows fuelled by alcohol, and McAlmon later claimed that Hemingway had made advances to him when they shared an hotel room.

In 1925, McAlmon introduced Hemingway to Lady Duff Twysden, an attractive, seductive English woman, later to become immortalised in literature as Lady Brett Ashley in *The Sun Also Rises*. Born Mary Smurthwaite, she got her title through a failed marriage. Now she was known around Montparnasse as a hard drinker who was at her best in male company. As such she was typical of the new liberated female expatriates in Paris in the 1920s. She soon became one of a group of assorted writers and others that Hemingway enticed to Pamplona for the *fiesta* that July.

After a week of heavy drinking, rows and sexual jealousy, Hemingway returned to Paris to start writing a novel that was eerily close to the reality of those Pamplona days, changing the names only to avoid libel.

As an epigraph to *The Sun Also Rises* Hemingway used the phrase 'You are all a lost generation,' a rebuke made to him by Stein in criticising him and his expatriate friends. It was an expression that has been used and misused ever since.

Asked by a writer friend if his novel reflected the 'Lost Generation,' Hemingway replied:

'Don't take what Gertie says too seriously. How the hell are you going to be lost when you've never been found?' [40]

It was Stein who passed on the phrase to Hemingway, but even she had not created it – much as she would have enjoyed the credit for doing so. She had heard the expression from the proprietor of an hotel in provincial France where she and Alice were staying. Impressed by the enthusiasm and speediness of one of his staff, Stein praised him to the hotelier, saying she had heard you could no longer get young men to work so efficiently. He replied that it was only those who had gone off to the war who were no good. 'C'est une generation perdue,' he said, referring to those young men who had returned disillusioned by what they had seen. Soon afterwards the phrase came to be used to symbolise the American expatriates in Paris who seemed to have lost their belief in life's values. [41] In its most recent incarnation, the phrase has been applied to those young people who grew up knowing only the good times and finding themselves at sea as the economic recession gripped ever more tightly.

In the early 1920s, the 'lost generation' of expatriates lost themselves in the bars and clubs of Montparnasse where the cost of living was becoming cheaper as the franc lost its value. In 1921 $1 was worth five francs; it bought 19 francs in 1924 and 21 francs the following year. A nice meal for two cost two to three francs. An American could live very well in Paris on $5 a day including hotel accommodation (about $50 today).

For Hemingway, who had started out in Paris in a cheap apartment, life became easier as he had short stories published in addition to his journalism. He drank most often at the Dome [42] and at the Dingo. He was capable of drinking as much as anyone, but he despised Americans who sat around in the cafés and drank and talked of what they were *going* to do. In a piece for the *Toronto Star Weekly*, he wrote: 'The scum of Greenwich Village, New York, has been skimmed off and deposited in a large ladlesful [sic] on that section of Paris adjacent to the Café Rotonde.'[43]

The Rotonde is one the best known of the numerous bars and cafés in Montparnasse. Situated where boulevard du Montparnasse meets boulevard Raspail, it faces the Dome across the street. Before the expatriates arrived in large numbers, the two establishments had attracted different types of clientele. The Dome was a small bistro with a horseshoe-shaped zinc counter to one side and a billiard table; it was frequented by working Frenchmen. Across the road the Rotonde, with its larger interior and marble-topped tables, drew a more international clientele, among them Slavs and revolutionaries from Russia and Eastern Europe. Both establishments had large terraces, which were increasingly attracting English-speaking visitors.

By the summer of 1924, this colourful mixture of nationalities and the excited intellectual discussion that ensued on the terraces drew the attention of local people as they made their way to and from the trains at Gare Montparnasse. Many Parisians resented the newcomers, seeing them (as Hemingway did) as lazy time-wasters; and some did not hesitate to show their annoyance. Arthur Power, who drank in both the Rotonde and the Dome, recalled seeing van drivers pull up on the curb and abuse the café clientele. One driver parked his van there every evening, ensuring his slogan - 'Extermination of rats undertaken' - could be clearly seen by the drinkers he so despised.[44]

The manager of the Rotonde, too, had little time for the expatriates, especially the independently minded young American women whom he regarded as little more than prostitutes. When one day he looked out and saw a woman sitting at one of his tables hatless and smoking –

at a time when women ought never to smoke in public and always wore a hat out of doors – he decided he would have to do something about it.

Approaching the woman, he told her that if she wished to smoke she must move inside.

'But why?' she asked. 'The sun is lovely. I am not causing any trouble. I prefer to stay here.'

A crowd gathered. People argued and took sides. Finally the young woman said that if she could not smoke on the *terrasse* she would leave. She walked across the street to the Dome where she asked the manager if she could smoke and sit without a hat in front of *his* café. The manager consented, thus causing the mass migration across the road of virtually the entire Anglo-American colony.[45]

On the weekend of 14 July 1923 (Bastille Day), as Parisians started leaving their city for holidays in the country and by the sea, McAlmon returned from Rambouillet where he had been putting the finishing touches to a novel. As he made his way along boulevard du Montparnasse towards the Dome, he came upon the aftershock of an 'event' that would be the main talking point in the bars and cafés for a long time.

An excited group of Americans, headed by Peggy Guggenheim and Laurence Vail, told him the American writer Malcolm Cowley had assaulted the manager of the Rotonde and had been arrested. Cowley was a radical who liked the Rotonde because it was patronised by revolutionaries, but he resented its *patron* because of the way he treated American women. It appeared that Cowley and the Dadaist Tristan Tzara had been drinking heavily at the Dome that day and the American decided he wanted to make a 'significant gesture of violence.' He crossed the street to the Rotonde where he struck the manager and was duly imprisoned.

The following day, McAlmon led a well-dressed and sober deputation of expatriates to the *gendarmerie* where they defended Cowley, swearing that the *patron* had started it all. McAlmon had little time for Cowley, whom he regarded as naïve and 'fairly slow on the uptake.' But he had less for the Rotonde's manager. In court, he told a judge that the *patron* was renowned for his evil disposition. With only his own waiters to back him – as against a dozen or so of McAlmon's 'detached observers' – the *patron* lost all credibility and Cowley was duly released.[46]

---

[1] Before the war Hemingway was a reporter with the Kansas City Star, whose style guide influenced his future writing.

[2] On the 9 January 1922. A few months earlier Joyce had been staying at Number 71, a hundred metres down on the opposite side of the street, in a flat lent to him by Valery Larbaud.

[3] Hemingway: *A Moveable Feast* 46.

[4] Fitch: *Sylvia Beach and the Lost Generation* 115.

[5] Shaw's letter was first published in Beach: *Shakespeare and Company* 52.

[6] Lynn: *Hemingway* 161.

[7] Idem. 458.

[8] Joyce regarded Hemingway's short story *A Clean Well-Lighted Place* as one of the best ever written. (Power: *Conversations with James Joyce* 123).

[9] Joyce interview with Danish journalist quoted in Ellmann 695.

[10] Djuna Barnes was the only person other than Nora who was allowed to call him Jim. (Sharon Benstock: *Women of the West Bank* 231).

[11] Fitch: *Sylvia Beach and the Lost Generation.*

[12] *Time* magazine 13 December 1954, quoted in Ellmann 695.

[13] Beach: *Shakespeare and Company* 78.

[14] Hemingway: *A Moveable Feast* 17.

[15] Stein: *How to Write.* Her writing broke all the rules: 'Now what is a sentence. A sentence hopes that you are very well and happy. It is very selfish. They like to be taken away. A sentence can be taken care of....'

[16] Mellow: *Hemingway*, page 149.

[17] Interview published in *The Paris Tribune*, 7 April, 1931.

[18] According to Stein, Djuna Barnes was to have introduced Joyce to her,

but she showed up at Stein's apartment without him (*Djuna Barnes Interviews*, Sun & Moon Press, Maryland, 1985).

[19] Ellmann interview Toklas 1954.

[20] Published in *A James Joyce Miscellany* by The James Joyce Society, 1957 and quoted by Kay Boyle in *Being Geniuses Together* 296n.

[21] Mellow: *Hemingway* 241.

[22] Dorman-Smith , who is regarded as the model for the hero of *Across the River and Into the Trees*, rose through the ranks to become Major commanding the British at the Italian Piave Front. He was demoted and when he retired to Cootehill, changed his name to O'Gowan (the Irish for Smith) and helped the IRA in their campaign against British troops in Northern Ireland. See Lavinia Greacen: *Chink– a Biography*.

[23] Greacen: *Chink: A Biography* 71.

[24] Born Ford Madox Hueffer, he changed his name in 1919 when German connections were unpopular. He had founded *The English Review* in 1928, publishing WB Yeats and Wyndham Lewis among others.

[25] In the magazine it ran for nine installments amounting to 111 pages.

[26] Quinn had already bought the manuscript of *Ulysses*. When the two met for the first time in October 1923, Joyce regretted the price at which he had sold the MS.

[27] Hemingway was among the contributors to Letter from New York while Philippe Soupault wrote Lettre de Paris.

[28] Poli: *Ford Madox Ford and the Transatlantic Review* 35.

[29] Coulter had an MA degree from Trinity College. He later worked for the Sinn Féin paper *An Phoblacht* and became one of the first journalists to join the *Irish Press*.

[30] Poli: *Ford Madox Ford and the Transatlantic Review* 123.

[31] The previous January Quinn had sold his *Ulysses* manuscript to a dealer named Rosenbach for $1,975 (just over $20,000 today).

[32] According to McAlmon, Walsh told him he had been born in Cuba of Irish parents and brought up a Catholic. He went on to father a child by Kay Boyle and died from TB in 1926.

[33] Hemingway also told Liam O'Flaherty that the magazine might publish a limited edition of one of his short stories. (Letter October 1929).

[34] Hemingway: *A Moveable Feast* 90.

[35] Idem. 93-95.

[36] Mellow: *Hemingway* 287.

[37] Idem. 315.

[38] It is thought that Hemingway wrote *The Torrents of Spring* in an attempt to break his contract with Boni and Liveright, Anderson's publishers, and move to Scribners, publishers of F. Scott Fitzgerald. If true. the ruse, in which Fitzgerald was a co-conspirator, worked.

[39] Mellow: *Hemingway* 337.

[40] Putnam: *Paris was our Mistress* 129.

[41] The American writer Mathew Josephson saw the period differently, describing it as 'the era of the Lost Generation that was never really lost but enjoyed a prodigious success.' (In a Forward to Ford ed: *The Left Bank Revisited*).

[42] In his short story *Mr and Mrs Smith* he wrote of the couple drinking at the Dome and 'avoiding the Rotonde across the street because it is so full of foreigners.'

[43] *American Bohemians in Paris a Weird Lot*, Toronto Star Weekly, 25 March, 1922.

[44] Power: *Conversations with James Joyce*, 30.

[45] Charters: *This must be the Place* 5.

[46] Smoller: *Adrift Among Geniuses*, 106-107.

Chapter Six
Moore Is The Man For It

Sylvia Beach was chatting to Joyce in her bookshop when she noticed a tall, elderly man with a large face and pink cheeks gazing at the books in the window. As he stepped into the shop, she left Joyce to greet her new customer who introduced himself as George Moore. He told her that their mutual friend, Nancy Cunard, had promised to bring him to meet her but he had to leave for England the next day and could not wait.

As she was talking to Moore she noticed him glancing several times at Joyce. But she did not introduce the two writers since Joyce, who was recovering from an eye operation, had told her he didn't feel like meeting anyone.

Eventually Moore left 'rather reluctantly,' according to Beach. Joyce asked her: 'Who was that?' and when she told him he said he would like to have thanked him for his kindness in obtaining for him the 'King's Purse' some years earlier.

Moore felt much the same. A few days later he wrote to Beach from London wondering if the man in the shop was James Joyce since he would like to have met him.[1]

McAlmon, who had been going through his post in the back of the bookshop, noticed the absence of engagement between the two writers:

> *Whatever either thought of the other's work certainly was not expressed. They were both past*

> *masters at the art of blague and blarney and*
> *courteous formality in the old Irish manner, and*
> *this would have prevailed.*[2]

It was May 1921 and Moore was on one of his frequent trips to Paris. Touching 70, he divided his time between his family mansion (Moore Hall in Co Mayo) and homes in Dublin, London and Paris (where he had first settled in 1873). Now an established author and raconteur, Moore was revisiting old friends, among them Édouard Dujardin, the French writer credited with developing the concept of the interior monologue, who was living at Fontainebleau. Joyce had long known that Dujardin was a friend of Moore's and it is likely it was his knowledge of their friendship that influenced him, while in Paris in 1903, to buy a copy of *Les Lauriers sont Coupés* - a decision which was to have a profound effect on his writing and on modern literature.

Moore enjoyed coming to Paris to see old friends, among them the artist Claude Monet and the writer Paul Valéry. But one writer he had no desire to contact was Joyce. Each kept the other at a distance. While there was no love lost between them – Moore was no Joycean disciple – their lives intertwined to such a degree that their connection cannot be ignored.

That relationship – if such it can be called – began in hostility in 1901. Moore had just moved to Dublin when one of his servants answered a knock at the door of his home in Ely Place and was handed a pamphlet. The young man who delivered it was Stanislaus Joyce, younger brother of its author. The leaflet was entitled *The Day of the Rabblement*. It featured an attack on the Irish literary theatre, in particular on WB Yeats and Moore, written by a 19-year-old university student, James Joyce.

Moore had been introduced to Yeats by his cousin, Edward Martyn (who lived at Tillyra Castle in Co Galway and was a neighbour of Lady Gregory). His interest in the literary renaissance deepened to the degree that he collaborated with Yeats and supported the Irish language movement although, like Yeats, he could neither write nor speak Irish.

Their work together led to considerable tension. Nancy Cunard, in her *Memories of George Moore*, recalled Moore telling her how the two men, both staying at Tillyra Castle, fought over their collaboration on *Diarmuid and Grania*, a play which both wanted to write in Irish yet were unable to do so. Out of frustration, Moore told Yeats he would rather write the play in French. In the middle of the night, Yeats came to Moore's bedroom, sat at the end of his bed and advised him to go ahead; Lady Gregory would then translate it into English, it would be given to Tadhg O Donnchadha[3] to translate into Irish, then turned into Hiberno-English by Lady Gregory after which Yeats would finally improve upon it.[4]

The literary movement did not appeal to everyone, however, and one of its critics was Joyce. He was closer to Europe than to Celtic Ireland. As a committed Ibsenite, he took heart in Yeats's claim that the Irish Literary Theatre would produce plays by continental as well as Irish dramatists. But when *Diarmuid and Grania* was performed Joyce wrote an article condemning the Theatre for its parochialism. Unable to have the piece accepted by the college magazine at the Royal University, Joyce published it himself (together with his friend Francis Skeffington who was having similar difficulties over an article advocating gender equality at the university). *The Day of the Rabblement* attacked the Irish Literary Theatre for succumbing to 'the trolls,' Yeats for being too fond of the aesthetic, and Moore for failing to keep up with the modern novel.

Joyce twisted the knife again in *Gas from a Burner*, his

1912 broadside against the publishers Maunsel & Company.[5] He wrote of Moore as a 'Genuine Gent/ That lives on his property's ten per cent.' He also had Malachi Mulligan, in *Ulysses*, refer to Moore as a 'lecturer on French letters to the youth of Ireland,' a snide reference to the older man's renowned promiscuity.

Unsurprisingly, Joyce was never invited to Moore's 'at homes' on Saturdays in Ely Place, something the younger writer resented, all the more because his friends Padraic Colum and Oliver St John Gogarty were regular guests.

George Moore told George Russell (Also popularly referred to as AE) he had not taken offence at Joyce's *Rabblement* pamphlet, finding it 'preposterously clever.'[6] But when, in 1916, it was suggested he might help get Joyce a Civil List grant, Moore was decidedly lacking in enthusiasm. The campaign was spearheaded by Pound. He persuaded Maud Cunard, mother of Nancy, to send copies of Joyce's books to the Prime Minister's office, and he managed to get Yeats to write a letter of tribute. With Moore, however, he was not so successful. Moore's letter praised little of Joyce's work - excepting the short story *The Dead* which he said he wished he had written - then went on to suggest that the best thing the Prime Minister (Asquith) could do for the Irish would be to treat them as the Pope did. Only in a post scriptum did Moore get round to what was to have been the point of his letter: 'PS I am sure, from a literary point of view, Joyce is deserving of help.'[7]

Despite his criticisms, however, Joyce admired both Yeats and Moore. He was so impressed by Moore and Martyn's collaborative play *The Bending of the Bough* that he borrowed the same theme for his own *A Brilliant Career*.[8] But while he made a point of meeting Yeats the following year, along with other writers of the literary renaissance, it was almost 30 years before Joyce was to talk to Moore, and then only when it was clear the older man had not long to live.

Moore had a distinguished and intriguing family history.
His great great-grandfather, a Protestant, converted to
Catholicism when he married an Irish Catholic in Spain
and, using his wife's connections with the Wild Geese,[9]
made a fortune in the wine import business. He used his
wealth to build Moore Hall in Co Mayo in 1792. His son,
a noted historian, wrote about the French revolution, a
book that was to influence hugely his great grandson
George Moore and to encourage him to become a writer.
The historian's son, the writer's grandfather John
Moore, could claim to have been the first president of
the Republic of Ireland - or at least of Connaught - for a
few days in 1798 after French forces had landed at Killala
and, assisted by local rebels, defeated the British at
Castlebar. The writer inherited Moore Hall and its 12,000
acres (with a rent capability of £5,000) when he was only
18. Such, briefly, is how George Moore the novelist came
to be one of the few Catholic landlords of his time.

It also explains why, when he left Moore Hall for Paris at
the age of 21, Moore did so (unlike Arthur Power)
accompanied by his valet. Like Arthur Power though, his
personal wealth gave him the freedom to pursue whatever
he wished. He, too, had been educated in England; and his
ambition was to become a painter. And like Power, he
would remain a bachelor for the rest of his days. Unlike
Power, however, Moore got a lot more value from his
bachelorhood, for he was to become renowned for his
relationships and sexual dalliances with numerous and
beautiful women. By another coincidence, one of the first
female friendships he enjoyed in his early days in Paris -
some 20 years before Arthur Power was born - was with a
woman who was directly descended from the Bonapartes
and indirectly from the Wyse family of Co Waterford -
neighbours with whom the Powers would later socialise.

Madame Marie Ratazzi was a granddaughter of Lucien

Bonaparte, Napoleon's brother. Her mother had been married to Thomas Wyse[10] of Waterford, a man who advocated a multi-denominational education system for Ireland and who was to become a significant figure in the history of Irish education.

Ratazzi was renowned for her affairs and was one of many aristocratic French women Moore sought out after he had decided against painting as a career. In 1876, she invited Moore to a masked ball in her Paris mansion. But she was not the one he bedded that night. Whoever it was, Moore wrote to his mother that he had been granted 'the most certain of all proofs' that a woman could love him. It was the start of a series of relationships that would last his lifetime.

As his friendship with writers such as Mallarmé and artists like Manet and Dégas developed, and as his own writing progressed, so did Moore's affairs with women. He dined twice a week at the Champs-Elysées home of the Princesse de la Temoille who adored him for his manners; then, if the evening ended early, he would make his way to Montmartre and the lowliest of Parisian cafés - the Nouvelle Athènes in Pigalle - where he would drink beer with artists and prostitutes and 'scream the beastliest and slangiest French to groups of bohemians.'[11] But Moore, who never over-indulged in drink, was observing everything around him. The café, he later claimed, was his 'academy of fine arts.'

Moore's first meeting with Ivan Turgenev in Paris almost exactly parallels Power's with Joyce. Moore came across the Russian writer in 1876 at a students' ball, most likely at the same dance hall where Power waited for his date, the Bal Bullier in Montparnasse. Turgenev wanted to talk to Moore about Swinburne but Moore had other designs. He preferred to dance with a young woman whose name was on his card. Afterwards, the two writers resumed their discussions. (Moore was to model *The Field* on Turgenev's *Sportsman's Sketches*.)[12]

The similarities between Moore and Power stop there, however, for Moore was by far the more complex person. Physically unattractive,[13] many women found him enchanting, mainly because of his impeccable manners, his ability to make brilliant conversation and his wit. Yet he could be extraordinarily vulgar, rude and offensive. He told one woman: 'How I regret, for your sake, that I'm impotent.' He asked another whose husband had just died: 'How are you enjoying your widowhood?'

He was always asking his women friends to tell him their innermost thoughts, imploring even those he had never met to treat him as a confessor. He corresponded passionately with a widow, beseeching her to 'write the thoughts that pass through your mind, however "naughty" they may be, and I hope they will be very naughty.' He told her she should have no fear that anyone else would see her letters - then read them to friends at dinner parties.

Moore's interest in women was instinctive and to him sex was something exquisitely beautiful and desirable. He explained his feelings about such matters in his autobiographical *Ave*:

> *I am penetrated through and through by an*
> *intelligent, passionate, dreamy interest in sex,*
> *going much deeper than the mere rutting instinct,*
> *and turn to women as a plant does to the light, as*
> *unconsciously, reading them through every pore,*
> *and my writings are my exhalations that follow*
> *the inspiration.*

Many women wrote to Moore asking him to give his opinion of something they had written and often Moore ended up collaborating with them. When John Oliver Hobbes wrote to ask if his novel might make a good play, Moore replied that it would certainly not. But when he heard that 'Hobbes' was in fact the nom de plume of an attractive American heiress, Pearl Craigie, he wrote another letter expressing great interest in her. The two subsequently met and, as almost invariably happened with Moore, he fell in love.[14]

He enjoyed the double entendre. When an American woman journalist asked him to write an article for the magazine she was writing for, he wrote back: 'J'aimerais tant etre sous la meme couverture que vous' ('I would so much like to be under the same cover as you'). [15]

Sometimes it was the women who did the seducing. Méry Laurent, mistress of Mallarmé and formerly mistress of Manet, invited Moore to visit her and discuss her difficulties in finding a real lover who would have the time to devote to her. As Moore told the story in *Memoirs of My Dead Life*, Méry led Moore to her bedroom. There, Moore seems to have been so distracted by the notion that he was being invited to lie in the same arms that both Manet and Mallarmé had lain that Méry grew tired of waiting and told him: 'I don't think I'll detain you any longer in my bedroom.'[16]

Many of Moore's 'affairs' found their way into his fiction, making it more difficult for those who knew him to separate the real from the imagined.

In his later years, Moore gained a reputation of being a 'dirty old man,' pinching women's bottoms and putting his hand inside their jacket to fondle their breasts. But as he looked back over the years he was proud to boast that there had been only one great love in his life: Maud Cunard.[17]

They met in 1894. Moore was 41, Maud a 22-year-old American beauty, and the love that ensued lasted until his death even as Maud moved in and out of other affairs.

Moore was flattered by her attention and wrote home to his brother Maurice: 'What she could see in me to rave about I cannot think - a blasé roué like me, rotten with literature and art to which Wagnerism has lately been added...'

Moore had been introduced to the music of Wagner by Edward Martyn. Another Wagner enthusiast was the French writer Édouard Dujardin who, like Wagner, was anti-Semitic, but Moore - who did not share his views - did not let that get in the way of a close friendship.

In 1894, the three went to Bayreuth for the annual Wagner music festival. But it was more than music that Moore had in mind, for he arranged to meet his latest interest on his return journey at the Savoie spa resort of Aix-les-Bains ('Aches-les-Pains' as Joyce appropriately punned it in *Finnegans Wake*).

Walking together in the hills above Lac du Bourget, he recalled later, Maud would stop and say: 'You can make love now to me if you like.' But it is unlikely the two had a full sexual relationship before Maud married the shipping magnate, Sir Bache Cunard, the following year. Much later he wrote in a letter: 'For a whole year I was the lover of an American girl and when she was married she was a virgin (technically).' The suggestion of sexual intimacy without total intercourse may be clarified by a comment he made to a woman friend several years later: '...kisses placed within the nest of love are more intimate and exciting than the mere act of love which grocers and their mates perform at midnight...'[18]

Maud's marriage, far from quenching Moore's desire, only served to inflame it. Within months the couple spent a few days together in Scotland and, seven months later, a girl, Nancy, was born.

It is unlikely that Moore was the father of Nancy - but he liked to believe so. Years later, when Nancy asked him about it, Moore answered that only her mother knew. But when Nancy said she intended to bring up the matter with Lady Cunard, Moore replied quickly: 'Oh my God! Never ask your mother that!'

In 1910, Maud joined Moore in Bayreuth, after which Moore's role as lover was supplanted by the affections of a man six years her junior - the musician Thomas Beecham. In a reference to both Beecham's career and his family dynasty, Moore described him as 'the owner of an orchestra whose father sells pills which rouse music in the insides of lady's maids...'[19]

Thereafter, the writer devoted more of his time to young Nancy, doting on her as if she were indeed his daughter.

Nancy married in 1916, but separated from her husband 18 months later. She had been unfaithful in her marriage and thereafter was regarded as a nymphomaniac. Her lovers included the surrealist painter Tristan Tzara and the writer/painter Wyndham Lewis. Moore was well aware of her promiscuity; it affected his relationship with Maud, who avoided meeting him since she could not bear to be told what she already knew about her daughter.

The relationship between mother and daughter deteriorated steadily to the point that, in 1920, Nancy decided to go and live in Paris.

Moore often visited Nancy in her apartment overlooking the Seine at rue le Regrattier on the Ile St Louis, decorated with sketches by Wyndham Lewis. There, Moore met up with Nancy's many friends, among them the American journalist Janet Flanner who was writing for the New Yorker and her fellow-journalist and lover Solita Solano. The three women went everywhere together, calling themselves 'three happily unmarried women' in reference to their previous marriages as well as their newfound friendship.

In 1923, Moore and Nancy spent Christmas together in Paris. Nancy arranged a celebratory dinner for twelve in honour of Moore in an upstairs room at the Café Rotonde. The group included Dolly Wilde, the sculptor Brancusi, the poet Tristan Tzara and a beautiful young American, Mary Reynolds (lover of Marcel Duchamp and later to be a friend of Samuel Beckett). Moore was in his element as he sat between two beautiful singers - Yvonne Georges and Clotilde Vail.

Nancy thought highly of Moore. Long after his death, she published *Memories of GM* - a warm account of their times together. One anecdote that remained unpublished describes, in a beautiful and entirely believable way, how once she stood naked before the old man, at his request. Moore's biographer, Adrian Frazier, suggests the incident may have taken place during the same Christmas time as the 1923 party in the Rotonde.

> *Now, suddenly, something within me said: 'Do this!' and without more ado, facing away from him, I took off all my clothes, standing motionless a few feet from where he sat. How lightly, how easily that came about. My clothes left me, lying in a graceful summer pool on the floor, as if they had slipped away of themselves.*[20]

Nancy said Moore had a 'fresh impulsiveness' which she associated with the Irish, although she did not see the same trait in either Yeats (whom she met only once) or Joyce (three times). She often asked Moore to tell her about Ireland, but he would not. 'Oh my dear Nancy, that is a subject I cannot go into.' She asked him about the burning of Moore Hall by republicans during the civil war in 1923 but 'only great sadness came into his face as he muttered something indistinct.'

In 1926, during a visit to Nancy's apartment, Moore met her latest lover, the Surrealist poet Louis Aragon. Moore could not restrain himself from attacking modern writers and artists but he left on good terms with Aragon who said the Irishman had expressed himself with such finesses.

Not so in the case of his friend, Monet. Calling to see him at Giverney, Moore was shown the artist's enormous canvases of water lilies. Afterwards, Moore commented, in a letter to a friend: 'It is difficult to discriminate between these paintings and wallpaper.... A little time is required.'

Moore could not take to Proust either. 'He writes like a man trying to plough a field with a pair of knitting needles,' he told Nancy. But he accepted that Proust would find his proper place in literature - and Joyce, too. But he wondered what readers in the year 2000 would think of Joyce.

While the *Rabblement* pamphlet incident left any relationship between Moore and Joyce considerably strained, over the years each admired and benefited from the other. It was Moore's *Vain Fortune* that gave Joyce the idea for writing *The Dead*. And while living in Trieste, Joyce started translating Moore's short stories *Celibates* into Italian. He gave one of the stories, *Mildred Lawson*, to Nora to read, hoping she would begin to appreciate his own writing since the story ended inconclusively. Her reaction: 'That man doesn't know how to finish a story.'[21]

One of Moore's most virulent and personal attacks on

Joyce happened only weeks after the publication of
Ulysses. Talking to the American playwright Barrett
Clark at the Restaurant Voltaire in Paris on 25 April,
1922, Moore described Joyce as 'a sort of Zola gone to
seed.' He told Clark: 'Joyce, Joyce, why he's nobody -
from the Dublin docks: no family, no breeding.' *His
Portrait of the Artist* was 'entirely without style or
distinction' – he had done the same things, but much
better, in *The Confessions of a Young Man*. On *Ulysses*,
Moore told Clarke he had been sent a copy of the novel:
'I was told I must read it, but how can one plow through
such stuff? I read a little here and there, but, oh my God,
how bored I got! Probably Joyce thinks that because he
prints all the dirty little words he is a great novelist. You
know, of course, he got his ideas from Dujardin?'[22]

There could be no denying that Moore's friend had
influenced Joyce. Éduard Dujardin's *Les Lauriers Sont
Coupés* had little plot but a lot of style in which the
narrator describes the stream of thoughts that are going
through his head. Dujardin, in turn, had developed his
'Interior Monologue' technique under the influence of
Richard Wagner.

Where earlier composers of operas used the aria to
describe the emotions of their characters, Wagner wrote
very long monologues. Dujardin, who was editor of the
Revue Wagnerien, was fascinated by Wagner's method
and saw the composer's monologues as an extension of
the Shakespearean soliloquy.[23]

Moore, too, was a Wagnerite and he experimented with
Dujardin's technique in his short story collection *The
Untilled Field*,[24] Moore had great respect for Lauriers but
later he described the Interior Monologue as old-
fashioned.[25]

Joyce used Moore's collection as a model for his own
short stories in *Dubliners*. He frequently acknowledged

Dujardin's influence on his writing but he had little time for the adulation of Wagner.

Moore and Joyce were spotted together in Paris on a couple of occasions in 1922 but the two communicated only with their eyes. One evening Moore was dining with Barrett Clark and his wife at Foyot's restaurant when Joyce entered and sat down. Joyce had a patch over one eye, but Moore was convinced the other eye was looking directly at him. Moore stared back, then inquired in a stage whisper if that was Joyce and if so how did he make his living.[26]

On St Patrick's Day 1929, Moore asked his friend William Magee (who wrote under the pseudonym John Eglinton) to include an article on Joyce in his series of Irish literary portraits. His request was not entirely gracious, for there was a sting in its tail. He suggested a comparison between Joyce and Yeats and he alluded to two types of Irish writers: 'Those who think of Ireland as a wash tub, into which all the neighbourhood dirty linen may be thrown, and those who think of it as a vase that collects nothing except perhaps a little dust.'[27]

When eventually the two men spoke to each other, it was neither in Dublin nor Paris but in London. Joyce and Nora were holidaying in England in September 1929 when they decided to visit Moore in his home in Ebury Street. He wanted to ask Moore for a preface for an English translation of Dujardin's *Lauriers* (Moore agreed but later reneged on his promise). Afterwards, Moore described their meeting in letters to William Magee and the French writer Louis Gillet.

> *[Joyce] was distinguished, courteous, respectful, and I was the same; he seemed anxious to accord me the first place. I demurred, and declared him first in Europe. We agreed that our careers were not altogether dissimilar, and he added "Paris*

has played an equal part in our lives."

A few days later the two men met again over dinner and they talked of their mutual friend Dujardin. Joyce was offended when Moore asked him how the action or the thought of *Ulysses* was advanced by associating the 'minor' acts of Bloom with those of *Ulysses*. Joyce answered: 'I see I am on my defense.' Moore apologised. When Joyce offered to send him a French translation of *Ulysses*, Moore accepted graciously, but added: 'I hope you don't mind me reminding you that I can read English.' To which Joyce smiled 'a hesitating smile, reminding me of La Gioconda.'[28]

Joyce sent the book anyway but Moore managed to read no more than 60 pages. It is likely he had not even read the novel in English, for he never referred in his letters to Joyce of his own appearance in Episode Nine (*Scylla & Charybdis*) where a character comments about the future writing of Ireland's national epic and suggests that 'Moore is the man for it.' Nor that 'Moore is Martyn's wild oats.'[29]

The two writers never met again. 'Old men have a right to their anger,' Joyce told Beach. The tension between them should have ended with Moore's death in 1933. But when Joyce sent a funeral wreath inscribed simply: 'To George Moore from James Joyce,' he was vexed that his gesture did not receive coverage in the newspapers.[30] After a flurry of letters to Weaver and others in London, Moore's executor apologised.

Few of Moore's friends attended his funeral.

---

[1] Beach: *Shakespeare and Company* 72.

[2] McAlmon: *Being Geniuses Together* 223.

[3] Cork-born Irish language poet and scholar (1874-1949).

[4] Cunard: *Memories of GM* 95.

[5] Maunsel & Company refused to publish *Dubliners* on the grounds that it was actionable. Joyce left Ireland and never returned.

[6] Frazier: *George Moore* 318.

[7] Joyce was awarded a Civil List grant of £100 in August 1916.

[8] Joyce wrote the play in 1900, dedicating it to himself. Only a fragment remains.

[9] Irish soldiers serving in armies of other nations during the 18th century.

[10] Sir Thomas Wyse, had left his native Waterford to do the grand tour of Europe. While in Rome he met Letizia Bonaparte, daughter of Lucien, whom he married in 1821. See Burke's *Irish Family Records* for 1976 and *The Spurious Brood* by Olga Bonaparte-Wyse. They had two boys, Alfred and William, both surnamed Bonaparte-Wyse. The marriage lasted only six years, after which neither Mr Wyse nor Madame Bonaparte-Wyse saw each other again. Madame's second marriage (to a British army general) resulted in further offspring, among them a daughter, born in 1833, who used the name Marie Studholmine Letitia Bonaparte-Wyse. As she grew older she became renowned for her eccentricities and her friendships with revolutionaries. As a result, Napoleon the Third expelled her to Aix-les-Bains in Savoie, then part of the kingdom of Piedmont-Sardinia. Her second marriage (of three) was to an Italian politician, Count Urbano Ratazzi, who was four times Prime Minister in Italy. She was a prolific writer - poet, novelist and biographer - and wrote articles under many pseudonyms.

[11] Letter to his mother.

[12] Frazier: *George Moore* 62.

[13] Manet, who painted Moore, described him as looking like a squashed egg yolk with a lopsided face. The American novelist Gertrude Atherton, who knew Moore in Paris, saw him as having 'a long colourless face that looked like a codfish crossed by a satyr.' Yeats described him as 'a man carved out of a turnip, looking out of astonished eyes.'

[14] Frazier: *George Moore* 231.

[15] Huddleston: *Paris Salons, Cafés, Studios* 246.

[16] Frazier: *George Moore* 170.

[17] Maud Cunard, née Burke, was the grand-niece of the Irish patriot Robert Emmett.

[18] Letter to Hilda Hawthorne, granddaughter of Nathaniel Hawthorne, November 1907.

[19] Letter to Dujardin, 25 August, 1910, quoted in Frazier.

[20] Frazier: *George* Moore 437.

[21] Joyce to Stanislaus Joyce, 19 January 1905 (Ellmann ed., *Letters of James Joyce Vol. 2*, 77).

[22] Clarke: *Intimate Portraits* (Ellmann 529).

[23] Dujardin explained his approach in a 1931 essay called Interior

Monologue: 'Just as a page of a Wagner score is most often a succession of undeveloped motifs, each of which expresses an impulse of the soul, Interior Monologue is a succession of short sentences each of which also expresses an impulse of the soul, being alike in that they are not linked together according to a rational order but according to a purely emotional order, irrespective of all intellectual arrangement.'

[24] Moore used the method in *The Lake*. *The Untilled Field* short stories first appeared in Irish as 'An tUr–Ghort' with his own name in Irish – Seorsa O Mordha – on the cover. He had written it in English, then had it translated. But when he had one of the stories translated back into English by an Irish scholar he was delighted with the improvement on his own English. However, Moore soon became disillusioned with his hope for a language revival. In 1888 he wrote to Dujardin that 'the Celtic Renascence does not exist – it is a myth…' (Declan Kiberd: *George Moore's Gaelic Lawn Party* published in *The Way Back,* Wolfhound Press, Dublin, 1987.

[25] In 1930 Moore told Joyce: 'I know nothing of the question which apparently agitates France, the discovery of the *monologue interieure*. In England we don't believe that any discovery has been made. We think, rightly or wrongly, that the *monologue interieure* existed from time immemorial.' (Letter from Moore to Joyce 30 May 1930).

[26] Hone: *The Life of George Moore* 376.

[27] Moore to Magee, 17 March, 1929 (Frazier 455).

[28] Frazier: *George Moore* 456.

[29] Idem. 457.

[30] Letter to Weaver 29 January, 1933 (Ellmann ed., *Letters of James Joyce Vol. 3,* 267). Joyce told Padraic Colum: 'Not only was all mention of this absent from the list handed to the press but no member of the family thought it fit within a month to acknowledge receipt of it.' (Letter to Colum, 19 February, 1933).

A Little Circle Of Kindred Minds

Chapter Seven
Padraic And Mary
What-Do-You-Colum

Padraic and Mary Colum were walking near the Eiffel
Tower when, turning a corner, they noticed another
couple coming towards them. Padraic saw it was Joyce
and called his name. Joyce looked up but it was obvious
he could hardly see and it was Nora who recognised them.
Joyce was delighted they were in Paris and explained that
he and Nora were on their way to keep an appointment.
But would they come to his apartment for dinner that
evening?

The Colums readily accepted the invitation. They had
both known Joyce in their younger days in Dublin, Mary
having matriculated with Joyce at the Royal University
in Dublin. Now, towards the end of 1924, they were
curious to see how exile had affected him, for they, too,
had in their own way become exiles.

Padraic Colum first met Joyce at an evening in Lady
Gregory's. In 1901, Dublin was a small city and the
young Colum had already heard about the arrogant young
student who, at the age of 19, had written a review of
Ibsen's *When We Dead Awaken* and a pamphlet entitled
The Day of the Rabblement attacking the National
Theatre. Now here was that same student, seated beside
his friend Oliver St John Gogarty, taking tea in the home
of one of the theatre's directors while she discussed future
productions with another director, William Butler Yeats.
Lady Gregory later asked Joyce to write something for
'our little theatre.' But it was to be Colum who would do

the writing, for, although Joyce aspired to an independent Ireland, he had no time for the 'Celtic revival'.

A certain degree of jealousy pervaded the early years of Colum's friendship with Joyce. When in 1903 Joyce heard that AE had predicted that Colum would be 'our principal literary figure in ten years' he approached Colum one evening as the two were leaving the National Library. Raising the issue of the literary revival, Joyce remarked contemptuously: 'I distrust all enthusiasms.' He asked to see a play Colum had written, returning it a few days later with the comment: 'Rotten from the foundation up!' However, Joyce later acknowledged that Colum was not without ability.[1]

So it is no surprise that Colum and Joyce went separate ways, one looking inward to folklore and nationalism, the other looking out towards modernism, experimentalism and internationalism. While Joyce lived 'in sin' in Trieste and then avoided the war by fleeing to neutral Switzerland, Colum - a devout and practicing Catholic whose father led the riots against Synge's *Playboy* in the Abbey Theatre in 1907 - joined the Irish Volunteers, collecting guns from Erskine Childers's yacht 'Asgard' when it landed at Howth. He married Mary Maguire, the nationalist and feminist daughter of a police inspector in Sligo, and they settled into their home in Donnybrook in south Dublin where they held 'reunions' in the French salon style (but whose emphasis gradually changed from literature and art to politics and self-government).

Despite the friction between them, Colum and Joyce kept in touch by letter and during fleeting visits Joyce made to Dublin, once while he was establishing the Volta cinema in 1909, another three years later during one of his difficult meetings with Maunsel & Company over the publication of *Dubliners*. On that occasion Joyce was expecting to be given a set of proofs for correction, since George Roberts of Maunsel's had promised to publish the book. Instead, Roberts reneged on the agreement, insisting the risk of libel action was too great.[2] Joyce enlisted the support of Padraic Colum, who had had work published by Maunsel & Company. The two met Roberts, who would not budge. Joyce offered to make cuts. The answer was No. When the discussion turned to Roberts's fear that the public houses named in *Dubliners* might initiate legal proceedings against him, Joyce offered to take the publisher by car to each of the pubs to get an undertaking that no action would be taken. Again the answer was no.

Joyce got further support from his old friend CP (Constantine) Curran and Arthur Griffith, then editor of *Sinn Féin*, but to no avail. Eventually Joyce learned that the proofs had been destroyed.

He left Dublin, stopping in London to see if Colum's publishers, Mills and Boon, would accept his book, only to receive another rejection. On his way to Trieste, in his fury he wrote *Gas from a Burner*. It was an invective against his country as much as Roberts, whom he derided in the first person.

That visit to Dublin was to be Joyce's last. It had drawn Colum and himself closer since both had been through a series of rejections of their work. Besides, Colum was a quiet, good-natured person and Joyce enjoyed his company.

He told Colum he was pleased to have left the city. The Colums left Dublin too - in their case for America. Like Joyce, Padraic was destined to travel but he regarded himself as a vagrant rather than an exile.[3]

Although born in Co Longford (where his father was master of the workhouse), Padraic was brought up by his grandmother in Co Cavan when his father lost his job. At the age of ten he went to live in Sandycove on the south side of Dublin where his father had become a railway clerk. He acted in and wrote plays for the newly founded Abbey Theatre. But he found it difficult to make a living as a writer in a city whose literary side he saw increasingly as pseudo-intellectual and second-rate (he never forgot his rural roots). Despite his ardent nationalism, Colum was under no illusion about the difficulties that lay ahead – that Ireland would have to struggle against poverty and ignorance long after freedom was won.[4]

And so in 1914, Padraic and Mary left for the United States where Padraic pursued his writing and gave lectures on the Irish literary revival while Mary developed her journalism. In 1919 they received a begging letter from Joyce (in Zurich where he had spent the war) saying he was in dire need of a $1,000 - this despite monies he had received from Harriet Weaver, John Quinn and the daughter of John D Rockefeller, Edith Rockerfeller McCormick, who was providing him with 1,000 Swiss francs a month. On Mary's initiative, the Colums succeeded in persuading Scofield Thayer, the wealthy editor of the literary magazine *The Dial*, to come up with the funds.

Mary had now become quite a Francophile. She had been encouraged by Yeats to specialise in French literary criticism and while in America got a job with a women's magazine reviewing French plays and translating articles on French fashion. The couple became very friendly with the French writer Jules Bois whom they met at the New York home of John Quinn. Bois had been sent by the French government to the US as a sort of literary emissary. He had known Yeats and Maud Gonne in Paris where he had also met George Moore. In fact, he admitted to Mary Colum, he even had the same mistress as Monsieur Moore![5]

The Colums left New York to return to Ireland after the

Treaty was signed. On the ship they learned of the deaths of Michael Collins and Arthur Griffith. Having left an Ireland whose future, he believed, was uncertain, Padraic had even graver doubts now. The couple did not stay long.

In Ireland, Mary - who was successfully establishing a career for herself as literary critic - was contacted by the American magazine *The Freeman* and asked to review *Ulysses*. Her piece, which appeared in July 1922, was one of three American reviews of the novel that Joyce liked.[6] But her opening remark - that within the next couple of decades many books would be published on Joyce and *Ulysses* - was dropped by the editor on the grounds that, were such a comment applied to other giants of literature such as Cervantes or Tolstoy on publication of any of their works, it would have amounted to an exaggeration.

A month earlier Padraic, in an article for *The New York Times*,[7] expressed surprise that Joyce, through *Ulysses*, had paid such homage to Homer, for in his youthful arrogance Joyce had claimed that the Greek epics were 'outside the tradition of European culture.' Joyce had always claimed that Dante's *Divine Comedy* was Europe's epic. Besides, for all his linguistic abilities, Joyce knew no Greek.

Or so the Colums thought. The first thing they saw on entering the Joyce apartment was a Greek flag on the wall in the hallway. Joyce noticed Padraic looking at it. 'The Greeks have always brought me good luck,' he told him. He had brought the flag from Trieste, where he had talked to Greek sailors and learned the vernacular.

The flat, at eight avenue Charles Floquet, was in a bourgeois district near the *École Militaire* and a short walk from the Eiffel Tower. It had been chosen by Nora and was a big improvement on the dingy hotel room at rue de l'Université where Joyce had finished writing

Ulysses.[8] Joyce would have preferred to live closer to rue de l'Odéon and Shakespeare and Company. But the new apartment was big and bright. Here Nora could entertain guests, something she enjoyed but had been unable to do since their arrival in Paris. And now that *Ulysses* was going well, he was content to indulge Nora's whims.

The Colums were the only guests that evening. Giorgio was out, but Lucia, now almost 16, was there, looking pretty. She spoke little, and then only in Italian to her parents. But she endeared herself to Mary Colum who noticed her eyes were set oddly, although she felt that did not take from her attractiveness. The two would develop a close friendship in the years ahead.

Nora was wearing a scarlet shawl and she and Mary talked about fashion most of the time, for Nora was now buying expensive clothes from one of the haute couturiers.[9] Mary found her beautiful, vivacious and humorous. It was generally known that she had little education, but Mary was impressed and considered it unlikely she had been working in a Dublin hotel when Joyce met her. That was just the sort of thing the Dublin gossips would say after she ran away with Joyce, she thought. Her reaction suggests more about her own middle-class upbringing than her awareness of Nora's.

Mary soon realised that Nora had no interest in her husband's writing. 'Don't you think that Jim is making things very difficult for himself by writing the way he does?' Nora asked her. And on the subject of her husband's celebrity status following the publication of *Ulysses*,[10] she was sarcastic: 'We should put him in a cage and feed him peanuts through the bars.'[11]

Over dinner, Joyce thanked the Colums profusely for their help in securing the gift of $1,000 from Scofield Thayer. 'It was a godsend,' Nora told Mary. And Joyce added that the money had been very welcome as he had been having financial difficulties in setting up an English-speaking drama group in Zurich.

After dinner the four chatted about literature and about *Ulysses*. Suddenly, Joyce turned to Nora: 'Do you think the Colums would like to hear that new thing of mine?' Whatever was Nora's response (the Colums never recorded it but it is not unlikely to have been another put-down), both guests assured him that they would, and Joyce began to read from his *Work in Progress*.

Joyce had started on the first page of his new book in March In June, Joyce's friend, the French writer Valery Larbaud, was the first to hear some of the book.[12] Now the Colums were being treated to an extract.

Mary in particular was fascinated as she listened to Joyce's melodious voice. She thought him more a musician than a writer.

As they talked about the new work, Joyce expressed delight when his guests recognised place-names and references that only those who knew Dublin and its environs could identify. He told them he had worked the names of over 200 of the world's rivers into this, his first draft.

'What is the name of the river by your birthplace?' Joyce asked Padraic. Colum told him of the river Camlin which flows through his native Longford.

'I'll put it in.'

Thus, the humble Camlin has joined the world's greatest rivers in one of the world's most famous books.[13]

Although the Colums' stay in Paris was short, that evening was the first of many occasions that they and the Joyces met in the French capital. Whenever they were in Paris Joyce phoned regularly to find out how they were. Mary regarded him as a reliable friend who would help her with anything from finding an apartment to planning a journey. But although theirs was a strong friendship, it stopped at intellectual discussion; Joyce even told her he had little time for intelligent women. She developed a warm friendship with both Nora and Lucia while Padraic attached himself to Joyce, with whom he had copious discussions on writing and whom he often helped with his *Work in Progress.*

It was four years before the Colums returned to Paris - five years after the first publication of *Ulysses* - and Joyce's epic was continuing to make waves. It had been selling well, thanks to Valery Larbaud and to Joyce's efforts to hustle friends and acquaintances into becoming subscribers.

Parts of *Work in Progress* were appearing in magazines like *transition*, to the praise, bemusement and criticism of its readers. Everyone seemed to be talking about James Joyce.

Shakespeare and Company's reputation had grown with Joyce's. The bookshop was Colum's first stop when he returned to Paris in 1927. Copies of *Ulysses* were prominently displayed in the window and the book was selling well. An elated Beach phoned Joyce to tell him Colum was in the shop. Joyce invited the couple to join him and Nora for dinner that evening at their then-favourite restaurant, Les Trianons in Montparnasse.

Joyce, now in his mid-forties, was better dressed than before. Due to his poor sight, he let Nora choose his clothes and she had a good dress sense. He wore a ring in which there was a large stone and he had a small tuft of beard on his chin. His abundant hair was beginning to grey, but he was still slender and erect. The pupils of his eyes had become enlarged following several operations, yet his gaze was attentive.[14]

The Colums were aware that if any of the Joyce family needed money they went to Beach for it. The sums she advanced them came out of royalties on the sales of *Ulysses*. The Joyces genuinely believed Beach was making a huge profit on the book.

Equally Joyce never felt he was well off. In a begging letter to Beach on St Patrick's Day 1927, he wrote: 'It is a grand thing, so I am told, to be a "genius," but I do not think I have the right to plague and pester you night, noon and morning for money, money and money. You are altogether overworked without my rapping at the door. I am almost inclined to let the bailiffs in and watch them walk off with the furniture and animals in the ark.' As Richard Ellmann put it: 'She had in fact become his banker, with his constant overdrafts to add to troubles she had of her own.'[15]

Mary Colum said Joyce expected to be helped financially. He was writing great works of literature and thought it fitting that those who had money should support him. But she blamed Weaver for giving him so much. If only she gave him an annual stipend instead of a lump sum. That had a bad effect on the family since none of them had much sense about money.

Beach, who knew more about Joyce's financial position than most, recalled the sense of relief when Weaver endowed Joyce with a lump sum, since it took financial pressure from her shoulders. But the respite did not last long. Weaver, she wrote, 'had given someone else to live on the rest of his life, but not Joyce. It wasn't long before he was again hard up and Miss Weaver came again to his help.'[16]

Beach made no bones about Joyce's financial demands in an interview in 1962:

She [Weaver] never wanted it to be known how much she gave him but I can tell you it was a perfect fortune.... But he was very demanding and spent money like water if he had it. He would come to me and say "Sylvia, it's my birthday and I have nothing for my guests, would you advance me something?" And of course I had to. But he wouldn't just give them sandwiches like anyone else – oh no, he had to have the caterers in. Every time he travelled with his wife and family, he always put up at palaces. He liked the grand style.[17]

During one of his visits to the bookshop, Beach told Colum: 'Mr Joyce wants to know when he can see you' (to Sylvia, he would always be Mister Joyce). Colum sensed she was putting a special emphasis on the 'you' and this was confirmed when she elaborated that *Anna Livia Plurabelle* was to be published as a booklet and that Mr Joyce thought it should have an introduction. Did he know anyone who might provide it? Colum said he would think it over and perhaps make a suggestion or two when he met Joyce.

When Colum joined Joyce for a walk, the two men talked of who might write the introduction and the conversation always came around to the need for someone who both understood the work and knew Dublin. Colum felt Joyce was trying to tell him something.

'Would you like me to do the introduction, Joyce?'[18]

'You're the man I have in mind,' Joyce replied, and they turned back to go home.

The booklet was subsequently published[19] in New York.

The two men often walked together in the afternoon,

during which they talked about his *Work in Progress*.
Early in their discussions, Joyce urged Colum to read
Vico, the Neapolitan philosopher. Later, after Colum had
at least read what he could of Vico in Encyclopaedia
Britannica, Joyce explained Vico's theory that history
was cyclical, and his *WIP* would be too. Its beginning
would be its end, since both were the same. In between,
the heroes of history would all become one person – HCE
or Here Comes Everybody.

They talked about Joyce's word play and how and why he
used certain expressions and names. Once, while talking
of their student days, Colum recalled being in a Dublin
music hall when students 'ragged' a female performer by
throwing at her feet a large corset. Joyce responded to
the story with delight, for he had already heard of the
incident. 'I have her in,' he exclaimed. 'She is the one
who is madjealous.' For Madge Ellis was the name of the
performer that evening.

Colum wondered in later years that, if Joyce had never
explained it to him, would even the cleverest literary
critic be able to detect what lay behind the word
'madjealous' in *Finnegans Wake* ?

During their conversations, Colum was given insights into
the technique of *Finnegans Wake* . and learned how Joyce
worked history and place-names into his work; how the
two cathedrals of St Patrick's and Christ Church become
the one that HCE builds; and how the Norse king's
desecration of the altar of Christ Church - by asking his
wife to sit naked upon it - becomes 'chillybombom ...
upon the altarstane.'

Around the same time, the two Colums were invited to
Joyce's apartment (they were now living at Square Robiac
in the seventh arrondissement) for a reading of *Anna
Livia Plurabelle*. Joyce complained that the 20 pages
cost him 'twelve hundred hours and an enormous expense

of spirit.' Among the two-dozen friends present were
Hemingway, McAlmon and Beach, along with a few
French writers.

As each guest arrived Joyce met them at the door,
anxious that they should receive his new work with
enthusiasm. The occasion was something of a trial, not
only for McAlmon – who sat throughout armed with the
whiskey Joyce had given him - but for many of the
others. Seated around the room with serious expressions,
they listened as Joyce started reading. The author's
mellifluous tenor voice was well received by his audience
but not all understood his words. Some nodded their
heads, others - like Mary Colum - smiled at comic
touches when Joyce would chuckle at his own witticisms.
Still others looked into space, perhaps afraid to show any
response. Hemingway told McAlmon afterwards that the
passage gave one the feeling of night and of the dark,
flowing River Liffey. But he could not commit himself to
Joyce's *Work in Progress*.

As he read, Joyce glanced from time to time at his
listeners to see how they were reacting. Fixing his eyes
on Mary Colum, he only added to her confusion; it was
not her first time to hear his new work yet she still found
it difficult to understand. So when, at the end of the
reading, Joyce went up to her and asked: 'Well, what do
you think?' she summoned up all her courage before
answering.

'Joyce, I think it is outside literature.'

Joyce said nothing. She knew what she had said was
pompous, but at least she had given him an answer. She
had no idea what the others told Joyce, but afterwards
learned that their responses, too, were quite pretentious.

It was not until a month later that Joyce gave his verdict
on her opinion. He told Padraic: 'Your wife said that

what I read was outside literature. Tell her it may be outside literature now, but its future is inside literature.'

Mary was satisfied that Joyce never held the judgment against her, for soon afterwards he indicated his approval of her honesty when, with a knowing smile, he told her: 'But you were the only one present who frankly said you did not understand it. I remember how you laughed at passages that were humorous - that was more than any of the others did.'[20] As if to further reassure her, Joyce invited her to accompany him to a talk by a priest who held the same theory that Joyce adhered to, that language had its origin in gesture (Joyce had often told the Colums: 'In the beginning was the rhythmic gesture'). The lecture was in a small hall and there were loud whispers from the audience of 'M'sieu James Joyce' as the two made their way to their seats.

Afterwards they walked to a café where Mary's husband was waiting to join them. As Joyce talked animatedly, the Colums noticed a young man hovering near their table. After a while, the man asked if he might join them for a few minutes. He was a lecturer in literature at an American college and was anxious to gather information about Joyce's technical inventions in *Ulysses*.

Joyce told the young American of his indebtedness to Édouard Dujardin and his monologue intérieure. As Joyce explained his stream of consciousness technique, the young man took copious notes with which, no doubt, he would impress students and fellow-academics on his return. Mary, however, regarded the whole episode as a huge Joycean leg-pull and, once the American had left, berated Joyce:

'Haven't you had enough fun with this? Haven't you pulled enough people's legs? And why deny your indebtedness to Freud and Jung? Isn't it better to be indebted to great originators like that than to...?'

But Joyce interrupted her flow. He had been shuffling about in his chair, clearly irritated by her intervention, and could hold back his anger no longer:

'I hate women who know anything,' he told her.

It was an abusive remark, to which Mary was prepared to respond head-on. Her previous contretemps with Joyce had given her confidence (if indeed she needed any) and she knew that the best way to take the wind out of his sails was to be frank and direct:

'No, Joyce, you don't. You like them.'

Joyce was silent for a few moments. Then a whimsical smile spread over his face and, as she recalled later, 'the rest of the afternoon was pleasant for the three of us.'[21]

The intellectual tension that existed between Mary Colum and Joyce may have its origin in his dislike of serious discussions with women in general. She noticed he got angry when she became friendly with French people who were Thomists, although Thomism played a significant part in both their lives at university in Dublin. But whereas Joyce had retained and expanded greatly on all he had learned, Mary Colum acknowledged that she had retained relatively little.

But her forcefulness more than made up for any memory shortcomings she thought she had; for Mary Colum was someone to be reckoned with. In 1931, when Joyce's sense of persecution was at its height (not without some cause), Mary Colum came across an article in the Catholic World, an American publication, which was highly critical of his writing and his family. It was written by a Dublin judge, Michael Lennon, who had been friendly with Joyce. Mary Colum knew that Joyce would be humiliated by the piece and she determined that he must never be allowed to see it.

Unfortunately Padraic had already told Joyce about the article (without having read it) and Joyce had insisted they hold a copy of the magazine for him. When Joyce phoned to ask for it, Mary told him she had lost it. Joyce did not believe her and said he would send around Giorgio for it. The young man stayed for an hour, insisting on being given the magazine but eventually had to leave without it. The following day Joyce himself arrived. He was as formal as ever.

'Mrs Colum, I want you to give me the copy of the Catholic World that you have.'

'I haven't it, Joyce.'

'Tell me where you left it and I will have it traced.'

'I don't know where I left it.'

Joyce would not take no for an answer. Mary finally had to be more honest.

'I won't give it to you, Joyce.'

'I'll stay here until you give it to me.'

Like his son, Joyce stayed a long time before leaving empty-handed. But Mary Colum had got her way. She could never be the one who would show the article to Joyce, although she knew that it had become one of his obsessions and that he would obtain a copy somehow. As for her own copy, she burned it.[22]

Joyce's friendship with her husband was more relaxed. Joyce needed Padraic more than he did Mary and both men enjoyed their walks and talks. Padraic knew that Joyce was not able to read much, due to his recurring eye problems, and he was sometimes surprised that Joyce was capable of talking at length about literature. There was

nothing pretentious or solemn in what he said. But
Padraic got a feeling that Joyce, conscious of what he was
reported to have said of certain writers, now wished to
use him as an intermediary in putting the record straight.

His disagreement with George Moore, for example, was
widely known and he told Colum how, when Moore had
given him one of his books, he wished it had been *Esther
Waters*, which he regarded as a first rate novel.

And Yeats: had Joyce really told him 'We have met too
late; you are too old to be influenced by me'? Joyce did
not deny he had made the remark that had been well
publicised in literary circles; but he emphasised his
admiration for Yeats's work.

He spoke about *Remembrance of Things Past*, but Colum
knew that, because of his poor eyesight, he could not
have read the entire book. However, Joyce did meet
Proust - once and briefly. There are several versions of
the occasion, which took place in May 1922, and it is
likely they have been embroidered somewhat. All
accounts of the meeting date from the 1950s, at least 30
years after the historic encounter took place. Even Joyce
himself told different versions of the story.

What is certain is that the two writers met at a supper
party thrown by an English writer, Sydney Schiff, for
Stravinsky and Sergei Diaghilev after the premiere of one
of their ballets. Joyce arrived late and apologised for not
wearing formal clothes (of which he had none at this
time) and started drinking heavily to cover his
embarrassment. The door opened and in walked Marcel
Proust. The two authors were introduced to each other.

According to what Joyce told Padraic Colum, the
conversation went like this:

Proust: Ah, Monsieur Joyce... You know the Princess...

Joyce: No, Monsieur.

Proust: Ah. You know the Countess...

Joyce: No, Monsieur.

Proust: Then you know Madame...

Joyce: No, Monsieur.

And that, according to Colum, terminated the conversation.[23]

The exchange between the two writers has been reported with subtle differences – but equally brief and trivial - depending on whom Joyce spoke to. According to what Joyce told Arthur Power, Proust asked Joyce if he liked truffles. Joyce replied: 'Yes I do.' As Power put it: 'Here are two of the greatest literary figures of our time meeting and they ask each other if they like truffles.'

Whatever happened inside, as Proust was leaving the apartment he asked the Schiffs to accompany him home in a taxi. Although not invited, Joyce got in too and the first thing he did was open the window noisily. Schiff immediately closed it out of deference to Proust's sensitivity to fresh air. When they arrived, Proust suggested Joyce take the taxi home. But a tipsy Joyce hung around while a hypochondriacal Proust rushed indoors out of the cold. Joyce afterwards wondered if only they had had a chance to talk...[24]

During the late 1920s, the Colums divided their time between Europe and New York, where they wrote and taught, and Hawaii where Padraic[25] was commissioned to record the island's legends. But they kept in touch with political and literary developments in Ireland and Europe and took every opportunity to visit Paris to see the Joyces.

Padraic saw much of Joyce around 1929. It was a good time for Joyce. He was due no further eye operations and his work was progressing well.

One evening, invited for dinner, he arrived at the flat to find Joyce alone with Herbert Gorman, an American writer whom he had asked to write his biography. Gorman greeted Padraic with delight, saying they had just worked his name into *Work in Progress*. Colum was not much impressed to learn that the reference was to a ship: the SS Paudraic.

The conversation was wide-ranging. They talked about publishing *Haveth Childers Everywhere*, a fragment of *Work in Progress*, and who might write an introduction. But it would not be Colum on this occasion, or any other writer. Instead it should be written by an architect or a builder or a mayor, since the episode concerned the building of a city. Joyce truly believed in the ordinariness and the public appeal of his new work, Colum felt, and that it did not require a writer to compose an introduction to it. Just like Joyce's slogan for Guinness stout: 'My brandold Dublin lindub,[26] the free, the froh, the frothy freshener.'

Colum helped Joyce by typing *Finnegans Wake* prior to publication. Sometimes Joyce asked him to suggest a word that would be more obscure than the word already there. Colum became fascinated at the way Joyce mixed together distorted words from various languages, thus bringing together peoples of different cultures. And what's more, he enjoyed it, often laughing aloud at the word that came up in their discussions.

When the two couples dined in Paris for the last time, Europe was moving closer to war. Politics, never Joyce's favourite subject, was difficult to avoid. He was quick to condemn Mussolini and to praise France, which he regarded as Europe's highest civilisation. 'Where else can you go out to dinner and have a cardinal on one side of you and a commissar on the other?' he asked. The Colums' last memory was of Joyce distracting Nora's attention while he ordered another bottle of wine; then of the waiters bowing before him as he tipped them extravagantly.[27]

---

[1] Colum: *OFJJ* 21.

[2] Roberts also quarreled with Yeats, Lady Gregory and James Stephens.

[3] In an oration at Colum's graveside in 1972, the writer Ben Kiely remarked: 'He could simply not exile himself anywhere from his fellow men. He had too much kindness, too much sympathy, too much understanding of the human condition.'

[4] Sanford Sternlicht, ed., *Collected Short Stories of Padraic Colum* XXII.

[5] Mary Colum: *Life and the Dream* 231.

[6] The others were by Edmund Wilson and Gilbert Seldes.

[7] *New York Times*, June 11, 1922.

[8] A doctor who visited Joyce at rue de l'Université was shocked at what he saw: the two Joyces sitting on the floor with a pan of chicken between them together with a half empty bottle of wine. Suitcases lay open and their belongings strewn around the room.

[9] Mary Colum: *OFJJ* 114-115.

[10] Joyce's status in his native Dublin was much different. In 1924 Liam O'Flaherty wrote that Joyce's followers were 'a very, very small clique and they have no power. The power among the literary people is wielded by AE and Lennox Robinson.' (Letter to Edward Garnett).

[11] Maddox: *Nora*, 282.

[12] Larbaud wrote to Adrienne Monnier: 'It's excellent Joyce, though the meaning of the whole escaped me.' (Ellmann 552).

[13] Joyce liked to think how, some day, in the remotest parts of the world, someone would be pleased to come upon the name of their home river. [Ellmann].

[14] Padraic Colum: *OFJJ* 119.

[15] Ellmann 651

[16] Beach: *Shakespeare and Company*, page 76.

[17] Beach in an interview with Peter Lennon, *Irish Times*, 9 April, 1962.

[18] Padraic Colum pronounced his name 'Jice.'

[19] *Anna Livia Plurabelle* was published in a signed, limited edition by Crosby Gaige, NY, 1928.

[20] Mary Colum: *OFJJ* 130.

[21] Idem.

[22] Idem. 195-196.

[23] Padraic Colum: *OFJJ* 151.

[24] Various sources quoted in Ellmann 509.

[25] Years later the author James A. Michener, who had met Colum in New York, described him as a 'small, fey and lovable Irishman' and 'a shy, diffident man who wore frayed tweeds, spoke in a high-pitched voice and bounded up and down when he lectured. He had a most engaging personality and obviously loved to associate with young people.' (*Irish Times,* 13 March, 1981).

[26] Lindub, an anagram of Dublin, is close to the Irish for stout, *lionndubh*, according to Dineen's dictionary (1927) which Joyce liked to consult.

[27] Padraic Colum, *OFJJ* 234.

Chapter Eight
Riot At The Champs-Elysées

4 October 1923 was no ordinary evening at the Théatre
des Champs-Elysées and few among the invited audience
of writers and musicians had an inkling of what was to
come.

The main item on the programme was a performance by
the Swedish Ballet. It would be preceded by the musical
début of the young American composer George Antheil.

Joyce was among the many personalities who had been
invited. He settled into his box alongside others in which
were seated Eric Satie, Darius Milhaud and some other
members of 'Les Six.' Ezra Pound was also in the
audience that evening. So were Sylvia Beach and
Adrienne Monnier. So was Pablo Picasso.

Even Stravinsky was there. It was he who had urged
Antheil, whom he had met in Berlin, to come to Paris,
much as Pound was responsible for bringing Joyce to the
city. Antheil greatly admired his musical mentor, but the
younger man's compositions went far beyond
Stravinsky's revolutionary music and involved the use of
several piano rolls playing simultaneously, sirens and
even airplane engines.

This was Antheil's first public appearance in Paris (he
had given concerts in London and Berlin) and most of
those in the audience, excepting Stravinsky and Pound,
would not have known what to expect. In the event, the

music was loud, with much thumping of the piano keys.

As Antheil played his *Sonata Sauvage*, there was an eerie silence in the auditorium. Then a man in the front row began to catcall. Someone punched him. A murmur of astonishment ran through the audience. A member of the orchestra jumped up: 'Silence! Silence!' he shouted, only adding to the confusion.

At the end of the next piece, Airplane Sonata, Satie stood up and applauded wildly. Milhaud tried to hold him back. Satie pushed his friend away. As Antheil played his third piece, Mechanisms, a full-scale riot seemed to erupt, much to the delight of the Surrealists among the attendance. People punched one another; others yelled or clapped. Satie shouted his approval: 'Quel précision! Quel précision! Bravo! Bravo!' Taking a lead from his friend, Milhaud started to applaud too.

A spotlight was turned on the audience. At one point it seemed to be aimed at Joyce, most likely hurting his sensitive eyes. Someone stood up in one of the boxes and shouted: 'You are all pigs!' Some people at the front lifted up their seats and dropped them into the orchestra pit. The police arrived. Arrests were made.

But it was all a plot. Joyce and the other luminaries in the theatre that evening did not know the riot had been carefully choreographed to produce just such a reaction. Even Antheil knew nothing about the affair in which he, as 'victim,' played a central role.

The riot was arranged for one of the earliest French silent films, *L'Inhumaine*, starring Georgette Leblanc. She played the part of a singer who, in one scene, is booed by an angry audience. Unbeknown to Antheil, the film's director, Marcel L'Herbier, had hired the theatre and invited over 2,000 people to attend in evening dress. Many of them were from the film world and were asked to play the part of an unruly audience. A small proportion consisted of fashionable socialites and well-known Modernist writers, artists and musicians.

L'Herbier got Leblanc and Margaret Anderson (friend of Antheil and editor of the *Little Review* whose extracts from *Ulysses* had been banned in the United States) to persuade Antheil to play his Modernist music in the hope that his dissonant compositions would stir up a confrontational mood in the audience. Then, when Leblanc appeared on stage, she would be greeted by wolf whistles, catcalls and general mayhem. Ten hidden cameras were strategically placed to record the audience's disorderly reaction.

None of this was apparent to Antheil as he played. At first he was concerned at the audience's response to his music and felt in his pocket for the pistol he usually kept there when he gave a performance in case things turned nasty. But as the noise from the auditorium got louder, he began to enjoy the effect his music was having. Beads of perspiration gathered on his forehead as he played with vigour, barely noticing the well-dressed woman (Georgette Leblanc) walking up to his piano as floodlights shone on them both.

Margaret Anderson later admitted to Antheil her role in the plot, saying she and Leblanc (who owned a half-share in the film) felt he would be too nervous if he knew beforehand that the audience had been planted and told how to react. She was confident he would benefit from the affair – and she was right. The performance received extensive coverage, one newspaper calling it the 'music of the future.'

'I was notorious in Paris, therefore famous,' Antheil wrote later.[1] Furthermore, Satie's endorsement ensured his successful career for years to come.

In fact the event had a happy outcome for everyone, including the Swedish Ballet whose performance followed the 'riot' (they were also in on the plot). The filmmakers too were delighted with the publicity in addition to the audience reaction they had sought.

Antheil was just a little disappointed that the audience was not really reacting to his music. Nevertheless there were those present who enjoyed his compositions. Joyce was interested in the music as a phenomenon and he was intrigued by the reaction to it by Darius Milhaud and Eric Satie.[2]

The concert marked the beginning of a friendship between Joyce and Antheil that would last for several years. It was hardly surprising since they had already met, having been introduced by Beach above whose shop Antheil and his partner Boski shared an apartment.

The flat was small and had no room for a piano, but Antheil took it anyway; he was pleased to be living above the shop of the publisher of *Ulysses*. The couple moved in and over the next two years Antheil composed a symphony, two violin sonatas, a quintet and his legendary *Ballet Mécanique* without the aid of a piano (though he sometimes practised in Adrienne Monnier's studio).

Short and delicate looking, with light hair, Antheil was good-natured and he got on well with Beach; both came from New Jersey. She did not seem to mind when, if he had forgotten his keys, he would climb to his first floor apartment with the aid of the Shakespeare sign that hung above the entrance to her shop.

Through Sylvia, Antheil got to know other writers including Hemingway and McAlmon (who gave him a $100 a month for two years). Sylvia introduced him to Ezra Pound who decided he would be his latest enthusiasm. Tall, lanky with red hair and beard, Pound (the 'complete expatriate'[3]) was always promoting someone. From his time in London, he had been encouraging Joyce, publicising his writing and securing a regular income for him from the Royal Literary Fund and the Civil Pension List. If it was Yeats who introduced Pound to Joyce it was through Pound that Joyce became 'adopted' by such patrons as the magnanimous Weaver and the Irish-American lawyer John Quinn.

Pound was effectively Joyce's unpaid literary agent. But his enthusiasm went far beyond Joyce. Besides being a mentor to Hemingway, he worked on *The Waste Land* with TS Eliot and helped Ford with the *Transatlantic Review*. All this time he was writing his *Cantos*, although it was only after *Ulysses* and Eliot's poem were published in 1922 that he really got down to finishing it. That was when he announced that the Christian era was over and the Pound era had begun.

Pound loved isms[4] and cliques such the Imagists (a group of poets to which HD and Desmond FitzGerald belonged) and Vorticism (the name Pound gave to the British art movement led by Wyndham Lewis) and easily became attached to Dadaism and Surrealism. It was only a short step from there to his enthusiasm for Antheil who, by the use of propellers and sirens, stretched Modernism in music to the limit.

Soon after they met, Pound borrowed some of Antheil's writings on music and published them as Antheil and the Theory of Harmony.[5] When the treatise appeared in Ford's *Transatlantic Review* in early 1924 it was preceded by a carefully-worded editorial comment: 'We are assured by competent musicians that this communication is of great value.'

Pound insisted that Antheil compose sonatas for his mistress, the violinist Olga Rudge. Later Pound got

Antheil to help him compose two operas – even though Pound's friends, including Yeats, felt he was tone deaf (so was Yeats). And Pound and Antheil co-operated on a 'Musical Supplement' to accompany the second issue of the *Transatlantic Review*.

Joyce helped the young composer too. After Beach introduced them in her bookshop, Antheil invited the writer upstairs for tea and to look at his music manuscripts. In return Joyce asked Antheil and Boski to his apartment at avenue Charles Floquet near the Eiffel Tower. Antheil thought it was a nice, up-to-date bourgeois Dublin apartment, which looked out of place in Paris.

He became a frequent visitor. He was very fond of Nora; it was clear she loved her husband without quite understanding his genius. Sometimes he would hear her scolding Joyce for not writing 'sensible' books.

Antheil became friendly with Lucia ('beautiful only as Irish girls can sometimes be beautiful – in a sort of fey way'[6]) and Giorgio who was attending singing lessons. Often Giorgio would sing while Antheil accompanied him on Joyce's piano. After a glass or two of white wine, Joyce could be persuaded to sing too.

Music was important in the Joyce household and the two men would talk about music late into the night. Joyce's knowledge was encyclopaedic; he told Antheil about rare music manuscripts hidden in museums in Paris.

They talked about literature too, and Joyce showed the younger man copies of each of the sections of his *Work in Progress* (which he assumed Antheil understood) as they were published.

Joyce was passionate about opera and he and Antheil would often go to the Paris Opera to see whatever was on. When Joyce heard that a wealthy French woman was giving performances of early French, Italian and English operas on Sundays, he suggested to Antheil that the two should try to attend. Unfortunately the musical salon was by invitation only and, since the woman had never heard of James Joyce, such an offer was not forthcoming.

Undeterred, Joyce decided he was going there, even if it meant gatecrashing the event. Anticipating some difficulty, he prepared a campaign, writing scenarios that he and Antheil rehearsed to enable them to get past anyone at the door that might stop them. The plan worked on two occasions. But on the third visit the French woman had them thrown out. Antheil said later he had never been thrown out of a better place and in better company.[7]

At this time Antheil had become an unenthusiastic agent for a German literary magazine, *Der Quershnitt*, but he succeeded in placing *Chamber Music* and Hemingway's *In Our Time* with the publication.[8]

Joyce helped Antheil by writing articles about his music in French magazines. In return, Antheil suggested writing an opera based on the *Cyclops* episode in *Ulysses*. Instrumentally there would be 13 electric pianos. There would be drums, steel xylophones and various other loud instruments. The score would be played at great speed with crescendos and diminuendos achieved by switching pianos on and off. The singers would be out of sight, singing into microphones attached to loudspeakers on the stage, and a *corps de ballet* would mime the action.

As with other planned collaborations between Antheil and Joyce, it came to nothing. There was to have been a symphony based on *Anna Livia Plurabelle*, then an opera based on Byron's *Cain*, which Joyce hoped would help promote the career of the Kerry tenor John Sullivan. However, Antheil did succeed in setting to music

Nightpiece, one of Joyce's poems in *Poems Pennyeach*, for the *Joyce Book* being compiled by Herbert Hughes; and he set *I Hear an Army* to music for voice and piano.

When Hemingway, in a review of Antheil's music, wrote that he 'preferred his Stravinsky straight,' the composer was devastated.[9] To cheer him up, Beach and Adrienne Monnier decided to take him to the Moulin Rouge, where Antheil danced with Monnier.

It may have been in a subsequent conversation that Joyce and Antheil conceived a wicked little scheme. They decided to bring Monnier back to the Moulin Rouge. But in addition to the performance on stage they hoped to orchestrate an audience reaction of their own – among the *poules* who frequented the area around the theatre in Pigalle.

Monnier liked to wear a long grey dress that went down to her ankles. It was bordered by a white collar and cuffs. She also wore no makeup or lipstick and her demeanour was calm. In short, she could be mistaken for a nun.

After the two men got Monnier into the Moulin Rouge, they went among the prostitutes outside, whispering to them that they had smuggled a nun out of the local convent and got her into the theatre to see the show.

The women were shocked by the news, even more outraged than the two had expected since French prostitutes, for all their social mores, held nuns in high esteem, people whose purity they respected.

With the help of the Anglo-Irish-American community, Antheil's music did not want for publicity, whatever its audiences thought of it. Pound had introduced the composer to Jean Cocteau, opening up French interest in his music, for Cocteau was eminent in Parisian theatrical circles.[10] Yet Antheil was concerned that people might not be interested in his new work, *Ballet Mécanique.*

Antheil was fascinated by things mechanical. His latest composition was scored for eight grand pianos, xylophones, percussion and three airplane propellers. When Beach told him the name he had given the music was similar to the French for a carpet sweeper – balai mécanique – he enjoyed the Dadaist connection.

To generate interest in his new work, Antheil decided on a bizarre publicity stunt. Taking Beach into his confidence, he borrowed money from her to go to Africa – allegedly in search of 'new rhythms.' Before leaving, he hired a music room for a preview of his new work. Publicity was arranged through his friend and pianist Bravig Imbs who worked for the *Paris Tribune* and through Beach who would spread the word among the expatriate community. Then he 'disappeared.'

With no sign of the composer returning, the preview, to which Joyce and Beach were invited among many others, would have to go on without him. Imbs would play the piano in his place.

The performance was greeted with delight. Joyce asked to hear a part of the second roll again. A reporter for the *New York Herald* was amazed that there were 17 pianolas. For days, Beach was besieged by reporters who wanted to know Antheil's whereabouts. The *Tribune* headline said he was 'Lost in African Desert.' Becoming alarmed at the extent of the prank, Beach sent Antheil a telegram: 'Come back to Paris immediately and deny this idiotic newspaper story lions ate you in Africa...' In due course he returned to Paris. In his memoirs he commented:

> *If you do not really die, you will be amazed by the number of your closest friends who will deeply resent your returning to the world of the living again – especially after they have copiously and*

publicly slobbered all over the place concerning you, what a great guy you had been etc., ad nauseam.[11]

The fuss generated by his 'disappearance' was nothing compared with the commotion on the first performance of the 'ballet.' All 2,500 seats at the Théatre des Champs-Elysées were taken up for the matinée performance. It seemed as if the whole of Montparnasse was there.[12] The Joyces had a box.[13] Pound was on the upper gallery. Eliot was also in the audience. Hemingway was out of town but Beach was there with Monnier.

The programme started with Handel, followed by Antheil's Second Symphony. Then it was time for the main item on the programme. *Ballet Mécanique* had , barely started when it was drowned out by yells and people started to punch one another. Objectors argued with defenders. When the huge electric fans were turned on (substituting for the airplane propellers which the score provided for[14]), programmes were blown away as were women's hats. A man seated near the front lost his wig. As the wind persisted, one man stood and opened his umbrella against it; others followed.

The riot ended with the music, 28 minutes later. Antheil was delighted. It was a Dadaist's dream come true. He was now the toast of Paris, even among those who could not understand his music.

The following year, Antheil and Boski got married. The composer, whose first string quartet had been premiered at Natalie Barney's famous salon, was now firmly established as a Modernist composer. Proud of his latest protégé, Pound invited Antheil to his Italian home in Rapallo where he met WB Yeats and the German dramatist Gerhart Hauptmann (both Nobel Prize winners).

Much of his time in Rapallo, Antheil recalled later, was spent talking with these literary giants about the latest murder mysteries. Becoming enthused himself, he decided to write one for them, basing his main protagonist on Pound. As he wrote, he got his newfound acquaintances to read over and correct his poor grammar. Eventually the book was published with the help of TS Eliot, then editor at Faber and Faber.[15]

Yeats asked Antheil to write incidental music to three dance-plays. The poet rewrote *At the Hawk's Well, On Baile's Strand* and *The Only Jealousy of Emer* (renamed *Fighting the Waves*) and marvelled at the revolutionary energy with which Antheil was working on them. 'There will be masks & all singing within the range of the speaking voice' he wrote to Lady Gregory.[16] He also enthused about the Anglo-Irish choreographer and dancer Ninette de Valois[17] whom he wanted for the leading part.

The production went on at the Abbey theatre in the summer of 1929. The critics, according to Antheil, 'decided that I was really an Irishman because the score (so they said) was so thoroughly Irish.'[18] However, according to Yeats's biographer Roy Foster, 'the combination of de Valois, Antheil, Cuchulain and Yeats was a shock to Abbey audiences.' *The Irish Times* called it 'an interesting experiment.'

Yeats himself remained convinced he had discovered 'a new form' of theatre by the combination of dance, speech and music.[19]

---

[1] Antheil: *Bad Boy of Music* 134.
[2] Ellmann 557.
[3] A description by Sisley Huddleston: *Paris Salons, Cafés, Studios.* He went on: 'Unquestionably he is a European although he was born in the United States.'
[4] He would eventually sympathise with fascism and anti-Semitism,

although he continued to have Jewish friends.

[5] In his autobiography *Bad Boy of Music*, Antheil claims that the book did him more harm than good. It contained many theories held by Pound, such as that melody is for twits because it does not exist.

[6] Antheil: *Bad Boy of Music* 153.

[7] Idem. 151.

[8] Idem. 148.

[9] Hemingway in the *Transatlantic Review*.

[10] Cocteau was one of the leading avant-garde writers of the day. He produced the ballet *Le Boeuf sur le Toit* by Darius Milhaud.

[11] Antheil: *Bad Boy of Music* 169.

[12] McAlmon wrote later: 'In those days we all delighted in attending such affairs; people moved en masse from performance to performance, but this did not mean that they dearly loved art.' (McAlmon: *Geniuses* 196).

[13] Joyce liked to attend performances of Antheil's music. In a review of his Symphony in F in October 1926, the Tribune reporter wrote: 'James Joyce sat in a loge at the right of the stage, in a characteristic pose of absorption and detachment, as if his mind contained the music and had taken it to a sphere seven times removed in order to enjoy it' - *Paris Tribune*, 17 October 1926 (*Left Bank Revisited* 222).

[14] Actual propellers were used in a performance at Carnegie Hall the following year.

[15] *Death in the Dark* was published under the pseudonym Stacey Bishop. Antheil claimed it was poorly written and was published only because the original MS contained copious corrections and footnotes by Yeats and Pound.

[16] Yeats to Lady Gregory, 9 March 1929 (Foster: *W B Yeats: A Life* vol. 2, 385).

[17] De Valois was born in Blessington, Co. Wicklow, the daughter of a British army officer. She danced with the Ballets Russes and founded the Royal Ballet.

[18] Antheil: *Bad Boy of Music* 229.

[19] Foster: *W. B. Yeats: A Life* Vol. 2, 389.

Chapter Nine
Portrait Of The Artist

In the spring of 1923, Joyce decided he wanted to have a portrait of his father, John Stanislaus Joyce. He asked Arthur Power if he would recommend someone and Power suggested the landscape painter Paul Henry who had also done portraits. Power went on to name a further eight artists, among them John Butler Yeats, Sean Keating and Harry Kernoff. Last on his list was a man called Patrick Tuohy. Power told Joyce he had reservations about the intense realism of Tuohy's works, but Joyce paid no heed. He had known Tuohy's father in Dublin. That was enough. It had to be Tuohy.

While Power had concerns about Tuohy as an artist, he might equally have had issues about the man himself. As Tuohy was establishing himself he was also becoming known for his irascibility. Maurice MacGonigal, one of Tuohy's students, remembered him as unpredictable, morose, angry and suspicious, although he admired him as a teacher.[1]

Tuohy's complex personality may have been due in part to having arrived in the world with a deformed left hand. Born in Dublin in 1894 to nationalist parents (his mother was a member of Inghinidhe na hÉireann, which had been founded by Maud Gonne), Tuohy was sent to St Enda's, the progressive and co-educational school founded by Patrick and Willie Pearse. There the young Tuohy became influenced by the founders' passion for an independent Ireland and by the literary influences of the teachers, among whom were Thomas MacDonagh and

Padraic Colum, both young poets and playwrights.

Patrick Pearse encouraged him to attend classes at the Metropolitan School of Art. Padraic Colum also encouraged him in his artistic endeavours and the two remained good friends throughout Tuohy's short life.

On Easter Monday, 1916, Tuohy and his father, who was a doctor, followed Pearse and others into the General Post Office in Dublin when Pearse declared an Irish Republic. Young Tuohy's role is not clear; his father, however, attended to the wounded. Both of them escaped from the building before the defenders were forced to surrender. As imprisonments and executions followed, Dr Tuohy sent his son to Spain where he would remain until things settled down. Thus Tuohy refined his art among the Goyas and Velasquezes of Madrid, teaching painting at the Colegio de las Madres Irlandesas run by the Loreto nuns. He returned to Dublin in 1917 and took up a part-time teaching post at the Metropolitan School of Art where he fell in love with one of his students called Phyllis Moss. Her family, which was Protestant and unionist, was horrified at the liaison and sent her to study art in Paris to separate her from Tuohy.

When Tuohy arrived at the home of Joyce senior in Fairview in north Dublin, he found a 73-year-old man, bedridden and living in cheap rented accommodation. John Joyce took a liking to Tuohy, despite the artist's persistence in following him into his bedroom to learn more about the man's 'inner self.' The resulting portrait captured the man's personality in all its sadness and irritability. It has been widely acclaimed as an exceptional work and one of the best Irish portraits of the 20th century.[2]

Before painting John Joyce, Tuohy had produced another outstanding portrait, this time of the writer James Stephens. Stephens was renowned as the author of *The*

Crock of Gold and *The Charwoman's Daughter* (both published in 1912) and was Registrar of the National Gallery in Dublin.

During the sittings with Stephens, Tuohy mentioned he hoped to go to Paris to visit his girlfriend. The sympathetic Stephens recommended that he also visit Joyce, whom Stephens had met many years before in Dublin, and gave him a letter of introduction. Tuohy had not met Joyce at the time he was commissioned to paint his father.[3]

In early 1924, Tuohy – a small, slim, moustached man of 28 - arrived at the Joyces' accompanied by 21-year-old Phyllis, who jabbered away nervously, irritating Joyce.[4] But the writer took quickly to Tuohy whom he regarded as 'very Dublin.'[5] The two men spoke at length about Dublin landmarks and family names. The artist was not yet showing signs of the depression that would propel him towards an early death.

Tuohy asked Joyce to sit for him and Joyce reluctantly agreed. Tuohy, meticulous as ever, spent much time with his sitter, insisting that he sat for him almost every day. Joyce was not finding it easy, and when Tuohy went on about his need to capture his subject's soul, Joyce snapped back: 'Never mind my soul. Just be sure you have my tie right.'[6]

Tuohy did not finish the portrait until 1927. Joyce was not particularly pleased with the result and Tuohy offered to paint a second portrait, but it turned out to be no better (nor worse) than the first.

Joyce revered the portrait of his father and it took pride of place in his home. He had strong feelings towards the old man yet he could never bring himself to visit him. He was however keen to recapture the idioms in his father's speech for use in his own writing and asked Tuohy to arrange for a stenographer (probably a court official or a journalist) to talk to his father and send back a transcript of the conversation.[7]

For most of his life John Joyce had squandered whatever money he had through drink and heavy borrowings. In his final years, deserted by most of his children, he was proud of his eldest son who sent him copies of his books – but little else. Learning of the success of *Ulysses*, he asked James for money. In a long detailed response, James explained that things were not as good as they seemed:

His gift from Weaver of about £9,000 gave him, when invested, an income of £450 a year. Since he had to support three adults plus himself in a very expensive city, his father was better off on his pension of £150. Besides, Joyce had to stoke the fires himself, as well as make up two of the four beds. The other two were made up by a *femme de ménage* who came in for three hours a day costing him £36 a year. Then the flat itself cost £300 a year... and his medical fees came to £100 a year... [8]

It wasn't easy being a famous writer in Paris with a family to support.

Around this time royalties started coming in monthly from a second edition of *Ulysses*. Four months later Weaver sent him £12,000.

Refusing to visit his father, Joyce urged his friends to keep an eye on him. Tuohy was back in Dublin, teaching at the Metropolitan School of Art, so he proved a natural choice and an excellent one since he and the older man got on very well together. A bonus for Joyce was that Tuohy sent back to Paris, not just reports on his father's welfare, but anecdotes of Dublin told in Tuohy's Dublinese, snippets that Joyce pounced upon for inclusion in his *Work in Progress*.[9]

Joyce had also asked McAlmon to look out for his father. McAlmon was in London where he and Bryher still kept an apartment and, in the autumn of 1925, decided to go to Dublin. McAlmon met up with Tuohy, whom Joyce had introduced to him the previous year, and the two went to see the older Joyce.

McAlmon and Tuohy sat at John Joyce's bedside and the three drank whiskey and talked. McAlmon said he had never seen a more intense face than that of the old man.

> *Before I left, Mr Joyce had become for me the street-corner politician and aged man about town as revealed in* Ulysses. *And I reflected that when I meet the Irish, I'm glad I have Scots blood, and when I meet the Scots, oh, bring back the Irish in me.* [10]

McAlmon did not think much of Joyce's native city. Dublin was 'grey and dull and meanly ingrown' and its people foul-mouthed. Its men had dirty minds towards women, especially towards whores, whereas to Frenchmen prostitutes were *poules* or *cocottes* or *petites amies*.

McAlmon also met up with some of the Dublin literary set, but felt they were 'back two generations' in their knowledge of English and American writing, for which he blamed the censors. Irish people had heard of Padraic and Mary Colum but didn't seem much interested in them.

Judge Kenneth Reddin,[11] who knew Joyce, Tuohy and Stephens and who was writing for the Abbey Theatre, invited McAlmon to his home in Howth from where there was 'a view as beautiful as any in Greece.' He met AE (George Russell) and was pleasantly surprised that he knew the characters and plots of stories McAlmon had written. But that seemed to be the one bright spot in his visit. He thought writers such as Sean O'Casey, Liam O'Flaherty and Sean O'Faolain were making little impact among Dubliners. Overall, the city left McAlmon cold and he could understand why so many of its people had emigrated. Doubtless with the Joyces, the Colums and others in mind he wondered: 'Do the Irish who have gone away and remained away awhile ever return to live contented in their homeland?'[12]

Joyce eventually did send his father money. With his letter of Christmas greetings in 1931 he enclosed a postal order for one pound. A day later, when he heard his father was dying, he telegraphed Dr Kerry Reddin, brother of Kenneth, asking him to provide the best medical attention and that he would pay for it. John Joyce died on 29 December. When Weaver heard the news she sent Joyce £100[13] (at the suggestion of Padraic Colum) to pay for the expenses of his father's illness and for the funeral.

Anxious to learn how his father had spent his last years, Joyce asked Colum (who was returning to Dublin) to call on the family with whom the old man had been staying (in those days it was normal for a man of a certain position to take board and lodging with a family for 25 or 30 shillings a week). Sadly, the picture that Colum reported back was of 'a battered shabby old man who had come to live with them after some kind of breakdown, either an accident such as befalls old men or a shock that had left him somewhat astray.'[14]

Tuohy spent much of his time during 1926 and early 1927 in Paris with the Joyces, doing portraits of Lucia (1927) and of Joyce's mother (drawn from family photographs) in 1926.

His unpredictability could embarrass those around him. Once, Arthur Power invited the artist and Joyce to a tea party along with some American friends. Tuohy, who was sitting by the door when Joyce arrived, started clapping in mock applause, annoying the writer intensely. Later during a conversation about Joyce's writings, Tuohy kept interrupting: 'Write a best seller, that's what you have to do, write a best seller.' (Power was later to admit that he, too, felt that Joyce should have written a 'best seller' rather than *Finnegans Wake*).

Life was not all despondency, however. Helen Nutting, a friend of the Joyces, wrote in her diary of a Christmas Eve party *chez* Joyce attended by Tuohy and Arthur Power among others. Joyce, a pink paper hat on his head, asked Tuohy to sing. Afterwards the artist asked Lucia to teach him to dance the Charleston. 'He never got the steps,' wrote Helen Nutting, 'but with infinite patience, with rosy cheeks and coattails at angles, he did his best. Lucia sweetly and most politely saying 'Now you must do this,' winking over his shoulder when his head was turned.' [15]

Tuohy's depression, however, gradually became more apparent and he often talked of suicide. He spoke of emigrating to America where he felt the financial rewards for his work would be greater.

The United States appealed to him also because his friend and former teacher Padraic Colum and his wife were living there. He passed through London on his way, calling to the offices of the *Connoisseur* art magazine which was edited by Thomas MacGreevy, later to become a particularly close friend of the Joyces.

Tuohy was 33 years old when he arrived in New York in April 1927. He visited the Colums where they were staying in Connecticut, then went on to visit Dr ECL Adams and his wife in South Carolina (he had met them at the Joyces and they had promised to arrange commissions in the US). He got a few commissions in the south but his conversations with sitters got him into trouble; he would often berate them over the position of African-Americans. As if that was not enough, he became over amorous towards some younger women. Made to feel unwelcome, he lost confidence in his work and became increasingly troubled in himself.

His commissions, however, paid considerably better than in Ireland and, with the help of the actress Ria Mooney (who was playing in *The Plough and the Stars* on Broadway), he found an apartment in New York and built up a circle of friends.

He returned once to Dublin to help get works for an exhibition in New York of contemporary Irish art, and intending to marry Phyllis Moss. He spent some time with Michael Scott (an actor then, later to become a celebrated architect) whom he asked to be his best man. But he never did get married. His depression was getting even worse.

On his return to New York in the spring of 1929 he exhibited alongside other Irish artists including AE, Paul Henry, Sean Keating and Harry Kernoff. Among Tuohy's entries was his portrait of James Stephens. The exhibition was highly praised with Tuohy, the only artist present in person, receiving much of the kudos.

For a while life seemed good for Tuohy who went on to paint some of his best portraits. But his depression returned. He often phoned Padraic Colum who tried to help by visiting him in New York. Joyce cheered him up when he sent him two signed copies of the first edition of *Ulysses*. Tuohy gave them to Mooney to bring back to Ireland for two of his close friends.

In late August 1930, Tuohy failed to keep an appointment with his psychiatrist. He also did not turn up for a meeting with Mooney and others. Concerned about his welfare, they asked his landlady to open the door of his apartment. They found the artist on a couch in a room full of gas. He had been dead for at least a week. He was 36.

When Joyce heard the news, he was not surprised. He told Power: 'He nearly made me commit suicide too.'

Padraic Colum and others arranged for the remains to be shipped home. Moss was among the large attendance at his funeral in the Pro-Cathedral in Dublin, as was Reddin who kept Joyce informed of the sad event. In a tribute in the *Sunday Independent*, Reddin wrote that he had never met a man who was more engrossed with life or more unhappy with it.

---

[1] Murphy: *Patrick Tuohy* 65.

[2] Idem. 77.

[3] Ellmann 565n.

[4] Hutchins: *James Joyce's World* 149 (an account of the meeting given by Phyllis Moss).

[5] Joyce to McAlmon May 1924 (Ellmann ed., *Letters of James Joyce Vol. 3*, 95).

[6] Budgen: *James Joyce and the Making of Ulysses* 362.

[7] Jackson and Costello: *John Stanislaus Joyce* 388.

[8] Ellmann 540.

[9] Hutchins: *James Joyce's World* 150.

[10] McAlmon: *Geniuses* 233.

[11] Writing in *Envoy* magazine in April 1951, Reddin wrote: The first time I met Joyce he was living in the rue de Grenelle. I went down armed with a box of Olhausen's black puddings. I did this on Paddy Tuohy's advice...' As a District Justice he heard driving charges against Samuel Beckett in 1937.

[12] McAlmon: *Geniuses* 234.

[13] Over £5,000 in today's terms. Thus the £1 postal order was equivalent to £50 now.

[14] Colum: *OFJJ* 201.

[15] Helen Nutting's diary quoted in Shloss: *Lucia Joyce* 172.

A Little Circle Of Kindred Minds

Chapter Ten
Literary Twins

James Stephens's eagerness to help Tuohy by giving him an introduction to Joyce sprung from the writer's characteristic kindness towards others. But his generosity took no account of the fact that, at the time he was talking to Tuohy, he and Joyce barely knew each other. They had met only once, twelve years previously, and the encounter had been decidedly cool. About all they had in common was distaste for each other's work. Yet, by the late 1920s, in a major literary u-turn, Joyce was asking Stephens to take over the writing of *Finnegans Wake* if he could not finish it himself.

Stephens was both surprised and flattered. The two were, in so many ways, opposites. In contrast with Joyce's middle-class family-oriented upbringing, Stephens had grown up an orphan. His father died when he was two and he was virtually abandoned by his mother who was disinterested in him. He was forced to attend an industrial school. His difficult upbringing does not appear to have left him with any ill-will towards his mother, although he seldom spoke about his early years. Still, he grew into a relatively balanced person, renowned for his wit, charm, kindness and an innate curiosity. Padraic Colum described him as 'the most exuberant of Dubliners.'[1]

He was also self-effacing. Describing Joyce as 'tall and slender with a finely cut face, beautiful hands and a lonely tenor voice,' he went on: 'I was the exact opposite to all that and had obviously been assembled rather hastily out of old boots held together by chewing gum.'[2]

His first short story, *The Greatest Miracle*, was published by Arthur Griffith[3] in his paper *The United Irishman* in 1905. The two men became good friends and Stephens became interested in nationalism and attended Gaelic League classes. He was transformed:

> *The Dublin I was born to was poor and Protestant and athletic. While very young I extended my range and entered a Dublin that was poor and Catholic and Gaelic – a very wonderworld.*[4]

As he moved around literary Dublin he went to Maud Gonne's 'at homes' on Monday evenings, the Colums' on Tuesday evenings and AE's on Sundays.'[5] He helped found and edit the *Irish Review* with Padraic Colum and Thomas MacDonagh.

> *I think I grew up among the wittiest conversationalists in the world, and every man-jack and woman-jill of them seemed to be writing verse, and reciting it at each other and at you… I think that if you lived in the Dublin of that day you had to write verse, or pretend to be a foreigner.*[6]

Stephens was easily recognised by his diminutive stature, resembling a leprechaun. He had a sad, deeply lined face with a small neck and a large head upon which sat a battered felt hat pulled down over his eyes. He covered the rest of himself in an old loose-fitting raincoat.

His big break came in 1912 with the publication of two novels, *The Charwoman's Daughter* and *The Crock of Gold*. That same year he met Joyce for the first time.

They met in Dawson Street in Dublin at a time when they were each having rows with George Roberts, the impossibly difficult managing director of Maunsel & Company. The strained background showed in their encounter, which came about when a friend accompanying Joyce introduced the two and then left.

Stephens made the first move. 'Come and have a drink.'

As they walked towards a hostelry in Grafton Street, Joyce was silent. Stephens tried to humour him by talking about the weather.

'An American holds that it never rains in Ireland except between the showers.'

'Ah,' said Joyce.

'But a French lady told me that it rains in Ireland whether there are showers or not.'

'Ah.'

They entered the first pub they came to. As their drinks of malt warmed them, Joyce began to come round. Looking down on the diminutive Stephens he remarked that he had read his two latest books and that, grammatically, he (Stephens) did not know the difference between a semi-colon and a colon. He went on to say that Stephens's knowledge of Irish life was non-Catholic and therefore non-existent... and that he should give up writing and take up a good job like shoe shining as a more promising profession.

Stephens replied that he had never read a word of Joyce's and that he never would do so unless asked to review it destructively.

The conversation could only improve after that. Soon, Joyce was singing one of his favourite songs, *The Brown and the Yellow Ale.*

As they left the pub, Joyce lifted his hat to Stephens, who remarked: 'You should engrave on your banner and on your notebook the slogan 'Rejoyce and be exceedingly bad.'

'Ah,' said Joyce, and they parted.

It would be seventeen years before they would meet again.

It took most of that period for Stephens to come round to Joyce's work. He found *Dubliners* 'interesting but unpleasant & must be counted among his many wild oats.'[7] Even the fuss that came with the publication of *Ulysses* failed to influence him. 'It is too expensive to buy, and too difficult to borrow, and too long to read, and, from what I have heard about it, altogether too difficult to talk about.'[8] *Chamber Music*, he believed, was Joyce's best work.

Equally, Joyce had little time for Stephens's writing. Of *The Crock of Gold*, he said: 'It's all right, but it isn't written. I don't see why anybody couldn't do that.'[9]

Shortly after his first meeting with Joyce, Stephens felt he should widen his literary horizons and decided to learn French. He went to language class each morning and took to wearing a French cavalry officer's cloak (in which his portrait was painted by Tuohy). He was often seen walking back to his flat in Mount Street in Dublin in the evening with a baguette under his arm.

He moved to Paris in 1913 with his long-term lover Cynthia Kavanagh (they married in 1919), finding a flat at eleven rue Campagne-Première, which he kept for the rest of his life. He considered Paris his second home, dividing his time between Dublin, Paris and London until the outbreak of the Second World War.

In that same year, 1913, he met Gertrude Stein who invited him to her home. He was enormously impressed by her art collection. 'She has about 150 pictures of Matisse, Picasso & the other men & to walk into her room where they hang is an experience,' he wrote to a friend.[10]

Paris during the Great War was a depressing city, dull and empty. Stephens did not mix much with French people, partly because of his limited knowledge of the language. Cynthia often went to Maud Gonne's Tuesday evenings with a friend. James used to take Gonne's son, Sean MacBride, for cake and ice cream after school.

Paris stifled him and he found it difficult to write, but he persevered, often jotting things down in cafés such as the Closerie des Lilas where Hemingway would write his novels a decade later. By 1915 he was finding it difficult to live on his royalties (by now *The Crock of Gold* had been awarded the Polignac prize, the gift of the Princess Edmond de Polignac) and he told his friends – he still kept in touch with AE and Padraic Colum – that he was looking for a job. They succeeded in getting him the position of Registrar with the National Gallery in Dublin – despite strong opposition from one of the gallery's directors, Dr J P Mahaffy, Provost of Trinity College, who mistook him for the Fenian James Stephens. Mahaffy was a snob who did not want someone of such humble origin appointed to the post.[11]

Stephens and Cynthia continued to visit Paris on their holidays. Cynthia would leave early to put the flat in order, then James would follow, often dining with the Kerry poet Thomas MacGreevy at the Royal Marine Hotel in Kingstown before boarding the boat.[12] Literature and art were their common interests; 35 years later, MacGreevy would become Director of the National Gallery.

On Easter Monday, 1916, Stephens was walking back to work after lunch when he saw a man being shot at a barricade. Stephens had no inside knowledge of the Rising, but the events of Easter Week moved him deeply, intensified his patriotic feelings and renewed his interest in old Irish literature. He attended Irish language classes.

Even in Paris, Stephens never lost his Irish pride. According to Paul Scott Mowrer, an American writer he sometimes met for lunch, Stephens was not concerned with the war. 'He was more given to expatiating on Cuchulain and Angus than on Joffre or Foch. To hear him, Ireland was the most ancient and only authentic seat of culture, from which all others had brazenly borrowed...'[13]

Stephens corresponded frequently with John Quinn, the New York lawyer who collected manuscripts of Irish writers, notably those of Joyce. Quinn paid Stephens £20 for the MS of *The Crock of Gold* in 1913. The topic of Joyce and his writings often arose in their letters. In 1922, after *Ulysses* was published, Stephens wrote: 'He [Joyce] has written, say, three books in prose – they are all the same book, and the man that he is at forty-five or six is only and merely the boy that he was at nineteen and twenty-five. If a tree doesn't grow it is no good, if a man does not grow he is no good.'[14]

By 1929, however, Stephens had changed his tune about Joyce. Re-reading his attacks on Joyce's works that he had written years earlier, Stephens added a postscript: 'Joyce has done great work, & has written beautiful prose. Time will judge him, & me, & us; & we, none of us, need to greatly mind it.'[15]

In 1924, Stephens resigned from his post at the National Gallery. He and Cynthia moved to England – to a little house in Kingsbury outside London. The move would become the catalyst for a new career – as a broadcaster for the BBC. Between the late 1920s and the time he died in 1950 he delivered numerous literary radio talks and, despite or perhaps because of his Irishness, became accepted in London literary circles.[16]

He still visited Paris and did lecture tours in the United States. The first of these was arranged by Padraic and Mary Colum in January 1925. Stephens refrained from using his eyeglass during the tour because he was told it made him look like an Englishman.

This was the time of Prohibition and Stephens was giving a talk in Cincinnati on St Patrick's Day when a considerable amount of liquor was consumed. He was in mid-speech when the door to the banqueting room burst open and a squad of policemen entered. His listeners were nervous but the police waited until Stephens was finished. There was much applause and before Stephens sat down the hard-boiled sergeant walked up to him and held out his hand.

'You've sure given me a whiff of old Ireland,' he said and he motioned to his underlings to retreat quietly.[17]

Stephens's close friendship with Joyce did not start until 1927 and came indirectly, through his friendship with the Colums. The Irish artist Sarah Purser was in Paris and got in touch with Mary Colum who arranged for her to stay in the small hotel in rue Montparnasse where she and Padraic were living at the time. Purser had trained in Paris in her youth, after which she became a highly successful portrait painter in London and Dublin. Now she was in her late seventies and she wanted to meet James Joyce.

Mary sent Joyce and Nora an invitation to join the three of them for dinner in a restaurant beside the hotel. She also invited James and Cynthia Stephens who were also in Paris. It was a good mix, for Stephens was well acquainted with Purser who was a governor of the National Gallery and had founded the Friends of the National Collections. Some years earlier Stephens had written her a letter of introduction to Gertrude Stein.

Stephens could not attend the dinner, however, having a prior engagement in London. In the restaurant, Cynthia sat beside Joyce throughout the meal. And while the author of *Ulysses* paid due attention to Purser – one of the literary and intellectual doyens of Dublin – it was Cynthia who made the bigger impression on him.

But it was her diminutive husband who was mostly on Joyce's mind these days. Joyce was going through a difficult patch with his *Work in Progress* and he began doubting his ability to finish it. Perhaps he should ask someone else to take on the task.

The opening pages of what would become *Finnegans Wake* had appeared in *transition* magazine. Mary Colum, reviewing it in *The New York Times*, found it almost entirely incomprehensible. Ezra Pound called it 'all a bad stunt.' Joyce's patron Harriet Weaver, on being sent an extract, wrote back: 'It seems to me you are wasting your genius.' Even Nora was unsympathetic: 'Why don't you write sensible books that people can understand?'

During this black period, Joyce became obsessed by a series of coincidences that pointed towards Stephens. He realised that, for years, he had been carrying in his pocket photographs of portraits Tuohy had painted of himself, his father and ... James Stephens. He was also taken by the writer's names, which corresponded, to his own first name and that of his hero in both *Portrait* and *Ulysses*. As if that was not enough, he learned, through enquiries he made in Paris in April 1927, that Stephens had been born in Dublin on the same date as himself – 2 February, 1882 – and at precisely the same time – six o'clock in the morning.[18]

They were, in effect, literary twins! He would ask
Stephens to take over finishing *Finnegans Wake* ! The
more he thought about the idea the more he liked it. The
collaboration would result in the letters JJ & S beneath
the title (the initials of the Dublin whiskey distillery,
John Jameson and Son).

Stephens wrote years later:

> *Joyce was strangely in love with his own birthday
> and with mine. He had discovered somehow that
> he and I were twins, born in the same hour of the
> same day of the same year in the same city. The
> bed it seemed was different, and that was the only
> snag in our relationship.*[19]

As was his wont, Joyce could not bring himself to
approach Stephens directly, instead asking Beach to 'get
into closer relations' with him. He also knew the
limitations of what he had in mind, but rationalised that
they could be turned to advantage:

> *Of course he would never take a fraction of the
> time or pains I take but so much the better for
> him and me and possibly for the book itself. If he
> consented to maintain three or four points which
> I consider essential and I showed him the threads
> he could finish the design... It would be a great
> load off my mind. I shall think this over first and
> wait until the opposition becomes more general
> and pointed.*[20]

Joyce mulled over the idea for several months. As the
coincidences piled on top of one another in his mind, he
could hold back to longer. He called to Stephens's
apartment but he was out. When Stephens returned, his
concierge told him a tall, beautiful, blind gentleman had

called and had left a note. In it, Joyce asked Stephens to meet him the following day. They were to see a lot of each other after that, but it took Joyce several months before he broached the subject of finishing the Wake. When he did, it came as a surprise to Stephens:

> *Well, I was astonished. I was admired at last.*
> *Joyce admired me. I was beloved at last: Joyce*
> *loved me. Or did he? Or did he only love his*
> *birthday, and was I merely coincident to that?*[21]

Stephens agreed to help with *Work in Progress* if necessary, but he was quick to tell Joyce he knew he would finish his book, adding: '*Anna Livia Plurabelle* is the greatest prose ever written by a man.'[22]

Even without Stephens's practical assistance, the little man's good-natured enthusiasm helped Joyce through this difficult period. The two men were frequently together and sometimes Colum would join them. 'No-one in the world had such spontaneity with so much gusto as James Stephens,' Colum wrote later, 'so much wisdom with so much nonsense, so much fantasy with so much poetry. If he had not been a poet and a storyteller James Stephens would have been a clown in the great style.'[23]

Stephens would visit the Joyces and entertain the family with his good humour and his singing – especially of Dublin street songs such as Molly Malone, his eyes closed, his hands clasped before him.

Colum had enormous admiration for both men. He observed the relationship between them grow closer, one complementing the other:

> *They had an occupational relationship; they were*
> *both of the company of a group of strolling*
> *players. I could see them in a booth or on a stage*

*in the open air, one appearing and singing some
great aria, then the other coming on with a
monologue composed of poetry and fantasy.
What a performance that pair could give!*[24]

The notion that Stephens should help him finish
Finnegans Wake remained with Joyce for a long time.
Apart from feeling flattered, Stephens did not take the
suggestion very seriously. The Joyces and the Stephenses
spent much time together in the summer of 1929 when
Joyce and Nora were in London. But the matter does not
seem to have arisen in any serious way.

Then, back in Paris the following November, two years
after he first thought of the idea, Joyce spent a week
explaining to Stephens the book's plan. Again, Stephens
consented, promising the author that, in Joyce's words,
'if I found it was madness to continue, in my condition,
and saw no other way out, that he would devote himself
heart and soul to the completion of it, that is the second
part and the epilogue or fourth.'[25] As Richard Ellman put
it: 'Stephens had by now become so much a part of
Joyce's phantasmagoria that Joyce could freely beguile
himself with the fancy of transferring authorship.'[26]

The 'literary twins' concept became established among
Joyce's friends who were invited to join the two Jameses
in celebrating their birthday on 2 February, 1931. The
dinner was held at the Trianons restaurant and was
attended by all the Joyces, James and Cynthia Stephens,
Beach, the Irish tenor John Sullivan who was singing at
the Paris Opera, and Mary and Padraic Colum. Joyce
asked the waiter to bring one of his favourite wines, *Clos
de Saint Patrice* which came from the region in the
Rhone valley where St Patrick is supposed to have stayed
after he escaped from captivity in Ireland (Joyce always
insisted St Patrick was born in France). 'He is the only
saint a man can get drunk in honour of,' he said.[27]

Afterwards the party adjourned to Joyce's apartment at Square Robiac. Giorgio and Sullivan sang. Joyce sang *The Brown and the Yellow Ale*. Then Joyce turned to Colum: 'John McCormack's voice and mine are so similar in texture – as are my son's voice and mine, in spite of the different pitch, and as are my own voice and my father's – that more than once when a disc of McCormack's has been on, the girl in the kitchen has thought it was me.'[28]

Stephens's daughter Iris became friendly with Lucia Joyce and the bond between Joyce and Stephens continued, surviving disagreements Joyce had with others, among them Weaver, Beach and Monnier. In May 1932, the 'jubilee year' of himself and Stephens, he translated a poem of his literary twin into five languages – French, German, Latin, Norwegian and Italian – hoping that Stephens himself would translate it into Irish (in fact Stephens's Irish was not good enough). The poem, entitled *Stephens Green*, was hardly worth the trouble of such extensive translation, but Joyce could not resist exploiting the unintended pun in the title.

Later that same year, both Stephens and Colum urged Joyce to accept an invitation from Yeats and Shaw to join their new Academy of Irish Letters, but he declined, telling Yeats: 'I see no reason why my name should have arisen at all in connection with such an academy.'[29]

It was only a matter of time before the literary twins would disagree on something. In September 1936, just back from a visit to Copenhagen, his thoughts full of Ibsen, Joyce urged Stephens to read *Little Eyolf*, a copy of which he lent him.

Two days later, Stephens posted his reply from his flat at rue Campagne-Première. He accepted that Ibsen was a competent stage manager. But that was as much a compliment as he was prepared to pay the playwright. In a scathing attack on Ibsen ('the most thorough-going liar, or falsifier of the truth'), Stephens continued in a vein that could hardly be more hurtful to a committed Ibsenite such as Joyce. 'If ever there was in literature a sadist such an one was Ibsen, and that anyone could ever have been taken in by him, critically or morally, remains for me as an inexplicable enigma.' [30]

Joyce replied a few days later and, in a line that suggested he was not prepared to let Ibsen come between his literary twin and himself, wrote: 'what you say is true but it is by no means all, in my opinion.' [31]

In the same letter, Joyce invited him to dinner.

---

[1] Colum: *Arthur Griffith* 94.

[2] Stephens: *James, Seumas and Jacques*.

[3] Stephens regarded Griffith as 'the greatest journalist working in the English language' (Calton Younger: *Arthur Griffith*).

[4] Stephens: *Memories of Dublin*.

[5] The writer Liam O'Flaherty wrote of one such evening at AE's: 'Stephens the novelist was there, nice fellow enough, but rather proud of himself... We got on well, however, which I effected by keeping my mouth shut and agreeing with him on every point...' (Letter to A. A. Kelly, March 1924).

[6] Stephens: *James, Seumas and Jacques*.

[7] Letter to Thomas Bodkin, 2 August, 1914 (Finneran, ed: *Letters of James Stephens*).

[8] Letter to John Quinn, 15 August, 1922.

[9] Elliot Paul: article in *Bookman*, May, 1932 (quoted in Ellmann 591).

[10] Letter to Thomas Bodkin, 9 July, 1913.

[11] Mahaffy once remarked: 'James Joyce is a living argument in favour of my contention that it was a mistake to establish a separate university for the aborigines of this island – for the cornerboys who spit into the Liffey.' [Gerald Griffin, *The Wild Geese: Pen Portraits of Famous Irish Exiles* (London, 1938) quoted by Ellmann in *James Joyce* 58].

[12] Pyle: *James Stephens* 91.

[13] Idem.

[14] Letter to John Quinn, 15 August, 1922.

[15] Letter to W. T. H. Howe, 14 August, 1929.

[16] Regardless of his strong sense of nationalism, he dissociated himself from Irish neutrality during the Second World War,

declaring himself 'an Irishman who wished to elect himself an Englishman for the duration.'

[17] Story told in *transition* magazine, May 1931, reprinted in Ford: *The Left Bank Revisited.*

[18] Stephens's date of birth is more likely to have been the 9 February, 1880. In keeping with the mystery he cast over his early years, he claimed it was the 2nd of February, 1882.

[19] BBC Radio talk 1948.

[20] Joyce to Weaver, 20 May 1927 Gilbert ed., *Letters of James Joyce Vol. 2*, 253).

[21] Stephens: article in *The Listener.*

[22] Joyce to Weaver, 16 July, 1929 (Gilbert ed., *Letters of James Joyce Vol. 2*, 281).

[23] Colum: *OFJJ* 166.

[24] Idem. 166.

[25] Joyce to Weaver 22 November 1929 (Gilbert ed., *Letters of James Joyce Vol. 2*, 286).

[26] Ellmann 619.

[27] Colum: *OFJJ* 182.

[28] Idem. 184.

[29] Among others who refused to join were Douglas Hyde, Sean O'Casey and Daniel Corkery. (Mathews: *Voices: A Life of Frank O'Connor* 95).

[30] Stephens to Joyce, 20 September, 1936.

[31] Ellmann ed., *Letters of James Joyce, vol 3*, 391.

Chapter Eleven
Man In The Middle

One evening in November 1928, the Joyces were having a dinner party in their apartment at 2 Square Robiac when the phone rang. Joyce picked it up. It was Tom MacGreevy,[1] a 35-year-old Kerryman who was teaching at the *École Normale Supérieure*. He would like to call round with a friend - also from Ireland - who was interested in meeting Joyce.

Most of Joyce's guests were surprised to see a sudden change come over him. No sooner had he put down the phone than he started suggesting one of them might like to leave... or did they know someone they wished to invite...? He sounded frantic. Those who did not know Joyce well thought he was pulling their leg. Others present, like Mary Colum - aware of Joyce's superstitious nature - knew how serious he was. The addition of MacGreevy and his friend would bring the number of guests to thirteen. Eventually, to Joyce's great relief, one did leave.

Far from bringing bad luck, the occasion proved to be one of the most propitious for Joyce. MacGreevy's friend was a Trinity College graduate from the middle-class Dublin suburb of Foxrock named Beckett.

It was what Joyce might have called 'a concatenation of circumstances' that brought these three Irish writers together in Paris. Arguably, Joyce might never have met up with MacGreevy and Beckett but for MacGreevy's friendship with the artist Patrick Tuohy. Tuohy had been recommended to Joyce – who was seeking someone to paint his father - by Arthur Power. Such was the network of friendships that was slowly transforming itself into the latest Joyce circle.

More significantly, MacGreevy, a poet of considerable standing in his own right, became a close friend of both Joyce and Beckett – straddling the literary and personal lives of two of Ireland's most outstanding writers.

Thomas MacGreevy was born in Tarbert, Co Kerry, in 1893. His father had been a policeman but it was his mother, a teacher, who influenced him the most by passing on a love of music and books. She even taught him French and how to sing the *Marseillaise*. After a national school education he entered the civil service at the age of 15. He worked in the Land Commission in Dublin before moving to the civil service in London. At the outbreak of the Great War, he was transferred to the Intelligence Department in the Admiralty. In 1916, he enlisted in the Royal Field Artillery and, after a lengthy training period as a gunner, received his commission as second lieutenant. He was sent to the front line at the Ypres Salient (where Arthur Power had fought the previous year).

MacGreevy could hardly be described as an enthusiastic soldier (years later he would graphically describe in his poems some of the horrors he witnessed). But he was trustworthy and conscientious and always acted out of a sense of duty rather than of anger or hatred of the enemy. As an artillery officer, MacGreevy was often more exposed to enemy attack than the rank and file gunners under his command.

It was his responsibility to leave the guns and go up to an observation post, which was usually just behind the front line, trench. Using field glasses, he would identify enemy soldiers and direct shelling at their positions. As a result, one of the priorities for the Germans was to put the observation post out of action. Wyndham Lewis, the

English writer and painter who would later become a drinking companion of Joyce in Paris, was a second lieutenant in the Royal Garrison Artillery. He later wrote of the work involved at the Observation Posts (O. Pips):

> *This O. Pip work was hard and often very dangerous... In an active part of the Front the telephone wires would never remain intact for long, as they would be cut by shell-fire. It might have been quite useful if the enemy had not persisted in destroying the wires, or if they had left the observation post itself in peace. But this they would not do. They spotted an observation post within a half-hour at the outside and would shell it to pieces.*[2]

But even the dirtiest of wars has its moments of routine and boredom - and humour. MacGreevy later described how, on occasions, each side would entertain the other:

> *I noticed that the soldiers on the opposing sides had ways of playing games with each other. Thus an English machine gunner might rattle off a few rounds to the rhythm of Dah, Da-Dah, Dah and stop. Back immediately would come the answering close of the rhythm from a German machine-gunner, Dah, Dah. Then there would be silence for another while.*[3]

MacGreevy was at home in Kerry, half way through army leave, when the Germans launched their spring offensive in March, 1918. Ordered to return, he made his way back to his brigade, now based at Saint Quentin in Picardy. The following October, wounded for a second time by shellfire, he was transferred to hospital in Manchester and, after the Armistice, to Athlone. He was demobbed in January, 1919.

As with Power, the war deeply affected MacGreevy. Its horrors and its meaninglessness tested his devout Catholicism. But it was events at home that were to have a more lasting impact. Like Power, the Ireland he returned to had changed dramatically since he had been there, an Ireland that was in conflict with the views of many of his British friends at whose side he had fought. As was the case with Power, he would have been made to feel uncomfortable as someone who had fought in the British Army at a time when his fellow countrymen were fighting that same army. There was no doubting where his sympathies lay in the War of Independence, however: he accepted and respected his country's right to self-determination.[4]

MacGreevy's service in the British Army gave him the opportunity to attend Trinity College Dublin by availing of a scholarship for former officers. This move was to influence his entire future - as a writer, poet, lecturer and connoisseur of art – leading ultimately to his appointment as Director of the National Gallery.

The irony of his decision to attend TCD was not lost on him: a Catholic nationalist attending what was then a predominantly Protestant unionist university.[5] He was one of a dozen Trinity students (all former British army officers) who petitioned the Provost to appeal for a reprieve for Kevin Barry, a medical student of the Catholic National University who was sentenced to death for taking part in an attack on British soldiers. The Provost refused to do anything.[6]

On 14 March, 1921, he joined 20,000 people who stood outside Mountjoy Jail in Dublin at dawn and prayed as six young men were hanged by the British. He often wondered if God had deserted his country, but he never lost his religion.

MacGreevy got an honours degree in politics and history

(specialising in the French Revolution) and wrote articles for *The Irish Statesman* and other publications. During this time he became friendly with several writers and painters in Dublin, among them the Yeats brothers, Mainie Jellett, Harry Clarke, Sarah Purser and the portrait painter Patrick Tuohy.

In May, 1924, he decided to visit Spain. Before leaving Dublin, however, Tuohy offered to introduce him to Joyce should he ever get to Paris. It was a year since Tuohy had painted Joyce's father, John Stanislaus Joyce, but he had never met the son. He was planning to go to Paris to see Phyllis Moss, the young art student with whom he had fallen in love, and while there he would avail of Stephens's letter of introduction and call on the Joyces.

Towards the end of May, MacGreevy arrived in Paris on his way back from Spain. When he went to Cooks agency to complete his travel arrangements, he was handed a note. It was from Tuohy offering to get him a room at the hotel where he, Tuohy, was staying and saying he would like him to meet Joyce who was 'a very nice person.'

MacGreevy had mixed feelings about meeting the author of *Ulysses*. He had read the novel but found parts of it puzzling and felt the author would be 'a detached kind of man.' He was unaware that Joyce had only just met Tuohy (who was accompanied by Phyllis Moss) and that Joyce was irritated by both.

In contrast, MacGreevy enjoyed Tuohy's company. The two often visited the Luxembourg Gallery together, where Tuohy was studying the French Impressionist paintings. One evening Tuohy suggested they join the Joyces for coffee after the family's evening meal at the Trianons restaurant. After being introduced to Joyce, Nora and Giorgio, the conversation moved quickly to news from Dublin, Nora asking MacGreevy to 'tell us about the swans' - a reference to Gogarty's presentation of a pair of swans

to the river Liffey in thanksgiving for his escape from
Republican soldiers (during the civil war) by swimming
across the river. But MacGreevy could only say that he had
not been there at the time.

Suddenly Joyce said coldly: 'I believe it was you told Tuohy
my father's Christian name was Simon.'

MacGreevy had to admit he had indeed done so. He never
knew John Stanislaus Joyce but his friend, the stained-glass
artist Harry Clarke, did, and always referred to the father as
Old Simon. MacGreevy assumed that was his name and told
Tuohy so when asked. Thus, Tuohy exhibited the painting
under the title 'Simon Joyce, Esquire.'[7]

It was not an auspicious start to a friendship. But the
inquisition was followed by a lighter side. Tuohy was
amused that MacGreevy had to defend himself, for to him
the title of the painting was much less important than the
portrait itself. And Joyce was pleased that he had got
something on Tuohy who was beginning to get on his
nerves (although MacGreevy thought at the time that
Joyce was quite fond of the painter). Besides, it pleased
Joyce that the name of his hero's father, Simon (Dedalus),
was reborn in reality.

Soon afterwards, MacGreevy moved to London where he
began writing criticism for newspapers and magazines,
among them the arts journal *The Connoisseur* of which he
became assistant editor. At the same time he acted as
deputy lecturer at the National Gallery in London. In
1926, he began to translate Paul Valéry's *Introduction á la
Méthode de Léonard de Vinci*. In the same year, he
published his first poem, *Aodh Ruadh Ó Domhnaill* - an
allegory on the 1916 Rising - which had been inspired by
his visit to Spain.[8] He also met TS Eliot.

Tuohy kept him informed of the Joyces' welfare as he
went on to paint portraits of all four members of the

household. MacGreevy, though, was - as he put it himself - 'far from being committed to the Joyce canon in literature,' especially in relation to the artist's 'silence, exile and cunning:'

> *I was not naturally given to silence, and Sunday after Sunday all through my years as a growing boy, I had heard our parish priest at home quoting Saint Augustine to the effect that open confession was good for the soul. I had had plenty of exile and did not think much of it. And the implications of the word 'cunning,' except in relation to the technique of art, were unpleasant...*[9]

Then, at the start of 1927, MacGreevy made a move, which was to catapult him into the centre of the Joyce circle. While working in London on the *Connoisseur* and freelancing for the *Times Literary Supplement* and other publications, a friend told him that the temporary post of *lecteur d'anglais* at the *École Normale Supérieure* in Paris was vacant and that his name had already been suggested for it. MacGreevy rushed across the Channel to Paris and was accepted for the job.

The *École* was a serious, third-level establishment with a superb scholarly reputation, whose students gained a place by virtue of a highly competitive entrance examination. To a student of TCD, and even to those at the nearby Sorbonne - where the privileged *normaliens* attended classes - the college smacked of elitism and seemed more *supérieure* than *normale*. Trinity College had a reciprocal arrangement with it whereby every two years an outstanding graduate of one college would go to the other as *lecteur* or assistant teacher.

Just days after MacGreevy moved into his room at the *École*, he wrote to Joyce to tell him he was in Paris. At 9.30am the next morning, Joyce was on the phone. Would he come round to his flat in Square Robiac that afternoon?

When MacGreevy called to the apartment, Nora answered his knock on the door. The Irishman did not recognise her, for he had not seen Nora for three years. The person before him was silhouetted against the light, which lit up her hair.

'Is it Miss Joyce? My name is MacGreevy.'

Nora was delighted and flattered by his mistake, which was excusable under the circumstances since he had not yet met Lucia. It was the start of a warm friendship that would become closer than his relationship with Joyce himself.

Years later, in his *Memoirs*, MacGreevy wrote of his more pragmatic relationship with Joyce:

> *Joyce was not interested in personal friendship or friendships. So far as people were concerned all that seemed to matter was whether they were prepared to be interested in the Work in Progress that was to be Finnegans Wake ... When new acquaintanceships turned up, I would say that his first and only consideration was whether they could be of use in relation to the still unnamed work.*[10]

Being 'of use' to Joyce's work meant being able to discuss with him anything that might become appropriate for him to put into *Finnegans Wake* - and that meant just about everything: history, geography, theology, literature... an endless list. A special emphasis, of course, was placed on anything Irish or, more specifically, relating to Dublin. And, as MacGreevy soon learned, being useful to Joyce also meant helping to transcribe his writing.

Joyce was going through mixed fortunes in early 1927. The first few chapters of *Finnegans Wake* were being published each month in Eugene Jolas's magazine, *transition*, and he was working on the *ALP* episode. But the strain it put on his eyes necessitated yet another operation - his tenth. At the same time he was involved in bringing legal proceedings against Samuel Roth's piracy of *Ulysses* in America. He was also in regular correspondence with his benefactor, Harriet Weaver, whose criticism of his writing upset him. But, thanks to Weaver - as well as royalties from *Ulysses* - he enjoyed a comfortable income of two thousand pounds a year (equivalent to about €120,000 today).

The circle of friends that Joyce was, consciously or unconsciously, circumscribing about him to help him produce his masterpiece was beginning to take shape and Tom MacGreevy would be the most important among them - for the moment at least. Joyce's speedy phone call to MacGreevy that morning was more than a casual call to someone who was from Ireland and who might be 'useful' to him. The two men got on well together from the beginning and it was not long before MacGreevy became accepted as a friend by the entire Joyce household. He no longer needed a phone call or letter to invite him to a meal or a singsong at the Joyces. He was one of the few people who could walk in unannounced. He enjoyed the company of Joyce's children, becoming Giorgio's best man at his marriage to Helen Fleischman.

The reason lay in MacGreevy's warm personality and character as much as his 'usefulness' to Joyce. Small and well dressed, the 33-year-old Kerryman was a good storyteller and had a lively sense of humour. He was deeply Catholic, a regular churchgoer, yet open-minded and tolerant of others (some of his anecdotes were quite risqué). He was self-confident and talkative, but also a good listener. He was knowledgeable and enthusiastic about painting and music, often singing to his own piano accompaniment at soirées in the Joyces. Exceptionally, he became a confidant of both Joyce and Beckett, albeit in different ways.

The fact that MacGreevy came from beyond the 'Pale' (the more anglicised greater Dublin area) appealed to Nora, who was from Galway. Joyce would confess: 'Thirty miles outside Dublin and I am lost.' But what pleased Nora above all was MacGreevy's dependability and moderation in drinking. Nora knew that if her husband was with MacGreevy he was in good hands.

True to their own drinking habits, Joyce's companions saw him in different ways. While McAlmon's memories of social evenings out with Joyce depict him as having to be poured into a taxi and helped up the stairs to his flat, MacGreevy remembered him, perhaps a little naively, as a man who drank in moderation:

> *He worked all day, ate a little and drank nothing*
> *until it came to dinner time… I think Joyce was not*
> *really a drinking man. If he took a second liqueur,*
> *one might feel he needed help getting to his taxi.*[11]

MacGreevy was delighted with the opportunity to meet up with the Joyces for more than intellectual and social reasons. His rooms at the *École* were spartan and the food served in the lecturers' dining room was poor, leading many of the staff as well as students to eat out as often as they could afford it.[12]

About once every two or three weeks, Joyce would call on MacGreevy unannounced, arriving by taxi at the gate of the *École* at about 8pm. MacGreevy's rooms did not have a phone and, whether Joyce telephoned the college or called, the concierge would shout up the message. MacGreevy would then either shout back his response from the window or run down the stairs to meet his guest.

As MacGreevy arrived at the gate, Joyce would ask him if he was free. If so, he got into the taxi and the two men would go to an *estaminet* or small Alsace-style pub on the rue Saint-Honoré that was owned by a Swiss. This was where Joyce would buy a bottle of one of his favourite wines - the Swiss Fendant de Sion. While they waited for the wine, the two stood at the counter and Joyce ordered apéritifs - a Dubonnet for himself and a light mandarin-curacao for MacGreevy which he would take with soda. (Once, Joyce ordered a Dubonnet for MacGreevy but he could not finish it).

Then, carrying the bottle of wine, the two would make their way to the Trianons restaurant to join Nora, arriving around a quarter to nine. The wine would be consumed with the meal, which would be followed by a liqueur. At 11.30pm or so, Joyce and Nora would get a taxi home, while MacGreevy would walk back to the *École*.

The timetable-like precision of the evening in itself illustrates the reliability, which Nora could place on MacGreevy.

Such an evening of relative moderation would often be followed by a phone call from Joyce at about half past nine the next morning, asking MacGreevy about something that came up in their animated conversation of the previous evening. Sometimes Joyce would ask him to call round to Square Robiac where they would elucidate on their discussion.

Nora felt sorry for MacGreevy on such occasions, feeling her husband was using him.

'Don't mind him, Tom,' she would say. 'If God himself came down from Heaven that fellow would find something for him to do.' Then, turning to her husband: 'You ought to be ashamed of yourself, Jim.'

Joyce would respond to her teasing with a smile. MacGreevy felt there was a perfect understanding between them.

If Nora was critical of the demands her husband made on MacGreevy, she was capable of making similar demands herself when the need arose. On one occasion she phoned MacGreevy and asked him to come over, saying she would explain everything when he got there. On his arrival, MacGreevy found Nora dressed in her finery. She had been invited to an afternoon party at the Ritz, but that morning she received a letter from her uncle in Galway, Michael Healy, saying he would be arriving the following day. Joyce wanted Nora to accompany him on a walk around the *quartier* in search of a suitable place for her uncle to stay; he was elderly and a daily communicant, so an hotel would have to be found near a church so that he would not have far to walk while fasting. Nora felt that Tom MacGreevy was just the man for this task and asked him to accompany her husband, whose eyes were bad at the time. As usual, MacGreevy was happy to oblige. Even then, Joyce was reluctant to let her leave. Eventually, in frustration, she departed with the words: 'For heaven's sake, Jim, let me go to my party and you mind your Ondts and Gracehopers till I get back.'[13]

Joyce and MacGreevy often chatted in the Joyce living room, which was surrounded by Tuohy's portraits of the family as well as those of Joyce's ancestors on his father's side, which he had brought from Dublin. But each viewed the pictures in different ways. Where MacGreevy saw the paintings as portraits, Joyce saw them as family - something that was of enormous importance to him. He had no illusions about his shortcomings in art appreciation and was puzzled by MacGreevy's knowledge:

'Where did you pick up that way you have of talking about painting?' he once asked MacGreevy. 'Yeats has it. Pound has it. I never had it.'

The admission was all the greater coming from a man some of whose closest friends were connoisseurs of art: Arthur Power, a painter, would become art critic of *The Irish*

Times... Tom MacGreevy Director of the National Gallery... and James Stephens had been Registrar of the same.

In fact, Joyce, who was having great difficulty getting published, never mind paid, envied painters' ability to sell their work virtually as soon as they had finished. He once wrote to Weaver (when feeling particularly low):

> *My position is a farce. Picasso has not a higher name than I have, I suppose, and he can get 20,000 or 30,000 francs for a few hours work. I am not worth a penny a line.*

The timing of MacGreevy's arrival in Joyce's world was fortunate, for he came when others were deserting him.

Even Joyce's own brother, Stanislaus, attacked his writing. He wrote wearily: 'You have done the longest day in literature, and now you are conjuring up the deepest night.' Weaver described his new work as 'wallowing in its verbiage' - but she continued to finance him.

Then, in April 1928, there came criticism from Sean O'Faolain of *Anna Livia Plurabelle*, which stung Joyce. It was accompanied by some good news but even that was not enough for Joyce. AE had reviewed *ALP* - the American edition for which Padraic Colum had written the preface - and amidst high praise described its author as 'a virtuoso in the use of words.' But the review, in *The Irish Statesman*, was attacked by O'Faolain in a Letter to the Editor, calling *Work In Progress* 'one of the most interesting and pathetic literary adventures I know, pathetic chiefly because of its partial success...'[14]

Joyce had had enough. It was time once more to go into action. He got Eugene Jolas (owner-editor of *transition*) and MacGreevy to bat for him by responding to the criticism in separate Letters to the Editor, which were published in *The Irish Statesman* at the beginning of 1929.

As if things were not bad enough for Joyce, his eyes were giving him further trouble and Nora was diagnosed with suspected cancer. She had an operation which was followed by radium treatment and, in February 1929, a hysterectomy.

But all was not bleak. MacGreevy was about to introduce another Irishman into Joyce's life – a young fellow Dubliner who would immerse himself in the older man's world before going on to plough his own deep literary furrow.

---

[1] The family name was McGreevy. He changed it to MacGreevy in the 1930s.

[2] Lewis: *Blasting and Bombardiering*, Eyre & Spottiswoode 1937. Calder 1982.

[3] MacGreevy papers. Manuscripts Department, TCD.

[4] MacGreevy sympathised with IRA members, but he resolved that he must work 'for an Ireland that could neither be made nor marred by guns.' (TCD MS Dept).

[5] Catholics were banned by their church from attending TCD until the late 20th century.

[6] Kevin Barry, a member of the IRA, was hanged on 1st November 1920, after which scores of students joined the organisation. (Macardle: *The Irish Republic* 392).

[7] The painting was exhibited at the Royal Hibernian Academy in Dublin and reviewed by AE in *The Irish Statesman*. He, too, referred to it as a 'portrait of Simon Joyce.'

[8] MacGreevy was in Spain with his friend Lennox Robinson and had been inspired by Red Hugh O'Donnell's final resting place there.

[9] MacGreevy papers, TCD.

[10] Idem.

[11] Idem.

[12] MacGreevy enjoyed the company of others and he was friendly with many of the staff members at the *École*, some of whom were homosexual. This fact, when viewed against his *Memoirs* (In TCD's Manuscripts Department, MS/8053 and MS8054) which describe his attraction to men rather than women as a young man, have led to suggestions that he was gay. There is no evidence, however, that he was actively homosexual and he was

devastated when a woman he was attracted to married his friend Lennox Robinson.

[13] MacGreevy papers, TCD.

[14] O'Faolain in *The Irish Statesman*, 5 January, 1929 (see also Susan Schreibman: *The Penman and his Bleaters*, The MacGreevy Archive online).

Chapter Twelve
Happy Days

On 1 November, 1928, Tom MacGreevy's stay at the *École Normale* was interrupted by the arrival of another graduate of Trinity College. Samuel Beckett, his successor as *lecteur d'anglais*, was exhausted, having travelled from Vienna in a third class carriage with wooden seats. But he had little time to rest, for when he arrived at his room he found his predecessor's belongings scattered everywhere.

The circumstances of this meeting between MacGreevy and Beckett would have tested anyone's nerves. Yet, the two men - poles apart in so many ways - were to become close friends for life.

A year earlier, MacGreevy - believing that no-one had been appointed to succeed him as visiting lecturer - had asked the Director of the *École*, Gustave Lanson, if he could stay on. MacGreevy got on well with Lanson (as he did with other members of the staff and with the students) and the Director led him to understand that there would be no problem.

Meanwhile, Trinity College appointed Beckett, an outstanding scholar, to the post. When Beckett's eccentric Professor, RB Rudmose-Brown, learned that MacGreevy planned to stay on, he accused the Kerryman of trying to take over a job to which he was only temporarily appointed. MacGreevy in turn pleaded innocence and asked to be kept on. After an exchange of letters between Paris and Dublin, Lanson defied TCD and agreed to let MacGreevy stay. But Rudmose-Brown persisted in his campaign on behalf of Beckett (he never had much time for MacGreevy) and it was finally agreed that the Foxrock man would take up the post a year later than expected.

It had been a difficult time for Beckett. He had spent the previous year teaching at Campbell College in Belfast and had been very unhappy there. Now, at last, he was in Paris to take up his position at the *École* only to find his predecessor occupying the room allocated to the *lecteur d'anglais*.

MacGreevy explained that he had been allowed to remain at the *École* for a further two years, although not as lecturer. He was doing some teaching, writing poetry and art criticism and had become secretary to the English edition of the French art magazine *Formes* - a position he got partly through his friendship with Joyce. He would simply move to another room at the *École* and Beckett could move in straight away.

It is a credit to MacGreevy's charm, honesty and straightforwardness that he succeeded in explaining the true position to his successor and smoothening his way - and to Beckett that he did not hold a grudge against the Kerryman for delaying his appointment.

The two men could hardly have been less similar. Apart from a ten-year age gap, there were major physical differences: the one small and dapper, the other tall, thin and awkward; the one dressed neatly in suit and bow tie, the other casually in Aran sweater and beret.

Their personalities were opposed: MacGreevy talkative, confident, gregarious, a storyteller; Beckett shy, solitary, moody, sometimes sullen. MacGreevy, of a rural Catholic and nationalist background, was a regular Mass-goer and daily communicant; Beckett, a southside Dubliner of Protestant Anglo-Irish stock, had become effectively agnostic. MacGreevy was a moderate drinker, with no interest in women. Beckett often drank heavily and was sexually charged.

What helped bring them together was a common tolerance and openness to the views of others. But their differences also attracted: Beckett, a loner, was delighted to meet someone who was a friend of Joyce and who might introduce him to that writer and to others he knew such as the Yeats brothers, Richard Aldington, Salvador Dali and Sylvia Beach. The sociable MacGreevy revelled in the company of a fellow Irishman of wide-ranging interests with whom he could discuss art and poetry.

They shared a disdain for what they had left behind; they were both relieved to be away from the bigotry and narrow-mindedness of the Irish Free State. In Paris they could explore the European traditions in the arts while immersing themselves in new ideas.

They also immersed themselves in the cafés of the Latin Quarter. They sat and drank and talked late into the evening at the Closerie des Lilas, the Dome, the Sélect and Les Deux Magots. They sometimes dined, when they could afford to, at the Cochon de Lait beside the Odéon Theatre, where Beckett loved to practice his Italian on the waiters. Afterwards, they went to the Café Mahieu, which was frequented by an Irish couple MacGreevy had become acquainted with in Paris. Alan Duncan[1] had been a major in the British army and knew WB Yeats. He and his tiny wife Belinda had lived near Foxrock, close to Beckett's home. They were to become good friends of Beckett with whom, he admitted later, 'we would swill beer in enormous quantities.'[2]

Beckett's consumption of alcohol increased steadily during his two-year attachment to the *École*. But, like Joyce, he had his own drinking rule: he seldom imbibed before a certain time in the evening - in Beckett's case,

5pm Often he did not get back to the *École* until well after midnight (when the gates were closed) and could be seen jumping over the railings and making his way unsteadily to his room.

Both men were 'night birds' who found it difficult to get up in the morning. Beckett sometimes played the tin whistle in his room at night, much to the annoyance of those trying to sleep nearby. Some days, if the two Irishmen did not set off somewhere for brunch, Beckett would go to MacGreevy's room where they would share bread and marmalade and tea to the accompaniment of Beckett's tin whistle or MacGreevy's records played on his gramophone. Once fed, they would start their days in ways that reflected their different personalities. According to MacGreevy:

> *Sam could go straight from his morning tea or coffee to his typewriter or his books, his biblical concordance, his dictionaries, his Stendhal. I, on the contrary, had to go out and make sure that the world was where I had left it the evening before.*[3]

Around the same time as MacGreevy introduced Beckett to Joyce, he brought him to rue de l'Odéon to meet Beach. Beckett had read *Ulysses* and was delighted to meet its publisher whom, he believed, was passionately devoted to Joyce (her passion was beginning to ebb at the time). He often visited Shakespeare and Company, but never, it seems, borrowed from Beach's lending library, probably since he had so many books to choose from at the *École*. He was often to be seen at the shop, his head in a book, aware of the presence of other English-speaking visitors such as Hemingway and McAlmon but never talking to them.[4]

Beckett's first pupil was named Georges Pelorson.

Beckett invited him to come to his rooms at 11am. But when the young Frenchman arrived he found his tutor asleep in bed. Henceforth, Beckett ensured that his tutorials were scheduled for the afternoon or evening. They met in the cafés of Montparnasse where they discussed the works of Joyce (one of Beckett's favourite subjects) and the French Surrealists (one of Pelorson's, who knew many of them). Thus began a close, long-lasting friendship. In due course Pelorson, too, would enter the Joyce circle. He also followed Beckett's footsteps in reverse, becoming the exchange French reader at TCD.[5]

Beckett had been in Paris only about a week when MacGreevy made that phone call inviting the two of them to the Joyces. Beckett was overwhelmed meeting the man whose works he so admired. He spoke little and it was MacGreevy who, as usual, did most of the talking. Joyce was delighted to meet someone from Dublin who knew its history and its streets and Beckett found the older writer very friendly from the moment they were introduced. He returned to the *École* exhausted but happy.

From that moment, Beckett took every opportunity to accompany MacGreevy on his visits to the Joyces. In due course, Beckett was invited to the flat at Square Robiac in his own right. And he, too, soon became enmeshed in the Joyce literary network. Besides meeting Giorgio and Lucia he would have come across Arthur Power, Robert McAlmon and Stuart Gilbert, an old colonial type who was making a study of *Ulysses*.[6]

Little by little, Joyce persuaded Beckett to do things for him, such as reading aloud from books that Joyce felt would help him with his *Work in Progress*. He was given books on Irish history and mythology to take away, read and report on. Sometimes Joyce, sitting with his legs crossed, one folded behind the other, dictated to the younger man - who gradually adopted the same seating posture.

During one of their dictation sessions someone knocked on the door and Joyce said 'Come in.' Beckett, who had not heard Joyce's rejoinder, included the phrase when he read back what he had written.

'What's that 'come in'?' asked Joyce.

'Yes, you said that' replied Beckett.

After a moment's hesitation Joyce said: 'Let it stand.'

Beckett told the story to Joyce's biographer Richard Ellmann who remarked of Joyce: 'He was quite willing to accept coincidence as his collaborator. Beckett was fascinated and thwarted by Joyce's singular method.'[7]

Beckett was only too happy to help Joyce with his work, although it took up much of his time. Such was his enthusiasm that he even suggested to the assistant director at the *École* that he register for a doctorate taking Proust and Joyce as its subject. But he was discouraged from doing so on the grounds of the French tradition that such treatises are undertaken only after a writer has died.

On Sunday mornings, the two would stroll along the quays of the Seine, but they did not talk much. Beckett said later:

> *There wasn't a lot of conversation between us. I was a young man, very devoted to him, and he liked me... I was very flattered when he dropped the 'Mister.' Everybody was 'Mister.' There were no Christian names, no first names. The nearest you would get to a friendly name was to drop the*

'Mister.' I was never Sam. I was always 'Beckett' at the best.[8]

When Nora was hospitalised with suspected cancer and Joyce stayed with her, Beckett devotedly transported Joyce's documents and correspondence between his apartment in Square Robiac and the hospital, which was the other side of the city. Later, he and his friend Alfred Péron translated *Anna Livia Plurabelle* into French. Joyce called it 'one of the masterpieces of translation.' But at the reading of the French version at Adrienne Monnier's bookshop, Philippe Soupault trivialised it as a first attempt (much to Beckett's annoyance) and produced a new 'improved' version.[9]

Despite his closeness to Joyce, Beckett never achieved the level of friendship with the Joyce family that his predecessor did. Beckett was useful to Joyce, who would often phone him at the *École Normale* to give him a task or two, be it to look up some reference or other or to escort him somewhere (because of his failing eyesight). He admired the younger man for his intelligence and, within a month of Beckett's arrival in Paris, appointed him one of his 'twelve apostles.'

Stunned by the criticism of his *Work in Progress*[10] that came from many different quarters, Joyce decided to counter-attack. He came up with another campaign, this time more intellectual, aimed at attacking his critics head-on. He would get certain people he could trust to each write an essay, which would explain the philosophies behind his work. Most of the essays first appeared in *transition* magazine, but Joyce got Beach to publish them under the word-playing title *Our Exagmination round his Factification for Incamination of Work in Progress*.

The twelve 'apostles'[11] included Eugene Jolas (who, with his wife Marie, was the owner/editor of *transition* that published extracts from *WIP*), Tom MacGreevy, Robert

McAlmon, Frank Budgen, Stuart Gilbert, William Carlos Williams and Samuel Beckett.

Joyce chose his apostles and then stood over them to ensure that they delivered what he had in mind: a riposte to his critics.[12] Each would write on the aspect of *Work in Progress* they knew best. Beckett's essay was entitled *Dante... Bruno. Vico...Joyce* and dealt with the role the Italian writers and philosophers played in the development of *WIP*. MacGreevy's essay was an answer to specifically Irish criticism of Joyce's work. Joyce liked the piece, which MacGreevy had called simply *A Note on Work in Progress*, but changed the title to *The Catholic Element in Work in Progress* to emphasise the Catholic roots in his writing.

McAlmon's essay, *Mr. Joyce Directs an Irish Prose Ballet*, described how Joyce freed language from past rigidities, making it 'sensible, musical and flexible.'[13] He also drew a relationship between Joyce's style and glaucoma. Afterwards, Joyce told him: 'You may be right, and do you think it has impaired my intellect?'[14] Eugene Jolas was excited by the essay and told McAlmon it was 'sensitive, very sensitive.' Or so said McAlmon.[15] Privately McAlmon, who was tiring of what he thought were Joyce's egocentricities, felt the writer was at the end of an epoch rather than the beginning and that he had carried words as far as they could go. Years later, he wrote of *Work in Progress*:

> *It was nice to hear him read it in that soothing 'Irish tenor,' but to read pages of that punning, sentimental-remembering, meandering-obscenities, was quite beyond my capacity.*[16]

Joyce thought that an unfavourable article should be included and asked Beach if she knew someone who would contribute. She persuaded one of her customers, a journalist, to write a piece and it appeared under the pseudonym of GVL Slingsby. It was not good criticism, she thought.[17]

Our Exagmination... did not sell particularly well (its title alone was enough to put off many potential readers) but Joyce was sufficiently enthused to follow it with a book of four essays on different aspects of his *Work in Progress*. The first was to be written by a young American named Harry Crosby[18] who, with his wife Caresse, had set up the *Black Sun Press* in Paris. Like many other small publishers, they were anxious to publish an extract from Joyce's *Work in Progress*. They had already met Joyce briefly, when Hemingway introduced them at a concert. In March 1929 they persuaded Stuart Gilbert to accompany them to Joyce's flat at Square Robiac. There they succeeded in getting Joyce to allow them publish *Tales Told of Shem and Shaun*. Joyce wanted Picasso to draw his portrait for the cover of the book, but the artist refused. He told Caresse he was not interested in Joyce.

A month later a contract was drawn up with *Black Sun Press* by Beach, who had Joyce's power of attorney, for the publication of three fragments which had already appeared in transition: *The Mookse and the Gripes*, *The Muddest Thick That Was Ever Heard Dump* and *The Ondt and the Gracehoper*.

Joyce and Harry Crosby worked well together. Joyce was nearly blind, stumbling into furniture in his own apartment. When Joyce visited the Crosbys to correct proofs they rigged up an enormous light bulb and provided a magnifying glass to help him see.

When the printer realised that the last page contained only two lines he asked Caresse if the author would provide a further eight or so. She laughed, saying the greatest writer of the age could not add words like a hack newspaper reporter. A day or so later she learned that eight lines had been found; the printer had gone straight to Joyce who was happy to provide the extra lines there and then.[19]

As Beckett's essay appeared in the June issue of *transition* (along with his first published short story, *Assumption*), Adrienne Monnier was arranging a celebration lunch for Joyce and his friends. 'Déjeuner Ulysse' was to mark, belatedly, both the publication the previous February of the French translation of *Ulysses* and the 25th anniversary of Bloomsday. It took place in the appropriately named Hotel Léopold in a tiny village near Versailles, Les Vaux-de-Cernay, on 27 June, 1929.

A chartered bus left from outside La Maison des Amis des Livres with the guests - mainly French and Irish. Among the more distinguished were Édouard Dujardin, Paul Valéry (writer and friend of Adrienne Monnier and Natalie Barney), Philippe Soupault (a former surrealist who had helped with the French translation), Léon-Paul Fargue (another of the translators) and Nino Frank (an Italian writer friend of Joyce). All four Joyces were there, as were Beach, Beckett and MacGreevy.

It was a bright, sunny day and, as the bus set off towards Versailles, an excited Adrienne Monnier persuaded her guests to sing in chorus to start the celebrations. Not all of them responded with enthusiasm, however, among them Beckett and MacGreevy for whom it was probably too early in the day. On arrival at the hotel, lunch was served - starting with Paté Léopold, which was followed by five other courses - accompanied by a wide selection of wines and ending with coffee and liqueurs. After the meal, presentations were made of the first copies of *Ulysses* in French. Fargue sang a comic song. He and Valéry called for speeches but Joyce objected. Beckett and MacGreevy, who had been indulging heavily in the wine and liqueurs, joined noisily in the demand, much to the annoyance of Joyce and the others.

A photograph of the luncheon party - apparently taken at the coffee stage - gives the impression of a serious, sober - even sombre - group. Appearances are deceptive, however. Beckett, when asked why he was not in the picture, answered that he was probably under the table (most likely he was in the toilet, too drunk to pose for the photographer).

Much has been made of the excessive drinking of the two young Irishmen on that occasion, but they were not alone in their obstreperous behaviour. The Italian Nino Frank, writing almost 40 years later, admitted to being among the younger members of the party (he was in his mid-twenties) who were out for a good time (as was the young Frenchman Philippe Soupault); and even Joyce joined in:

> *Were we the youngest, then? I don't know, but we were suddenly the wildest. The torpid gaze of the other guests rested on us, at first complacently, then with consternation, as we romped around engaging in all sorts of absurd antics. And Joyce, who was called back to the table, if not back to order, obstinately joined in with his awkward gait; one might have thought him the smallest and clumsiest of a bunch of kids, trying to ape the older ones.* [20]

A worried Monnier quickly arranged a group photograph, then hurried the party back to the bus. On the return journey, Beckett, MacGreevy and Frank continued to make themselves heard, singing loudly and cracking silly jokes. Joyce, however, joined in their singing. But it was a long journey and Beckett - egged on by MacGreevy - implored the driver to stop at a café under the pretext of the need to answer a call of nature.

In the twinkling of an eye there were five of us,
including Joyce, lined up at the bar drinking
white wine, all seized by the incomprehensible joy
that comes from who knows where and that will
never be forgotten.[21]

As the five serious drinkers - Beckett, MacGreevy, Frank, Joyce and Soupault - climbed back on the bus, there was a clear expression of annoyance on the faces of the other guests. The driver, however, was more sympathetic and, when they tried their trick a couple more times, he joined them for a drink. The remaining guests tried to remonstrate with Joyce, but in vain. Nora stayed in her seat and said nothing. It was not the first time she experienced such behaviour and it would not be the last.

The reception that Nino Frank got on returning to the bus was most likely replicated among the other drinkers:

Once back in my seat, I turned around and saw
the disgusted eyes and austere lips of Jean
Paulhan, undoubtedly a water-drinker. I think he
even scolded me in convoluted phrases to which I
replied with a particularly foolish grin.[22]

The last straw was when Beckett, genuinely anxious to relieve himself, became enraged when the bus would not stop; it did eventually slow down to let him get off, but continued without him. By this time the group had arrived on the outskirts of Paris and the travellers watched as he disappeared into the crowd.

Joyce, who found the entire episode more amusing than most of those present, later recalled how Beckett 'fell deeply under the influence of beer, wine, spirits, liqueurs, fresh air, movement and feminine society and was ingloriously abandoned by the Wagonette in one of those temporary palaces which are inseparably associated with the memory of the Emperor Vespasian' (ie a toilet).[23]

---

[1] His mother, Ellen Duncan, was the first curator of the Municipal Gallery in Dublin. With Countess Markievicz she founded the United Arts Club.

[2] Knowlson: *Damned to Fame* 100 (from interview with Beckett).

[3] Idem. 144.

[4] Fitch: *Sylvia Beach and the Lost Generation* 278.

[5] He later adopted the *nom de plume* of Georges Belmont.

[6] Gilbert became a close friend of Joyce, helped translate *Ulysses* into French and edited Joyce's letters.

[7] Ellmann interview with Beckett in 1954 quoted in *James Joyce*.

[8] Knowlson: *Damned to Fame* 108 (Interview with Beckett).

[9] Idem. 130.

[10] *Finnegans Wake* was published in 1939 to mixed reviews. The *Irish Times* felt it inconceivable that Joyce should spend so many years on a hoax. Gogarty called it the 'most colossal leg-pull in literature.' The book was praised by Harry Levin and Edmund Wilson.

[11] Joyce referred obliquely to his apostles in *Finnegans Wake* : 'Imagine the twelve deaferended dumbbawls of the whowl abovebeugled to be the contonuation through regeneration of the urutteration of the word in pregross. (Finnegans Wake 284).

[12] In a letter to Larbaud, 30 July, 1929, Joyce admitted 'I did stand behind those twelve marshals more or less directing them what lines of research to follow…' (Gilbert ed., *Letters of James Joyce Vol. 2*, 282).

[13] Smoller: *Adrift Among Geniuses* 200.

[14] Ellmann 613.

[15] McAlmon : *Geniuses* 254.

[16] Idem 253.

[17] Ellmann 613.

[18] Harry Crosby came from an upper-class Boston family and caused a furore when he married a divorcee. In 1929 in New York he shot himself in an apparent suicide pact with another woman. His death symbolized the end of the expatriate era.

[19] Wolff: *Black Sun* 250.

[20] Nino Frank: *The Shadow that had Lost its Man*, in *James Joyce, Portraits of the Artist in Exile* 85.

[21] Idem 86.

[22] Idem 86.

[23] Joyce to Larbaud, 30 July, 1929 (Gilbert ed., *Letters of James Joyce Vol. 2*, 282).

A Little Circle Of Kindred Minds

Chapter Thirteen
Unsuitable Suitors

Beckett continued to help Joyce with his work, visiting the flat at Square Robiac almost daily. Occasionally he would be invited to Joyce's soirées, which were more like Irish 'sing-songs.' Often, MacGreevy would be there too, or Arthur Power or the Colums or McAlmon. There would be singing and dancing and Joyce would accompany himself on the piano. He was even known to improvise a dance while Giorgio or Beckett played for him.[1] The Joyces came across as a naturally talented family: Giorgio was having his voice trained and Lucia attended dancing classes.

Beckett never became as close to the Joyce family as did MacGreevy. Nevertheless, being ten years younger and coming midway in age between Giorgio and Lucia, he was often invited to family occasions that involved the younger members.

In April 1929, the Joyces asked him to join them for Giorgio's public début as a singer. The concert was at the Studio Scientifique de la Voix, where Giorgio had been attending singing lessons over several years, and he sang two songs by Handel. Unlike his father's tenor voice, Giorgio's was a deep bass/baritone. But he suffered from stage fright and kept clearing his throat nervously. Giorgio did not work hard at his singing - nor did he have to: he had married a wealthy American divorcee, Helen Fleischman. He had also started drinking excessively.

The following month, the Joyces asked Beckett to

accompany them to watch Lucia dance in an international competition at the Bal Bullier in Montparnasse - the dance hall where, nine years earlier, Arthur Power had encountered Joyce for the first time.

In contrast with her brother, Lucia took her dancing very seriously and had attended classes by various teachers, among them Raymond Duncan, brother of the famed Isadora. She also studied under Lubov Egorova, a former principal dancer with the Ballets Russes. Zelda Fitzgerald, Scott's wife, was also attending private classes with Egorova at this time, although by all accounts she was a less accomplished dancer than Lucia.[2] The Fitzgeralds would meet the Joyces two months later.

MacGreevy was also invited to watch Lucia dancing, as were Alan and Belinda Duncan who were now also friends of Beckett who adored the diminutive Belinda.

Lucia came on stage dressed as a fish. It was a clever costume designed by herself, tight-fitting and made from shimmering silver material, with one leg covered to give the impression of a fish tail. When the result of the competition was announced, Lucia was not the winner. But the impact she made on the audience was such that many of them protested aloud: 'Nous réclamons l'Irlandaise! Un peu de justice, messieurs' ('We're calling for the Irish girl! Be fair, gentlemen').

Joyce was disappointed but delighted with the response and immediately brought his party off to celebrate. Beckett, too, thought her dancing was excellent. But then he had been an admirer of Lucia ever since he first saw her six months earlier when MacGreevy brought him to the Joyces.

Lucia was an attractive young woman, tall, slender, with dark curly hair and a slight turn in one eye that some found alluring. A tendency towards mood swings may have been one of the indications of the mental illness that was to come. Her life had not been easy. She and Giorgio had been in a constant state of moving, having been born in Trieste and educated there and in Zurich and Paris; she was barely coming to grips with one language when it was necessary to learn another. She had developed a keen ability to draw but would eventually lose interest in whatever she was pursuing (she gave up dancing later that year). Now, at 23, one year younger than Beckett, she was developing an almost uncontrollable interest in young men.

She was vulnerable at an age when many young men were finding her attractive. Arthur Power has revealed how the writer Liam O'Flaherty, who attended soirées at the Joyces' flat in Square Robiac, pointed Lucia out to him: 'See that girl over there? I'm going to meet her at the Gard du Nord.' To which Power replied in horror: 'Don't you know who that is? That's Joyce's daughter.'[3]

It was clear that she fancied Beckett. She was often the first to greet him on his arrival during his frequent visits to the apartment to help Joyce. She was lonely and sought every opportunity to talk privately to him. For his part, Beckett took her out to restaurants and the theatre. He found her very good-looking, but did not reciprocate her deep feelings for him. For Beckett, being with Lucia was a way of being close to the person he most admired, her father.

Often when Joyce was dining out *en famille* he invited MacGreevy and Beckett to join them. Then when Giorgio became involved with Fleischman Beckett was asked to partner Lucia to make up three couples. Beckett welcomed this opportunity to be close to Joyce. But his constant presence among the Joyces did not go unnoticed and literary Paris was now anticipating an engagement between Joyce's daughter and this young, wiry Irishman.

It was difficult for Beckett to avoid Lucia. But at the beginning of 1930, he began making a special effort to distance himself from her. He took to going alone to the left bank cafés of the Dome, the Coupole and the Select; sometimes he went with MacGreevy to the cafés near the *École Normale* where MacGreevy introduced him to an English writer he had met at the Joyces' flat, Richard Aldington.[4] They in turn became good friends and the three would sometimes dine at the Café Mahieu with Alan and Belinda Duncan.

Lucia was persistent. In May, while her parents were in Switzerland, she invited Beckett to meet her for lunch in a café opposite the Luxembourg Gardens where he had often dined with her family. Not wishing to be alone with her, Beckett brought along George Pelorson, who knew nothing of his friend's concerns. When Lucia arrived, in full make-up and wearing a new dress, she was bitterly disappointed to find she was not alone with her 'lover' who she probably hoped would propose to her. She behaved strangely during the meal, in the middle of which she moved towards the door in obvious distress. Beckett felt he ought to be straight with her. He told her he came to the flat only to see her father, not her. Lucia was distraught.

When her parents returned from Zurich, they were shocked to see their daughter in a deep depression. Nora accused Beckett of leading her daughter on in order to ingratiate himself with her husband. She then told Joyce of her concern. He in turn told Beckett he was no longer welcome at Square Robiac. When Lucia told her parents that all the young men who called to the flat had seduced her, Joyce reacted by sending them all away. The ban included - most unfairly - the pious and well-mannered MacGreevy, who took it very badly.

Beckett was devastated. Joyce meant everything to him; he was at the centre of his very existence. He and

MacGreevy consoled each other, MacGreevy telling Beckett that Joyce would have to come to terms with his daughter's strangeness and that, when he did, he would recognise that Beckett had behaved honourably.

There was little Beckett could do but throw himself into his work to distract himself from his exclusion by the Joyces. One afternoon in June, MacGreevy called to his room to tell him he had just been talking to his friend Richard Aldington who, along with Nancy Cunard, was running a literary competition. They were offering 1,000 francs (about €1,000 euros in today's money) for a poem of no more than 100 lines on the theme of time. The winning poem would be published by Nancy's *Hours Press*.

Aldington had told MacGreevy that he and Nancy were disappointed with the standard of submissions so far. MacGreevy suggested to Beckett that he might enter the competition but that he would have to hurry - the deadline was midnight.

Motivated as much by the prize money as the by the chance of getting published, Beckett set to work. After his 'split' with the Joyces, he had spent more and more time researching the life of the philosopher René Descartes; now he thought he would write a poem around that subject, with time as an element in it. He wrote the first half before dinner (a salad and Chambertin at the Cochon de Lait), then returned to the *École* and finished it at about 3am, following which he walked to the *Hours Press* where he dropped the poem in the letterbox.

The poem of 98 lines, entitled *Whoroscope*, impressed Nancy and Aldington who awarded Beckett the prize. He was presented with the money the next day. When the poem was published, MacGreevy urged Beckett to send a copy to Joyce, who grudgingly went along with MacGreevy's enthusiasm for it.[5]

It was not enough to reconcile him with Joyce, however. The two men would not see much of each other for several years, but that was partly because of Beckett's travels to Dublin, London and Berlin. During this period, despite ill health, he wrote his first novel, *Dream of Fair to Middling Women* and most of *Murphy*.

While at home he appeared in court in Shankill on a dangerous driving charge. The judge was Kenneth Reddin, the writer and friend of Joyce who had entertained McAlmon at his Howth home twelve years earlier. He knew Beckett was a writer and could not resist remarking in court that the defendant cut corners in literature with a certain finesse, but perhaps did not do so with equal skill while driving. He fined him £1.

Two months later Beckett was in court again, this time in the High Court as a witness in a libel case. The Sinclair family, who were related to the Becketts through marriage, had taken the action against the writer Oliver St John Gogarty. Gogarty lost and the trial cost him £2,000. Beckett, however, felt he too was the loser since he had been bitterly attacked and humiliated in court. For someone who abhorred his country's narrow-mindedness and bigotry, this was the last straw. He could hardly wait to return to Paris.

When he did, in an effort to renew old acquaintances he called into Shakespeare and Company where Beach introduced him to Hemingway. Hemingway felt Joyce was wasting his time with *Finnegans Wake*: 'We mustn't be too hard on the old man,' the American told him. '*Ulysses* tired him out.'[6] Beckett never wanted to meet Hemingway again – nor did he.

He didn't wish to meet Lucia either and the absence from her life of MacGreevy and himself did nothing to help her condition. Nora believed that what her daughter needed was a husband; but who might be suitable? Beckett was out. MacGreevy seemed like a confirmed bachelor. Arthur Power was too old for her. McAlmon had proposed to Lucia after he divorced Bryher, but he was homosexual. Others who had expressed an interest were either engaged to someone else or married.

Joyce, heavily involved in *Work in Progress*, stood back from such discussions. Mary Colum - never afraid to speak her mind - told Joyce he should arrange a marriage with a dowry, French style, to prevent Lucia chasing after unsuitable young men. The conversation was overheard by Nora who, observing a certain lack of interest on her husband's part, uttered: 'You have never really known your daughter.'

'Allow me to say,' responded Joyce, 'that I was present at her conception!'

Pressure was coming on James and Nora to legalise their relationship after 25 years of what the Irish Catholic church regarded as 'living in sin.' It was not the taboo that bothered them; they were concerned about the illegitimacy of their children. Lucia had begun to use her status as a way to attack her parents during her increasingly frequent rows ('If I am a bastard,' she shouted at her father on several occasions, 'who made me one?'). James Stephens's daughter Iris, who was friendly with Lucia, believed the trauma of illegitimacy caused her breakdown.

More significant for Joyce was that Giorgio (also upset when he learned he was illegitimate) and his wife were expecting Joyce's grandchild - an occasion, Joyce had told Padraic and Mary Colum, he longed for. But the fact that his grandchild would be born to an illegitimate father worried him. He was also advised that, if he were temporarily domiciled and married in England, his children would be legitimised and his wife could inherit his estate.

The marriage of James and Nora Joyce took place in a registry office in London on 4 July 1931 in a ceremony that both tried to keep secret (Joyce never even mentioned it when he wrote to Padraic Colum two days beforehand). But a couple of newspapers got wind of the event by checking with the registry office the day before and carried stories and a photograph. Joyce was furious. When told later by Colum that one of the reporters was Irish, he said bitterly: 'I expected he would be.'

Arthur Power was in London at the time and, reading of the marriage, tracked down Joyce and jokingly referred to the publicity he had received. Joyce was not amused. 'If you want information about this, see my solicitors,' he snapped.

The marriage was clearly the right decision for Joyce and his wife. Immediately after it, he made a will leaving the income from his royalties to his wife until her death and thereafter to his children and then grandchildren. But he never anticipated the furore that ensued from their marriage. Nora's mother and the rest of the Barnacle family in Galway were shattered, having always believed that Nora had married Joyce in Trieste in 1904 (as Joyce had put about).

Far from improving after the marriage, Lucia's mental health continued to worsen as it had over the previous decade. The Dublin-born artist Stella Steyn[7] had noticed a significant difference between 1926 – when she first met Lucia – and 1929. Steyn had been given an introduction to Joyce by Patrick Tuohy, her teacher in the Metropolitan School of Art and family friend.

'Joyce encouraged a friendship between us as we were of an age,' she wrote in her memoirs. 'Lucia was a dancer and had been studying since the age of sixteen and seemed to be absorbed in dancing as I was in art.' But Steyn was shocked when Lucia told her that her father wanted her to give up dancing and take up art.

> *I don't think Joyce knew much about*
> *women...He also said that it was enough if a*
> *woman could write a letter and carry an*
> *umbrella gracefully... I am sure he loved her*
> *more than any other human being and wanted*
> *nothing but her happiness. But he had no interest*
> *in the visual arts...*[8]

Steyn was rather afraid of Joyce (she was after all a year younger than his daughter). Once, while she waited for Lucia, Joyce came into the room and, ignoring her, sat at the piano and sang melancholy Irish songs in a low voice.

'You must miss Ireland,' she suggested.

'I do.'

'Would you not like to go back?'

'No. They jeer too much.'[9]

The Joyces had given up their flat at Square Robiac before their marriage in London so that when they returned to Paris they moved home again - this time to a hotel near the Champs-Elysées. Lucia did not wish to stay with them - natural enough for a young woman of 24 – and went to live with Giorgio and the expectant Helen. She sometimes visited the Colums who were now living on rue de Sevigné, not far from Notre Dame.

Near neighbours of the Colums were Stuart Gilbert and his wife Moune, who kept them informed of developments within Joyce's circle. He was an English literary scholar and admirer of *Ulysses* who, with his French wife, became close friends of the Joyces.[10] Through them the Colums learned of the Joyces' anxiety about their daughter. They also learned that Joyce had taken Mary Colum's advice and settled a dowry on Lucia, who was now engaged to be married.

Her fiancé was Alex Ponisovsky, brother-in-law of the man who was now at the centre of the Joyce circle, Paul Léon,[11] secretary to Joyce. Alex[12] - a friend of Giorgio's - had taught Joyce Russian and had introduced the writer to his brother-in-law in 1928. Léon was totally devoted to Joyce (although he never read *Ulysses* nor understood *Finnegans Wake*) - so much so that he persuaded his wife's brother (who had been dating Lucia) to propose marriage - which he did mainly from a sense of duty.

Joyce was pleased with the engagement. But Nora knew Lucia was not ready for it. The Colums foresaw difficulties, too. They had seen Lucia deteriorate progressively. They had noticed how she would slip from English into French, then into Italian in a matter of seconds. Her behaviour was also causing her parents considerable grief. One day Lucia threw a chair at her mother. When the Colums invited her to join them, she warned that she would leave if the subject of her father came up in conversation. When Padraic mentioned to her that her father had difficulties of his own, she answered: 'I saw him crying when he found he couldn't see to write,' but she said it without sympathy.

Lucia's behaviour often deeply embarrassed her parents. In April, 1932, the Joyces decided to spend some time in England (as part of their effort to claim English domicile for inheritance purposes). They intended bringing Lucia with them, for they felt she was in no condition to be left behind.

At the Gard du Nord, with all their luggage, hat boxes and boxes of books already loaded into their compartments, Lucia became hysterical. She howled loudly as she stood with her parents in the middle of the station. Joyce and

Nora knew they could neither take her on the train nor leave her behind. They booked into a hotel and Lucia went to stay with the Léons.

The following day, Padraic Colum was in Shakespeare and Company when Beach told him, without going into details, that the Joyces never got away after all. Padraic thought it funny and typical of Joyce whose unpredictability was becoming something of a joke. He was laughing when Joyce emerged from another room in the bookshop, clearly offended. Joyce told Colum what had happened. For the first time, Colum thought, Joyce now realised the extent of the crisis he was facing.

The close friendship between the Joyces and the Colums took a somewhat clandestine turn following the birth, in February 1932, of Joyce's grandson. The birth of Stephen James Joyce was a proud moment for Joyce and a source of great comfort as it followed the death of his own father by less that two months. But when the question arose of having the baby baptised, Joyce would have none of it. He had not had his own children baptised. 'There are a hundred and twenty religions in the world,' he said, 'They can take their choice.'[13]

Giorgio had not taken such a choice; he had no religious affiliations. But Helen wanted her baby baptised. The problem was: how to achieve this without Joyce knowing?

The subterfuge that followed required the co-operation of the Colums and Eugene Jolas, all of whom were sworn to secrecy. The Colums were asked to be godparents. It was a good choice since both parents were unfamiliar with the rite of baptism and they knew they could rely on the Colums' Catholic background to help them out.

They could not have taken into account, however, Padraic's poor French. Despite some coaching from his wife prior to the ceremony, he still managed to get the responses wrong, confusing 'Je renonce' with 'J'accepte.' When the priest asked whether - on behalf of the child - he renounced the Devil and all his work and all his pomp, Padraic answered 'Non.'[14]

The secrecy of the ceremony was nearly blown when, during polite conversation afterwards, the priest asked 'Est-ce que l'enfant est le petit-fils de Monsieur James Joyce, l'écrivain célebre?' The Colums were concerned that news of the ceremony would reach the newspapers and through them an angry Joyce, thus threatening their close friendship. But they need not have worried. It was some years before Joyce heard of his grandson's baptism when Mary Colum accidentally revealed to Joyce that the ceremony had taken place. By then the news did not seem to bother him.

He was more concerned at his daughter's obvious unhappiness at home. Joyce asked her where she would like to go, to which she replied she would like to stay with Mary. Mary was happy to oblige. Not only was she fond of Lucia but she had seen the despair and unhappiness in Joyce's face and wanted to ease the burden on him. Despite her own ill health at the time, Mary took Lucia into her flat at rue de Sevigné that had been lent to them by Maria Jolas. Afraid that the young woman would harm herself, Mary slept in the same bed, even pinning their nightclothes together.

Lucia got on well with the Colums, both of whom took a close interest in her. One Sunday, as Padraic was leaving for Mass, Lucia said she would like to accompany him. While they were out, Joyce phoned and was told where she was. 'Now I know she is mad,' was Joyce's response - although he had not yet come around to accepting her true mental state.

He was sufficiently conscious of her illness, however, to

arrange for a psychiatrist to visit her at the Colums' apartment every morning. Mary convinced Lucia that the psychiatrist was in fact treating her - Mary - but that Lucia could help her to answer some of the questions. Seated together on a couch, the two women would talk to the psychiatrist but every now and then Mary would excuse herself, leaving Lucia to continue the conversation alone.[15]

Joyce visited Mary Colum regularly to talk to her about his daughter. When Mary repeated the psychiatrist's remark that 'Mademoiselle seems to have been hearing a good deal about sex,' Joyce was aghast. 'She never heard about it from us,' he replied. Mary readily accepted his word, for she had never heard Joyce say anything that would embarrass a nun.[16]

Lucia was not allowed to go out in the evenings, but sometimes, her fiancé Alex would visit her in the Colums' flat. On one such occasion, a row ensued between Lucia and Padraic when Lucia insisted on going out to the theatre. By the time the verbal battle was over, Alex had disappeared. It seemed he had had enough.

The episode did not help Lucia. Mary blamed her husband for being so authoritarian.

The time came when, due to deterioration in her own health, Mary Colum could no longer look after Lucia. At the end of May, she and Giorgio brought her to a clinic at L'Hay-les-Roses. She stayed there for several weeks, during which time her illness was diagnosed as a form of schizophrenia.

Even without Lucia's illness, it was a difficult time for Joyce. His relationships with other women were deteriorating. Beach was tired of being his 'banker' and she and Adrienne Monnier were annoyed with him over his efforts to have future editions of *Ulysses* published in

London. Harriet Weaver had again told him he should be living within his means. Now, on top of all that, he was full of remorse for not having recognised his daughter's state of mind sooner.

With Lucia in full-time care and Mary Colum under doctor's orders, Joyce came to the Colums' flat almost daily. He knew the apartment well, having visited the Jolases there. The grand piano was one he had often sat at and played in happier days. He played it again now, alone except for Mary Colum. He accompanied himself in sad arias and poignant Irish ballads. Then the two would talk, always about Lucia.

Joyce's eye problems continued. In July, he and Nora brought Lucia to Feldkirch in Austria (where she stayed with a nurse-friend close to where the Jolases were holidaying) while they went on to Zurich for yet another consultation.

Dr Alfred Vogt told Joyce he required two more difficult operations. Journeying between the eye clinic in Zurich and Lucia and the Jolases in Feldkirch, Joyce wrote letters continuing to promote among his friends and acquaintances his daughter's work on her decorative alphabet for *Pomes Pennyeach*.

On the return journey to Paris in the autumn of 1932, James and Nora brought Lucia with them to the Cote d'Azur. The Colums and the Joyces continued to keep in touch. Mary Colum posted a cheque to their hotel in Nice, payment she had received for submitting Joyce's poem, *Ecce Puer*, to a couple of magazines abroad. Following major surgery, Mary asked Nora to book herself and Padraic into an hotel nearby where she might recuperate. On their first day the two couples met - Padraic and Mary spotted the Joyces relaxing on deck chairs outside their hotel. The four could chat only briefly, for the Joyces were about to return to Paris.

The Colums, however, remained in Nice for almost a year, continuing to keep in touch by post with the Joyces. Lucia's condition had not improved. But the letters from Paris spoke highly of her illustrations for Joyce's *Pomes Penyeach*, published that autumn. One art critic compared her designs to the Book of Kells.

Delighted though he was with the news, his daughter's illness was weighing heavily on Joyce. One evening, distracted by his thoughts, he left an entire manuscript destined for *transition* in a taxi. He had no copy.

For Beckett, tragedy struck in a more dramatic way in the streets of Paris during Christmas 1937. As he walked home from a restaurant with Alan and Belinda Duncan he was stabbed by a passing pimp. He was rushed to hospital with serious wounds to his chest, close to the heart.

The next day the Duncans got in touch with the Joyces to see if they could use their influence to ensure Beckett got the best of treatment.

James and Nora Joyce arrived at the hospital as Beckett was coming out of a coma. 'When I came to, the first thing I remember was Joyce standing at the end of the ward and coming to see me,' remarked Beckett.[17] 'It was thanks to Joyce and his crazy woman doctor, Fontaine, that he got me a private room.'

Joyce behaved generously. Besides asking his own doctor, Thérèse Fontaine, to look after Beckett, he paid for the hospital room. He and Nora visited frequently and brought food and flowers while the Duncans kept reporters at bay. One of his visitors was a woman with whom he had played tennis, who would later become his wife.

Shortly before the stabbing, however, Beckett had become involved with the American heiress Peggy

Guggenheim. Their relationship kicked off one evening when they both dined with the Joyces at Fouquet's. Beckett escorted Peggy home and spent the night with her and all of the following day in an orgy of sex and champagne.

Joyce knew Peggy through her cousin Helen Fleischman, Giorgio's wife. Peggy had been married to Laurence Vail in a wedding that the Joyces had attended in 1922.[18]

Peggy accompanied Beckett to Joyce's 56th birthday celebrations a month after the stabbing. She gave Joyce a gift of a blackthorn stick; Beckett brought some Fendant de Sion. The celebrations started at the Joyces' flat where family and friends listened to a special broadcast from Radio Éireann.

The transmission was called 'A James Joyce Programme' and featured a biographical note by Herbert Gorman (Joyce's biographer), readings of Joyce's poems and songs (including *She Weeps over Rahoon* by Herbert Hughes). A critical assessment of Joyce's work was made by Professor JJ Hogan. The programme included a 'personal sketch' of Joyce by his old friend CP Curran.[19]

Curran's daughter Elizabeth attended the celebrations, which moved on from the Joyces' to the Jolases' 'in a taxi full of bottles of wine and cheese, crackers and records and us, of course, singing.'[20] Fifteen people attended the dinner, among them Beckett and Guggenheim, Nino Frank and Joyce's latest obsession, the tenor John Sullivan. The centrepiece on the dinner table was a cake (with 56 candles) in green and white with representations of the Liffey and of Joyce's new book, still publicly unnamed.[21]

In a letter home Elizabeth Curran wrote of guests pulling crackers and wearing paper hats, drink flowing, the piano being played and Joyce singing come-all-ye's and

Siubhail a rúin. 'And then Joyce sang Phil the Fluther and danced and pretty well went on dancing until after three.' Sullivan and Jolas 'bawled their heads off,' according to Beckett.[22]

The man from Foxrock was now firmly re-established within the Joyce circle. He helped Giorgio to correct proofs of parts of *Finnegans Wake*, amounting to about 15 hours' work. Joyce paid him 250 francs (about $7 at the time) for his effort, then supplemented it with an old overcoat and five ties. 'I did not refuse,' Beckett told MacGreevy. 'It is so much simpler to be hurt than to hurt.'[23]

---

[1] A glimpse of these occasions may be got from Stuart Gilbert's diary entry for New Year's Eve 1929: 'At 2.30, Joyce [was] very gay and dancing a jig to *Auld Lang Syne*; Mrs Joyce, indignant, compels all to leave. She thinks he is 'making a fool of himself.' – but I disagree; he is a nimble dancer. If Joyce had not been a writer he'd a been a meistersinger; if not a singer, a ballerino.' (Gilbert: *Reflections on James Joyce* 16).

[2] For Zelda, like Lucia, dancing gave her a sense of identity. But the similarity doesn't end there. Both were later diagnosed with schizophrenia and recuperated separately at the same clinic in Switzerland.

[3] Maddox: *Nora* 333.

[4] Aldington described Beckett as a 'splendidly mad Irishman….. who wanted to commit suicide, a fate he nearly imposed on half the faculty of the *École* by playing the flute…..'

[5] MacGreevy papers, TCD.

[6] Knowlson: *Damned to Fame* 254.

[7] Stella Steyn first went to Paris in 1926 and spent most of the following five years there. She often visited the Joyces. At Joyce's request she supplied illustrations for *Finnegans Wake* which was then appearing in instalments in *transition*.

[8] Stella Steyn: *An Autobiographical Memoir*, Gorry Gallery, Dublin, 1995, ed. S. B. Kennedy.

[9] Idem.

[10] Browsing at Shakespeare and Company some years earlier, Gilbert noticed mistakes in a French translation of *Ulysses*, and drew these to the attention of Sylvia Beach who promised to inform Joyce. Gilbert then joined Valery Larbaud and August Morel in the translation of the novel

which was published by Adrienne Monnier in 1929.

[11] Paul Léon would play a major role in Joyce's affairs until the outbreak of war. As the Nazis approached Paris, Léon saved Joyce's personal papers for posterity. He was later interned as a Jew and killed.

[12] In 1940 Alex and Giorgio were instrumental in getting Peggy Guggenheim's art collection out of Paris.

[13] Frank Budgen in an interview with Ellmann.

[14] Padraic Colum: *OFJJ*.

[15] Mary Colum: *OFJJ*.

[16] Idem.

[17] Knowlson: *Damned to Fame* 260 (interview with Beckett).

[18] Joyce had no idea why he had been invited and told McAlmon: 'I scarcely know him though I think I met him or her somewhere.'

[19] Constantine Curran was a model for Gabriel Conroy in *The Dead*, according to Richard Ellmann.

[20] Curran: *James Joyce Remembered*, 90.

[21] Joyce had hoped *Finnegans Wake* would be published on his 56th birthday but he had to wait another year.

[22] Letter to MacGreevy 11 February 1938 (MacGreevy papers TCD).

[23] Idem.

Chapter Fourteen
Beautiful And Damned

Francis Scott Fitzgerald worshipped Joyce. He was so much in awe of the Irishman that he could not bring himself to approach him, instead asking Sylvia Beach to introduce them. His wife, Zelda, on the other hand, was quite indifferent to Joyce. She was also indifferent to her husband for by 1928 she was experiencing the symptoms of schizophrenia, an illness she shared with Lucia Joyce. Both women recuperated at the same clinic and, by an even stranger coincidence, they liked to dance and - independently of each other– took lessons from the same ballet teacher.

Fitzgerald was already an acclaimed writer when he met Joyce. His first novel, *This Side of Paradise* (1920) had proved very popular with Beach's book-borrowing customers. He had also published *The Beautiful and Damned* (1922) and *The Great Gatsby* (1925). He had read Joyce's main works, although he expressed himself 'puzzled and disappointed' by *Ulysses*.

The Fitzgeralds and their daughter Scottie sailed to France four times during the 1920s, bringing up to 17 pieces of luggage each time. When he called in to Shakespeare and Company in the summer of 1928, Fitzgerald enjoyed discussing books with Beach and got on well with her and Adrienne Monnier.

Beach described him as 'one of our great pals,' although she was well aware of his shortcomings: 'Poor Scott was earning so much money from his books that he and Zelda had to drink a great deal of champagne in Montmartre in an effort to get rid of it,' she wrote sarcastically.[1]

Nevertheless the blue-eyed writer with fair wavy hair charmed the women of rue de l'Odéon and had no difficulty in persuading Beach to introduce him to Joyce.

By now, well used to bringing together writers of different backgrounds and nationalities, Beach and Monnier invited Joyce and the Fitzgeralds to dinner at their apartment at 18 rue de l'Odéon on Wednesday, 22 June. They also asked along a young French writer, André Chamson, and his wife Lucie. There followed an evening, which Fitzgerald depicted in a sketch, which he drew inside Beach's copy of *Gatsby*. Entitled the 'Festival of St James,' it shows a dinner table and guests, with Beach and Monnier at either end portrayed as mermaids (possibly intended to be interpreted as sirens) and Fitzgerald on his knees paying homage to Joyce who is seated beside him beneath a halo.

So overawed was Fitzgerald by being close to the Irishman he so admired that he called him 'sir' and offered to jump out of the window as a demonstration of his esteem. Joyce would have none of it, declaring: 'That young man must be mad – I'm afraid he'll do himself some injury.' [2]

Afterwards Joyce wrote, in a formal and sarcastic way, to Fitzgerald:

> *'Dear Mr. Fitzgerald: Herewith is the book you gave me signed and I am adding a portrait of the artist as a once young man with the thanks of your much obliged but most pusillanimous guest. Sincerely yours, James Joyce.'* [3]

Fitzgerald was fascinated by Joyce's working pattern, which seemed to produce a finished novel about every 15 years. Under pressure from his own publisher (Maxwell Perkins of Scribner's) to send him a manuscript, Fitzgerald wrote back in mitigation of himself that Joyce didn't expect to finish his *Work in Progress* for another three or four years 'and he works eleven hours a day to my intermittent eight.'[4]

Within weeks of the dinner party, Fitzgerald wrote to Hemingway in Wyoming that he had been seeing 'a good deal of Joyce.' It was an exaggeration. The Fitzgeralds had indeed invited Joyce and Nora to their apartment on rue Vaugirard. Perhaps Fitzgerald, who sometimes felt inferior to the more macho Hemingway, wished to show that he too could be close to the famous Irish writer.

Fitzgerald found Chamson[5] more congenial than Joyce. The two were closer in age and they met several times that summer. On one occasion, visiting the Chamsons in their sixth floor flat, Fitzgerald climbed out onto a balcony and, balancing himself, shouted 'I am Voltaire, I am Rousseau.' Drunk and depressed by the failure of his marriage, he had to be dissuaded by Chamson from jumping to the street below.[6]

Fitzgerald seemed to have inherited his jump-threatening tendency from his mother, Mollie McQuillan. The eldest daughter of two Irish-born parents, she once threatened to jump into the river if her husband to be, Edward Fitzgerald, did not propose marriage.

Mollie's wealth came from her father. Philip McQuillan had emigrated from Co Fermanagh in 1843. He was only nine years old and settled with his parents in Illinois. As a young adult he worked as a shop assistant before moving to St Paul where he started a small grocery store. The business grew into a grocery wholesaler. He married an Irishwoman and built his business into a thriving concern, dying a millionaire in 1877 at only 43.

Mollie, the eldest of his children, was born in 1860. She later married Edward Fitzgerald who had moved from Maryland to St Paul. He could trace his family back to the earliest colonial times. He had literary ambitions and encouraged young Fitzgerald in his writing. But he was unsuccessful in business and depended on his wife for financial support. Fitzgerald, who was born in 1896, would later unfairly compare the two sides of his family.

Although the McQuillans had been one of the most prominent and respectable Catholic families in St Paul, Fitztgerald seemed ashamed of his origins, regarding his maternal grandfather as a mere Irish immigrant rather than admiring his achievement. He often referred to his antecedents as 'straight 1850 potato-famine Irish' and told a friend that the combination of being Irish and middle-class 'depresses me inordinately.'

In later life he said: 'I am half black Irish and half old America stock. The black Irish half had the money and looked down upon the Maryland side of the family who... really had... breeding.'[7]

In fact, Fitzgerald was more Irish than he admitted. His paternal grandfather, Michael Fitzgerald, had also emigrated from Ireland, yet Scott always denied this. 'I'm not Irish on Father's side,' he wrote to the critic Edmund Wilson.[8]

Wilson was one of several critics in the 1920s that could not take Fitzgerald seriously, with the result that it was another 30 years or so before his works – which were commercially very successful - were critically acclaimed. Wilson also believed it was Fitzgerald's insecurity as an Irish Catholic that led to his 'erratic social behaviour' – a euphemism for his frequent drunkenness. And he analysed him further:

> ... *Fitzgerald is partly Irish, and that he brings both to life and to fiction certain qualities that are not Anglo-Saxon. For, like the Irish, Fitzgerald is romantic, but also cynical about romance; he is*

bitter as well as ecstatic; astringent as well as lyrical. He casts himself in the role of playboy, yet at the playboy he incessantly mocks. He is vain, a little malicious, of quick intelligence and wit, and has an Irish gift for turning language into something iridescent and surprising.[9]

While Fitzgerald was pleased to acknowledge the Irishness on his mother's side, he was embarrassed by her social awkwardness. But her money ensured he had a first-class education.

She sent him to a Catholic school in New Jersey, then to Princeton. There he came under the influence of a priest, Fr Cyril Fay, who was friendly with the Anglo-Irish writer Shane Leslie[10] – a Catholic convert and first cousin of Sir Winston Churchill – whose descendants still live at Castle Leslie in Glaslough, Co Monaghan. Both Leslie and Fay are credited with having given young Fitzgerald a sense of a Catholic elite. Shane Leslie had been to Eton and Cambridge. He was interested in the plays of Synge, Yeats and Gregory. His romantic sense of Irish nationalism stirred Fitzgerald's interest in his own ancestry.

The two kept in contact. In 1917, Fitzgerald showed Leslie the first draft of a novel he was writing and which he would call *This Side of Paradise*. Leslie recommended revisions, which Fitzgerald carried out. The novel's publication in 1920 made Fitzgerald an overnight success.[11]

When he arrived in Paris for the first time in May 1921, Fitzgerald was one of 6,000 Americans in the city , many of them refugees from Prohibition and provincialism and fired with enthusiasm for a more liberal and creative environment. Fitzgerald, however, was not impressed by what he saw. He had little time for his compatriots: 'This city is full of Americans,' he wrote to Edmund Wilson,' most of them former friends – whom we spend most of our time dodging, not because we don't want to see them but because Zelda's only just well and I've got to work.'

American women were worse: '... these preposterous, pushing women and girls who assume that you have any personal interest in them, who have all (so they say) read James Joyce and who simply adore Mencken.'[12]

He wrote to Leslie: 'France is a bore and a disappointment chiefly, I imagine, because I know no one here.'

He and Zelda, who was pregnant, did little to ease their integration. They made a nuisance of themselves in their hotel when Zelda tied the lift to her door so that it would be available when she'd finished dressing.

Their second visit, in May 1924, was more successful. In that year the number of Americans in Paris had grown to 30,000 and there were 60,000 British. Among the migrants were artists, writers and musicians who rejected the commercial world of the 1920s and who, as Malcolm Cowley put it, '... sailed for Europe as soon as they had money enough to pay for the steamer tickets.'

In Paris they met Gerald and Sara Murphy, a wealthy American couple who had decided to settle in France. Gerald was a painter in the Cubist style and was friendly with Picasso. American writers and artists also befriended them, including Hemingway. The characters of Nicole and Dick Diver in *Tender is the Night* are based on the Murphys, whose villa at Cap d'Antibes became a focal point for visiting American writers and artists.[13]

In 1925 the Fitzgeralds again crossed to France and in April Fitzgerald and Hemingway met for the first time. This was the start of what Fitzgerald called 'the summer of a thousand parties and no work.' The encounter took place in the Dingo bar in Montparnasse. Fitzgerald is reported (by Hemingway) to have drunk too much. A few days later the two men met again - at the Closerie des Lilas – and thus began a relationship that was at times either close or turbulent.

It was an unequal friendship. Fitzgerald was a recognised writer, author of two novels and earning over $18,000 a year. Hemingway had one book published (by McAlmon), *Three Stories and Ten Poems*, which earned him practically nothing. He still depended on his wife's money to survive. They were different in other ways too: according to a biographer of Hemingway, 'Fitzgerald, in brief, enjoyed getting drunk, whereas Hemingway enjoyed getting laid.'[14]

Each believed the other was the better writer. Fitzgerald hero-worshipped Hemingway and introduced him to his own publishers, Scribner's. Hemingway brought Fitzgerald to meet Gertrude Stein and they got on well. Scott also met Edith Wharton who was living in Paris at the time.

Eventually the friendship between the two men would be torn apart by Fitzgerald's heavy drinking bouts during which he would embarrass those around him. On one occasion Fitzgerald was the cause of Hemingway being kicked out of his apartment because Fitzgerald insulted the landlord, urinated on the porch and tried to break down the door in the small hours of the morning.

Writing aside, Fitzgerald was attracted to the qualities in Hemingway that he himself lacked: confidence, athleticism and good looks. Hemingway described his compatriot as a man 'who looked like a boy with a face between handsome and pretty. He had very fair wavy hair, a high forehead, excited and friendly eyes and a delicate long-lipped Irish mouth that, on a girl, would have been the mouth of a beauty... The mouth worried you until you knew him and then it worried you more.'[15]

Stories of the erratic, drunken behaviour of the Fitzgeralds became legendary around Montparnasse. They partied most evenings, drinking heavily at the Dome, the Coupole, the Deux Magots or the Closerie des Lilas. They drank with anyone they could, sometimes with Dolly Wilde, who lived near them on rue Vaugirard. Dolly smoked opium and injected heroin and drank at the Surrealist nightclub Le Boeuf sur le Toit. Once she made a pass at Zelda. Fitzgerald was furious. The Fitzgeralds argued increasingly.

Fitzgerald's drinking got worse when Zelda took up ballet lessons and became progressively more obsessed with dancing. No longer having a constant drinking companion, Fitzgerald visited the bars on his own, frequently over-indulging and often ending up in jail for his drunken behaviour. On one occasion he commandeered a three-wheeled delivery cart and drove it around the Place de la Concorde, pursued by two gendarmes on bicycles.

Hemingway believed Zelda encouraged her husband's heavy drinking so it would interfere with his writing. As a writer of magazine articles rather than novels, she was becoming jealous of Fitzgerald's success.[16] She was also jealous of her husband's affection for Hemingway and even accused him of having a homosexual relationship with him. She saw through the macho image that Hemingway liked to portray and she even thought he might be gay.[17] She called him 'a pansy with hair on his chest.'

Hemingway, in *A Moveable Feast*, recalls Fitzgerald telling him he was concerned about the size of his penis since Zelda had said it was too small to satisfy her. Hemingway took him to the toilet for an examination and tried to reassure Fitzgerald, with little success, that all was quite normal.

Years later, Hemingway described Fitzgerald as 'completely undisciplined, and he would quit at the drop of a hat and borrow someone's hat to drop. He was fragile Irish instead of tough Irish.'[18]

One of the reasons the Fitzgeralds returned to Paris in April 1928 was so that Zelda could enrol in lessons with Madame Lubov Egorova who had established a dance studio as a 'feeder' for the Ballets Russes. Lucia Joyce also took lessons from Egorova (one year later, after her appearance at the dancing competition at the Bal Bullier). Both women started ballet lessons too late in life, putting them under considerable physical and psychological pressure. And both began to show similar signs of the schizophrenia that would engulf them in the years ahead.

Zelda's lessons cost her $300 a month. She insisted on paying for them herself (from her journalism earnings) in order to be independent of her disapproving husband. Friends began to notice changes in her behaviour – confusing remarks, inappropriate smiles, etc. In 1930 she was admitted to Les Rives de Prangins at Nyon near Zurich. Three years later the Joyces were visiting Zurich when Lucia's symptoms worsened and she was advised to recuperate at the same clinic. She and Zelda never met.

Before leaving for the United States, the Fitzgeralds met Padraic and Mary Colum during the winter of 1929. The Fitzgeralds had not been directly affected by the Wall Street crash in October as Fitzgerald had not played the market and he had plenty of money put by. Between 1920 and 1929, his writings earned almost $250,000 (close to €3m today).

The war of words between Fitzgerald and Hemingway continued, even on the other side of the Atlantic. In New York, McAlmon slandered Hemingway in a conversation with Maxwell Perkins of Scribner's. When Fitzgerald heard about it, he wrote to Perkins: 'McAlmon is a bitter rat and I'm not surprised at anything he does or says. He's failed as a writer and tries to fortify himself by tieing up to the big boys like Joyce and Stein and despising everything else...'

Fitzgerald told Hemingway of the slander and when

McAlmon returned to Paris, Hemingway beat him up outside a bar in Montparnasse, saying: 'Now tell that to your goddamn friends!' Hemingway said later that McAlmon was too pitiable to be beaten to a pulp.

The arguments between Fitzgerald and Hemingway continued well into the 1930s. Much of the war of words was conducted in correspondence between the two writers and Maxwell Perkins. Mary Colum, then a literary critic in New York, was lunching with Perkins and Hemingway when Hemingway made a passing remark about the wealthy people he knew: 'I am getting to know the rich.' It was probably the sound of smug self-satisfaction in his voice that prompted Mary Colum to respond that 'the only difference between the rich and other people is that the rich have more money.' Hemingway then appropriated the quip, and used it devastatingly in a fictionalised attack on Fitzgerald in a magazine version of the story *The Snows of Kilimanjaro*.

---

[1] Beach: *Shakespeare and Company* 116.

[2] Ellmann 581.

[3] Joyce to Fitzgerald, 11 July, 1928 (Ellmann ed., *Letters of James Joyce Vol. 3*, 180).

[4] Fitzgerald to Perkins, 21 July, 1928.

[5] André Chamson, who became a member of the Académie Francaise, later wrote: 'Sylvia carried pollen like a bee. She cross-fertilised these writers. She did more to link England, the United States, Ireland and France than four great ambassadors combined.'

[6] Fitch: *Sylvia Beach and the Lost Generation* 275.

[7] Letter to Edmund Wilson.

[8] Letter, January 1922. Wilson had shown Fitzgerald an article he had written, before publication, citing Irishness and the Midwest as key influences on Fitzgerald's work. Wilson also cited alcohol as an influence but Fitzgerald asked him to leave it out.

[9] Edmund Wilson: *The Shores of* Light 31.

[10] Sir Shane Leslie (1885-1971) was interested in the Irish revival and had nationalist sympathies. He wrote biographies of Swift and Cardinal Manning among others.

[11] Leslie was less literarily astute in his review of *Ulysses*. He dismissed

Joyce's novel as an 'abomination' (*Dublin Review*, Sept. 1922) and campaigned to have it banned in Britain.

[12] Letter to Wilson.

[13] The Murphys were credited with making the French Riviera fashionable in summer. Prior to that it had been considered unhealthily warm and the well-off summered in the northern resorts of Trouville and Deauville.

[14] Lynn: *Hemingway*.

[15] Hemingway: *A Moveable Feast* 107.

[16] Hemingway's memoir of his Paris period was written about three decades later and should be read with caution. In the Preface, Hemingway wrote: *This book may be regarded as fiction. But there is always the chance that such a book of fiction may throw some light on what has been written as fact.*

[17] McAlmon, envying the success of Hemingway and Fitzgerald, also spread rumours that both were gay.

[18] Letter to Arthur Mizener, 1950 (*Selected Letters of Ernest Hemingway*).

A Little Circle Of Kindred Minds

Chapter Fifteen
A Night at the Opera

When the Colums returned to Paris in 1930 Padraic performed his usual ritual, calling first into Shakespeare and Company on rue de l'Odéon. As always he was greeted warmly by Sylvia Beach.

'Joyce wants you to do something for him' she told him, a twinkle in her eye.

Colum got the impression that he was not the only one being sought by Joyce and, turning to Ernest Hemingway who was in the shop at the time, said: 'Joyce operates like a general.'

'Like a general of the Jesuits,' replied Hemingway.

Joyce was indeed mobilising the troops. His cause: a Cork-born tenor named John Sullivan. His aim: to promote the singer as widely as possible. His method: by getting his friends to use their influence to publicise him.

Joyce had first heard of Sullivan in a letter from his brother Stanislaus in Trieste where Sullivan had been singing. What caught Stanislaus's attention was not his voice but the fact that the tenor was reading his brother's *Portrait of the Artist*. It was late 1929 and the singer was about to take up an appointment as a leading tenor at the Paris Opera. Stanislaus suggested he might look up his brother while there. The two met, and Joyce's fondness for his fellow-Irishman turned close to an addiction from the moment he first heard him sing in *Tannhauser*. He wrote to a friend:

*I do not believe there can have existed in the past a
greater tenor than his and as for the future I think
it doubtful that human ears (the kind they breed
nowadays) will ever hear such another until the
Archangel Michael sings his grand aria in the last
act.*[1]

Joyce booked seats for every opera in which Sullivan was
performing - *Samson*, *Les Huguenots*, *La Damnation de
Faust* and *William Tell*. A tenor himself, Joyce followed the
score and counted with glee Sullivan's high notes, for the
Cork man reached high Cs with remarkable ease -
something no other tenor was capable of at that time.

It did not take long for Joyce's enthusiasm to become an
obsession. He met Sullivan frequently; he invited him to his
home and introduced him to his friends. He had himself
photographed together with Sullivan and James Stephens,
suggesting afterwards the caption: 'Three Irish Beauties.'

Padraic Colum had been considerably less impressed. He
had heard Sullivan sing one evening at the Joyces' but,
having a poor ear for music, lacked Joyce's unbridled
enthusiasm. Neither was he impressed by Sullivan's
Irishness, for the singer never once mentioned his native
country. In fact, as Colum saw it, he had little to say about
anything and what he did he said in French.

Colum had heard that Joyce had been in touch with friends
they had in common in connection with Sullivan and he
knew it was only a matter of time before he too would be
contacted. Sure enough, Joyce phoned. What were the
Colums doing that evening? Would they go to the opera?
He would meet them there during the interval. No, another
evening would not suit because Sullivan was singing and it
was the last chance to see him for some time...

Colum seems to have been more impressed by the Opera

House than by the opera, savouring the presence of smartly dressed dignitaries with chains and women bedecked with wraps and jewels. When the opera - *William Tell* - started, he watched Sullivan come on 'looking bulky in brown habiliments,' but he was more impressed by the action – in which *William Tell* shoots an apple off his son's head - than by the singing. Colum later remarked how Joyce always skipped the third act of William Tell because Arnold, the character played by Sullivan, does not appear in it.[2]

At the interval, the Colums met Joyce who was with some friends. Joyce told them Sullivan would be joining him later for supper. Would they come too? But the Colums declined the invitation, preferring instead to have a snack of sausages and a beer on their own before returning to their hotel.

The following day, Colum visited Square Robiac where Joyce talked of nothing but Sullivan. Colum tried as best he could to contribute to the discussion about the previous evening's performance but knew he could not match Joyce's knowledge or enthusiasm.

Joyce's zeal stemmed from several factors, among them his own undoubted ability as a fine tenor (he had sung with John McCormack in Dublin in 1904[3] and had once considered a career as a singer); his son Giorgio had just embarked on such a career and he felt Sullivan could help promote it; and his father John Joyce had been born in Sullivan's native county of Cork. Then of course there was his innate enthusiasm for anything that came out of Ireland.

Now, he told Colum, he saw in *William Tell* the theme he had used in *Ulysses* - of a father's search for his son and the son's search for his father. As usual, Joyce kept the main point of his conversation until last. As Colum was leaving, he said: 'You have connections with a good many journals.

I want you to write something about Sullivan.'

Colum agreed, although he wondered where he would start. In due course he wrote an article on Sullivan for the *Irish Independent*. Following its publication, he received a note from the Irish Minister (ambassador) in Paris, Vaughan B Dempsey, who said he would like to meet Sullivan and could he arrange a meeting. When Colum told a delighted Joyce the news, the author of *Ulysses* immediately invited Dempsey and his wife as well as Padraic and Mary to have dinner with Nora and himself, during which the ambassador was left in no doubt about Sullivan's ability and achievements. Joyce's close friend, Stuart Gilbert, wrote in his diary: 'JJ is now all Sullivan.'

Shortly afterwards, Sullivan was invited to sing at the inauguration of a church in Killarney, but he was disappointed at the reception he received there. Madame Sullivan found Ireland very provincial.

John O'Sullivan (Joyce persuaded him to drop the prefix 'for the love of music') was born in Cork of Kerry parentage. His grandfather owned the Lake Hotel in Killarney. He spent most of his 50 years in France, having left Cork at the age of 12 to go to Rouen. He made his singing debut at Toulouse in 1911 and, by the time Joyce met him in 1929, was a leading tenor at the Paris Opera. He was married to a Frenchwoman, sang under the name of Jean Sullivan and generally spoke only French, even when talking to fellow-Irish in Joyce's home. He also had a mistress. Arguably, he was more French than the French themselves.

Yet, besides his voice, it was the Irishness in him that appealed to Joyce. In a letter to Harriet Weaver, he described Sullivan as having the body of a member of the Dublin Metropolitan Police and looking as if he had escaped from a boarding school at the age of 59.

In temperament, he is intractable, quarrelsome, disconnected, contemptuous, inclined to bullying, undiplomatic, but on the other hand good-humoured, sociable, unaffected, amusing and well-informed.

Sullivan, like Joyce, had a persecution complex. He believed the world's top tenors - most of them Italian - were conspiring to prevent him from appearing at key venues such as Covent Garden and the Metropolitan Opera. This great injustice, as Joyce saw it, led him to adopt the singer as a *cause celebre*.

Others did not see it that way. To Padraic Colum and Wyndham Lewis, Sullivan was more an *idée fixe*. A more perceptive and rational explanation of Joyce's obsession with Sullivan is given by the writer's biographer Richard Ellmann:

> *...Joyce saw Sullivan as an alter ego who had pursued the career he himself had rejected, and had then encountered the same opposition in music which Joyce had encountered in literature. Roused by the challenge of making another career, now vicariously in another art, Joyce extended to Sullivan an almost motherly solicitude.[4]*

Whatever his motivation, Joyce effectively implemented single-handedly a public relations campaign on behalf of John Sullivan that would be the envy of many a 'spin doctor' today. As he had done with the Colums, his campaign involved inviting friends to the opera, then to meet the tenor at a café where they would be asked to write articles or otherwise promote Sullivan as best they could.[5] One of the 'troops' was Samuel Beckett who avoided going to the opera as much as possible. But Joyce insisted. During one performance, Joyce in his enthusiasm shouted 'Up Cork!' Afterwards, Beckett and his fellow-guests were treated to a champagne dinner at the Café de la Paix.

Among others who were treated to opera and dinner by Joyce were Richard Aldington (the Imagist poet who had once been married to Hilda Doolittle), George Antheil, Sylvia Beach, Adrienne Monnier, Philippe Soupault, Stuart Gilbert and Eugene Jolas. Those who would not write articles were expected to write letters to patrons of the arts, urging them to offer engagements to, or otherwise support, Sullivan.[6]

Philippe Soupault recalled Joyce's enthusiasm for opera:

> At the theatre, seated in the first row - presumably because of his very bad eyesight - he carefully watched the action and listened closely to the performers. Only children are as passionately attentive as Joyce was. He was always the first to applaud and to shout 'encore' after the great arias.[7]

Joyce's secretary and close friend, Paul Léon, and his wife went to Rossini's opera with Joyce and Nora. After the first two acts, the party adjourned to the bar since Sullivan would not be on stage in the third act. They resumed their seats for the fourth and final act, which resulted in such rousing applause for Sullivan that Joyce got carried away: 'Bravo Sullivan... Merde pour Lauri-Volpi,' he cried, in a reference to Sullivan's rival tenor. Joyce's excessive enthusiasm led a member of the distinguished audience to exclaim: 'Il va un peu fort celui-la' ('He's coming on a bit strong, that fellow').[8]

When the same Lauri-Volpi received rave reviews for his role of Arnold in another production of *William Tell*, Joyce felt attack was the best form of defence. A letter was dispatched to the press in the name of Sullivan - but clearly written by Joyce - attacking Lauri-Volpi for taking shortcuts:

*...M Volpi has permitted himself to cut out a little
over half of his part, suppressing the recitatives,
diminishing the trio, and completely avoiding the
perilous duel with the final chorus...*[9]

The letter went on to publicly challenge the Italian to sing
the part of Arnold the way Rossini had written it 'and in
the way I have myself sung it hundreds of times in the
principal cities of France, Belgium, and even of Italy...'
Such an event would take place at a Paris concert hall
where both tenors would sing the part. The music critic of
the Paris edition of the *New York Herald* would be the
adjudicator.

The musical 'duel' never took place. But two days after the
letter was posted, a much sought after engagement, which
Sullivan had in Covent Garden, was mysteriously cancelled.
This, too, energised Joyce. He had just had another eye
operation, during which he had recovered a certain amount
of his sight. He decided he would use this happy outcome to
good effect in his great publicity campaign – and in a most
dramatic way.

The occasion was yet another performance of *William Tell*.
Seated in his box at the Paris Opera, having waited until
the final act, he suddenly leaned forward, raised his dark
glasses from his face and announced: 'Merci, mon Dieu,
pour ce miracle. Aprés 20 ans, je revois la lumière'
('Thanks be to God for this miracle. After 20 years, I see
the light again').

Members of the audience were stunned, many of them
recognising the Irish writer. The effect was as dramatic as
if a pilgrim had thrown away their crutches. One newspaper
reported: 'The audience were witnesses of a dramatic scene
which exceeded in intensity the drama being played on the
stage.'[10]

The 'miracle' received extensive publicity and, as journalists questioned Joyce about it, he ensured that Sullivan received plenty of praise; he even contrived that his Swiss eye specialist, Dr Alfred Vogt, [11] got due mention.

Things did not always go according to plan, however. One day, Colum called to Square Robiac and found Joyce particularly low. He had persuaded the American journalist and publisher Bill Bird, a friend of McAlmon's, to write an article for the *New York Sun*, but in his enthusiasm had suggested to Bird that John McCormack had been quite unhelpful in getting singing engagements for Sullivan. He even blamed McCormack for a boycott of all Irish tenors by the Boston Opera House, saying McCormack had arranged the boycott out of jealousy.

Joyce the publicity agent had become Joyce the spin doctor, but his story was now spinning out of control. Following publication of the article, the Boston Opera House denied any such boycott. Bird felt foolish. Joyce, who valued his friendship with John McCormack, feared a reprisal that would backfire on Sullivan. [12]

Colum tried to reassure Joyce that in New York news was soon forgotten. 'The hardest thing to find in New York is a morning paper in the afternoon,' he told him. 'An item of that kind just won't stay in the public mind.' Joyce cheered up.

At that moment, Nora entered the room. Colum knew that the subject of Sullivan was taboo in the Joyce household; Nora had once asked MacGreevy not to mention the singer's name and to ignore it if Joyce did. So the conversation turned to other things. Later as he left, Joyce put his hand on Colum's shoulder: 'Keep your shoulder to the wheel about Sullivan.'

Soon afterwards, Joyce decided it was time to make approaches towards influential musicians who might be persuaded to hire Sullivan. One such person was the renowned English conductor Sir Thomas Beecham, long-time friend of Lady Maud Cunard . Her Ladyship was in Paris and Joyce could have made contact with her directly. Instead, once again using a circuitous route, he decided to approach her daughter, Nancy, who was living at her *Hours Press* publishing address near the Pont Neuf.

The fact that Nancy, whom he had not yet met, was confined to bed with a sore throat did not deter Joyce, who called on her, groped his way to a bedside chair and introduced himself. He got straight to the point. He had come about John Sullivan, a great Irish tenor who was not getting the recognition he deserved... Lady Cunard was a close friend of Sir Thomas Beecham... Could she, Nancy, use her influence with her mother to encourage Sir Thomas to engage Sullivan forthwith...?

Joyce had no way of knowing that relations between Nancy Cunard and her mother were at an all-time low and that she had little or no influence with her. Since moving to Paris in 1920, Nancy had led a bohemian existence that did not go down well with Her Ladyship. She had associated with the Surrealist movement and had taken up with the French communist poet Louis Aragon (thus earning herself the nickname 'La Cunard Sauvage'[13]).

Lady Cunard did not approve of her daughter dressing in men's clothes and associating with the lesbian Natalie Barney and bisexual Djuna Barnes. And she was disturbed that she was now involved with an African-American jazz musician she had met in Venice - Henry Crowder - and went about Paris with ebony bracelets up her arms.

Joyce, however, was not prepared to accept that Nancy was incapable of influencing her mother. Under pressure, Nancy promised to inform Lady Cunard that Joyce had come to see her about the matter, but that was the most she could do. When she told Joyce that he could contact her mother directly, he brushed the matter aside. She wrote later:

> *I did not feel like recalling to him that she had been very instrumental indeed, in 1917 or so, in obtaining public recognition for his great talent as a writer, recognition that could not have been more official, and on a financial plane, too.*[14]

Nancy pointed out that her mother was in Paris, Sullivan too, that Sir Thomas, if he wasn't in Paris already, would be there soon, and that he - Joyce - could bring them all together if he really wanted to. But Joyce insisted that his approach would have to be through Nancy.

Joyce left, obviously disappointed, but two weeks later he called back. This time he had another trick up his sleeve: bribery. Again he was persistent. Sullivan simply must be engaged. In fact, he added, if an engagement resulted from her overtures to her mother or Sir Thomas, some work by a famous author might find its way to the *Hours Press* for publication etc. etc...[15]

Much as she wanted new work to publish, Nancy felt she could do little but inform her mother of the matter. Joyce continued his Messianic work on behalf of Sullivan during a summer visit to London (where he importuned the Irish High Commissioner and members of the Guinness family).

On his return to Paris, he learned that Beecham had agreed to attend a performance of *William Tell*, along with Lady Cunard. A delighted and highly expectant Joyce accompanied them.

Beecham was impressed that evening. He agreed that Sullivan had 'certainly an amazing voice' and promised to do all he could to bring the tenor to London.

This only served to galvanise Joyce into further action. He

approached Antheil and asked him to compose an opera
especially for Sullivan. Joyce told him it should be based on
Cain (Byron's unfinished dramatisation of the Old
Testament). He would suggest what cuts to make.

Would he rewrite it? Antheil asked him.

'I would never have the bad manners to rewrite the text of
a great English poet,' Joyce replied.

But how could he, as a composer, insist that Sullivan be
chosen to sing the tenor part? The opera house could have
someone else in mind.

Joyce was unfazed. Antheil should write the part 'in the
pure tenor tradition.' That would exclude all tenors except
Sullivan.

'I believe you have here the great opportunity of your
career as a composer,' Joyce told Antheil. 'A magnificent
subject never treated before in opera, the work and name
of a great poet and the most remarkable operatic voice in
the world of our time.'[16]

But Antheil was too busy with other commissions.
Eventually Joyce had to accept the composer was not
going to write the opera he had in mind. A weary Joyce got
Paul Léon to write the final letter to Antheil, saying he
was too exhausted to carry on a long correspondence and
effectively ending the plan, but adding, with a large dose of
flattery:

> *He [Joyce] has had offers to entrust with the writing
> of this opera [from] Milhaud, Honegger, Prokofiev
> and Stravinsky but has not approached them
> because he knew you and estimated that you would
> better achieve the great task of handling Byron's
> great work.*[17]

Shortly afterwards, Sullivan went on tour and Joyce's campaign lost its momentum. He kept in touch with the singer, however. Two years later he took the trouble to go to Rouen to see him in an opera there. And he sent Sullivan a postcard from Copenhagen when he visited the Danish capital in August 1936.

But his blind obsession with promoting the Irish tenor had left him. Too many other things were happening in Joyce's life. Lucia's illness was increasingly worrying him and absorbing his time; he was drinking more than he should; and petty bickering was eating away at his friendship with two of the most important women in his life, Beach and Weaver.

Besides, Sullivan was now in his mid-50s and his voice was losing its timbre. Joyce had met him too late.

The irony of the 'Sullivan' period in Joyce's life is that the singer himself did not seem to be concerned about all the fuss that was being made on his behalf. Padraic Colum never once heard Sullivan talk about Joyce. But he recalled Stuart Gilbert telling him: Joyce doesn't have to worry about Sullivan; he has a devoted wife, a charming mistress, and a girl in every town he sings in.[18]

---

[1] Unpublished letter to Herbert Hughes quoted in Ellmann 620.

[2] Padraic Colum: *OFJJ* 172.

[3] Joyce sung in a Feis Ceoil competition that McCormack won. Joyce sang well but only received a bronze medal, possibly because he refused to read a piece of music because of his poor eyesight.

[4] Ellmann 621.

[5] In a letter to Weaver Joyce listed the coverage he got for Sullivan: 'I got him very fine notices in the *Morning Post* (twice), *Daily Telegraph*, *Daily News*, *Manchester Guardian*, *Irish Independent*, *Irish Statesman*, *Chicago Daily Tribune*, *New York World*, *New York Sun* (twice), *Daily Mail*, *New York Times* with photograph, *L'Intransigeant* and *La Rampe* of Paris.' (18 March, 1930).

[6] This was not the first time Joyce helped an opera singer. In 1919 in

Zurich, he arranged for a baritone, Augustus Milner, another Corkman, to give a concert of Irish music in the town hall.

[7] Philippe Soupault: James Joyce (article in Potts ed., *James Joyce, Portraits of the Artist in Exile*).

[8] Ellmann 625.

[9] Letter signed John Sullivan, 18 June, 1930 (Ellmann ed., *Letters of James Joyce*, Vol. 3, 199).

[10] Ellmann 624, based on newspaper accounts of the time.

[11] Eamon de Valera was also a patient of Vogt. He had to pay the specialist while Joyce was treated free of charge. It is possible that Joyce and Dev were once treated in Zurich at the same time, but they never met.

[12] Years previously Joyce had attended a recital by McCormack in Paris and wrote to the singer to tell him how much he enjoyed the concert. (Letter to McCormack 8 December 1920).

[13] Aragon had been known as Le Canard Sauvage before he met Nancy.

[14] Nancy was referring to her mother having used her influence with the office of Prime Minister Asquith in 1916 (under pressure from Yeats and Pound) when Joyce was duly awarded a Civil List grant of £100.

[15] Letter from Nancy Cunard to Ellmann 1957.

[16] Letter to Antheil, 7 Sept. 1930 (Gilbert ed., *Letters of James Joyce,* Vol. 2, 292).

[17] Idem.

[18] Performing in Dublin in 1930, Sullivan called on Joyce's father at James's request. Reporting back, he quoted the old man on the new Irish government: "That blackguard Lloyd George knew what he was doing when he gave them the Free State; he knew they'd make a mess of it." (Ellmann interview with Sullivan in 1953).

Epilogue
The End Of The Affair

It is difficult to say exactly when the party ended. As with all good parties, the guests slipped away in twos and threes. But for many the cry of 'last orders' came with the Wall Street Crash of October 1929.

What happened on Wall Street was not confined to the United States. The after-shocks of the Crash reverberated across the Atlantic just as the excesses that led to it had brought many along the same route years before. Even the French were not immune to the boom and the bust. The presence of English-speaking writers in Paris in the 1920s had provided the city's painters with a steady income and valuable publicity – thanks to journalists like Arthur Power who wrote about them in the European editions of American newspapers. So when *la crise* happened they were very conscious of the falling market. As a result painting became more commercial and art dealers stood outside their galleries like prostitutes inviting inside anyone who looked interested.

From 1929 the number of Americans drinking on the café terraces began to decline. Some of them received letters from home telling them their allowances had been stopped. Others simply felt they had had enough and left in the wake of their friends.

The collapse of shares on Wall Street was not the only catalyst for the exodus. The times were changing and some of the principles that had propelled Americans across the Atlantic in the early 1920s were no longer valid at the turn of the decade. Those still drinking at the Dome were reading in newspapers and magazines of an America that was different from the one they had fled. Its former shallowness was replaced by a new seriousness and they felt uncomfortable that they were not a part of it.[1] They had become more politically aware in Europe where debates about Left and Right were everyday occurrences (they saw Aragon move to the far Left and Pound to the far Right). They believed they could bring something new to American journalism and society. The Lost Generation was beginning to find itself.

By the mid-1930s the Depression had sent most of the Americans home to a society that was demanding a kind of revolution but with a face of humanity that had not been there when they had left.[2] Writing and art were no longer 'precious.' People had 'rights.' In New York, Malcolm Cowley and Samuel Putnam were among 100 returned exiles that went to the Port Authority to demand a writers' project, something that would not have occurred to them before.

Few writers brought back with them much of the Gallic culture they had been immersed in. The war, for those who had experienced it, was still their most significant influence. But they had benefited from being more cosmopolitan in outlook and many kept up their contacts with French poets and writers. Some, like Hemingway and Fitzgerald, continued to produce outstanding literature; others became book reviewers or literary editors, occasionally producing a novel or a collection of poems.

The biggest influence abroad was that of the little magazines of which *Transition* (now spelt with a capital T) was the most respected. In keeping with the darker mood in Europe as war seemed to be unavoidable, its editor Eugene Jolas, who had started the Revolution of the Word, came up with a new manifesto: the Language of Night. Jolas had always been an enthusiast of Joyce's *Work in*

Progress, which was soon to emerge as *Finnegans Wake*, Joyce's 'night book.'[3]

Politics did not bother Joyce. When Nancy Cunard sent him a questionnaire seeking his views on the Spanish civil war, Joyce phoned her in indignation. 'I won't answer it because it is politics,' he replied. 'Now politics are getting into everything.'[4]

Joyce was working long hours on *Finnegans Wake* but *Ulysses* was still very much on his mind. Its success in the United States (because of, rather than despite, being banned) led to pirated versions. Joyce had a very litigious nature but, as he had done in the past, he got someone else to do his dirty work. He turned to Sylvia Beach to wage war on his behalf. The most notorious pirate was Samuel Roth and Joyce even suggested to Beach that she might relocate Shakespeare and Company to New York so she could pursue Roth through the courts.[5] Eventually Judge John M Woolsey of the US District Court declared the novel was not obscene and could be sold. Joyce received so many congratulatory phone calls that the hubbub irritated Lucia who cut the line.

Meanwhile the tension between Joyce and Beach was mounting. It was not made easier by the Depression, which struck France in the early 1930s. With so many of Shakespeare and Company's customers gone, money was scarce and Joyce could no longer depend on Beach for day-to-day borrowings. Joyce presented her with a contract entitling her to exclusive rights to print and sell *Ulysses* anywhere in the world (something to which she was already entitled). That was Joyce's way of ensuring that Beach would be liable for legal and other fees incurred through the courts. As always, Joyce was in control.

He never told her about the American publishing firms that were making offers to publish *Ulysses* now that it was no longer banned. He told his US agent that Beach was his representative rather than publisher. So when his American lawyer asked him for a balance of $2,000 due to him in fees incurred in the Roth case, Joyce claimed he was not the owner of *Ulysses*, implying that Beach should pay. It was her companion Adrienne Monnier who insisted she refuse, telling Joyce that while his standard of living was extravagant, 'we're now third class and soon we'll be riding the rods.' Joyce was indignant. He paid up, but in a letter to Harriet Weaver he referred disparagingly to Beach's 'more intelligent partner' and their lesbian relationship.[6]

In her memoirs, Beach wrote:

> *People imagined, perhaps, that I was making a lot of money from* Ulysses. *Well, Joyce must have kept a magnet in his pocket that attracted all the cash Joycewards... It was all I could do to prevent my bookshop from getting sucked under.*[7]

The matter did not end there and once again Joyce got someone else to bat for him. Unknown to Beach, he had entered negotiations with an American publisher. He got Padraic Colum to persuade Beach to relinquish her claims to *Ulysses* and Colum called to Shakespeare and Company almost daily to try to wear her down.

'But what about my contract?' asked Beach.

'There's no real contract. It doesn't exist' replied Colum, who eventually came out with the truth: 'You are standing in the way of Joyce's interests.'

A shocked Beach phoned Joyce within hours and relinquished all claims to his book.[8]

Some time later, when Random House published an American edition, Joyce told Beach he had already received $45,000 in royalties (over €300,000 today). Sylvia, in her memoirs, did not feel bitter:

I know how desperately he needed the money...
After all, the books were Joyce's. A baby belongs to
its mother, not to the midwife, doesn't it?[9]

But it was the end of the Joyce/Beach relationship. Taxis
now brought Joyce's files and documents from Shakespeare
and Company to the apartment of the man who was now
acting as secretary to Joyce and handling his legal affairs.
Paul Léon, a Russian Jew trained in law and literature,
refused payment for his dedicated assistance to Joyce,
which would last until the war.

With Joyce no longer around and fewer English speakers,
business at Shakespeare and Company became less frantic.
Beach's reputation as publisher of *Ulysses* attracted new,
younger visitors, some hoping she would publish their
work. Unfortunately for Beach, *Ulysses* was listed in book
catalogues under 'erotic' alongside *Fanny Hill* and *The
Perfumed Garden*. An Irish priest who bought a copy of
Ulysses asked her: 'Any other spicy books?'[10]

Among the new generation of writers, Henry Miller called
to the bookshop with his mistress, Anais Nin, asking Beach
to publish *Tropic of Cancer*. DH Lawrence wanted her to
bring out *Lady Chatterley's Lover*. Beach always declined.
Some years earlier she had been visited by the Irish writer
Frank Harris who hoped she would publish *My Life and
Loves*. He told her his new book would go much further
than *Ulysses* and claimed he was the only writer in English
who was able to get 'under a woman's skin.'[11] Beach
refused him too, but Harris continued to visit the
bookshop. Once, when he asked if he could borrow
'something exciting' to read on a train journey, Beach
decided to play a trick on him. She handed him *Little
Women*, which he grasped with delight, probably thinking
of the meaning behind the French *petites femmes*. Beach
often wondered how he got on with Louisa May Alcott's
'hot' book.

While many expatriates had left, some of the old faces were still around into the late 1930s. Janet Flanner stayed until the outbreak of war. Natalie Barney kept her Friday salons going. Gertrude Stein still lived with Alice Toklas at rue de Fleurus. She and Joyce continued to ignore each other.

Joyce was becoming increasingly preoccupied with the welfare of Lucia who was receiving treatment at various clinics and asylums in France and in Switzerland. So distracted was he about his daughter that he became impatient and even antagonistic towards many women who were offering to help him, among them Mary Colum, Maria Jolas and even Harriet Weaver. Nora and Lucia were now virtually the only women in his life; he was spending heavily on medical fees for his daughter – for hospitalisation and for specialists such as the Swiss psychiatrist Carl Jung - and on extravagant *haute couture* for his wife. Eventually Lucia was institutionalised for the rest of her life. Joyce visited her until his death in 1941 but Nora, who lived until 1951, never saw her daughter again.

Joyce returned to Shakespeare and Company in May 1938 at the request of a photographer who wanted to take a picture of him with Beach and Monnier. He would hardly have done so but his *Work in Progress* was nearing completion and he wanted to ensure as much publicity as possible. The book, finally known as *Finnegans Wake*, arrived in time for his 57th birthday on 2 February, 1939. It had taken 16 years to write.

Joyce was concerned that, with war expected soon, no one would read his new book and he told Beckett he would not make any money from it. The reviews were mixed; some critics praised it, some said it required further study while others dismissed it as a bad joke.

Paris was now preparing itself for war. Gas masks were issued and there was a siege mentality about. In the cafés, customers were asked to pay when served in case an air raid siren emptied the tables. Candles were at a premium and metal shutters came down on the shops. It was a city of darkness again.

As the Germans got closer the roads became crowded with refugees. Stein and Toklas set off in their car for their country home at Bilignin in the Rhone Valley where they would spend most of the war. Both were Jewish and escaped deportation through their friendship with a collaborator with the Vichy regime who had connections with the Gestapo.

With *Finnegans Wake* finally published, Joyce was free to leave the city that had been his home for 19 years. He, Nora, Giorgio and Stephen moved to Saint-Gérand-le-Puy near Vichy where Maria Jolas ran a language school. Soon afterwards they were joined by Paul Léon and his wife Marie.

Léon helped Joyce correct misprints in *Finnegans Wake*. When his wife decided to return to her job as a journalist with the *New York Herald Tribune* in Paris, he followed her.

One of the tasks Léon set himself was to rescue Joyce's books and papers from the flat the family had hurriedly vacated. He even bought back furniture and paintings that the landlord had auctioned off to recompense him for the rent he had not been paid. Léon brought it all to Count Gerald O'Kelly, the Irish Ambassador to occupied France, and gave him instructions that, on Joyce's death or his, the papers should be kept in the National Library of Ireland and not opened for 50 years.[12]

In December 1940, Joyce and Nora moved to Zurich where they had spent the previous war. In January 1941, he died after an operation for a duodenal ulcer.

Later that year, Léon was arrested by the Gestapo and interned near Paris before being deported to Silesia where he was killed.

Not every foreigner left Paris. Peggy Guggenheim still drank champagne at the Dome and went from studio to studio buying paintings at knockdown prices. Her taste in art had been influenced by her former lover Beckett who had urged her to consider the Modernists rather than the Old Masters. Over the decade she spent $250,000 on a collection that, some years later, would be worth $40m.

Beach also stayed put. She and Monnier wept as they watched refugees making their way into Paris and out the other side. A short time later they watched German tanks and soldiers enter the city.

As the Occupation settled down, many who had survived the exodus returned to Paris and Shakespeare and Company was as busy as ever. When the United States entered the war, Beach was obliged to register at the Commissary once a week (Jews had to sign every day). One day she had a visit from a high-ranking German officer who had seen a copy of *Finnegans Wake* in the window. Speaking perfect English he said he wanted to buy it as he was very interested in Joyce's work.

'It's not for sale,' replied Beach.

'Why not?' asked the German.

Beach explained she was keeping the book for herself.

When he had gone she removed the book from the window.

A fortnight later the officer returned, demanding the book. When Beach said she hadn't got it, he was furious.

'We're coming to confiscate all your goods today.'

When he had gone she and her friends carried all the books up to the third floor, stripped the shop and painted over its signage. The Germans did not return or, if they did, they could not find the shop.

It was the end of Shakespeare and Company. The day after the German surrender of Paris in August 1944, Beach heard jeeps on the street and an American voice calling her name. It was Hemingway. He had come, he said, to liberate rue de l'Odéon.

---

[1] Putnam: *Paris was our Mistress* 240.

[2] Idem 244.

[3] Joyce claimed the book was his experiment in interpreting 'the dark night of the soul' (Ellmann 546).

[4] Letter from Nancy Cunard to Ellmann, 1957 (Ellmann 704).

[5] Wiser: *The Twilight Years* 25.

[6] Fitch: *Sylvia Beach and the Lost Generation* 322.

[7] Beach: *Shakespeare and Company* 201.

[8] Beach 204 and Fitch 322. According to Fitch, the Colums were privately critical of Joyce and sympathetic to Sylvia.

[9] Beach: *Shakespeare and Company* 205. Her biographer, Noel Riley Fitch, wrote: 'Although the original agreement had been that 66 percent of the profits would go to Joyce, letters and ledgers suggest he received all the profits.' (*Sylvia Beach and the Lost Generation* 129).

[10] Idem 90.

[11] Idem 92.

[12] The National Library of Ireland made the papers available to the public in 1992 and published a summary of them as *The James Joyce Paul Léon papers*.

Afterword
Full Circle

Samuel Beckett was in Ireland when the Germans entered Paris. He rushed to France and joined the Resistance. After the war he worked with the Irish Red Cross in Saint-Lô in Normandy. He was decorated by the French government and was awarded the Nobel Prize for Literature in 1969.

Robert McAlmon was interned in France in 1940 but his family used political influence to have him freed. He returned to the US where he worked for his brother in Arizona, selling medical equipment. He moved to Desert Hot Springs, California, where he died in 1956. His neighbours were surprised to learn of his prominent role among the expatriate community in Paris.

After divorcing McAlmon, Bryher (Annie Winifred Ellerman) married Hilda Doolittle's lover, Kenneth MacPherson, before all three settled into a bizarre *ménage a trois* in Geneva. Before the outbreak of war she helped over 100 Germans escape Nazi persecution before fleeing herself to London where she lived with Doolittle and wrote historical novels.

Gertrude Stein and Alice B Toklas returned to their home

in rue de Fleurus just before the Liberation. Stein became ill with stomach cancer. As she was wheeled into an operating theatre for surgery, she asked Toklas: 'What is the answer?' When she got no reply, she asked: 'In that case what is the question?' She died in 1946.

Nancy Cunard got revenge on her mother who had disinherited her (over her relationship with Henry Crowther) by writing *Black Man and White Ladyship*. It went into detail about the feud and brought in Sir Thomas Beecham and George Moore. Nancy was actively anti-fascist and later campaigned for civil rights in the United States.

George Antheil moved to Berlin but his avant-garde music was not welcomed in Nazi Germany. He went to Hollywood where he composed many film scores.

Ezra Pound's friendship with Joyce cooled after Pound's negative reaction to *Finnegans Wake*. He embraced fascism and broadcast Nazi propaganda during the war. Afterwards, he was indicted for treason in America but was declared insane.

Padraic and Mary Colum moved to New York where they taught at Columbia University. Padraic received many honours and awards. He died aged 90. He had been the last living link with Yeats, Synge, Lady Gregory and the early days of the Irish literary revival.

James Stephens gave a series of talks on the BBC, which continued through the war and afterwards. He denounced Irish neutrality and declared himself an Englishman for the war's duration.

Thomas MacGreevy returned to Dublin at the outbreak of war and became art critic with *The Irish Times* (1941-44). In 1950 he was appointed Director of the National Gallery, a post in which he excelled.

Arthur Power farmed for a while in Waterford before selling up and moving to Dublin where he started to paint and write his memoirs. He too was art critic with *The Irish Times*.

A Little Circle Of Kindred Minds

Bibliography

Ackroyd, Peter, *Ezra Pound*, London, Thames & Hudson, 1980.

Adam, Peter, *Eileen Gray: Architect/Designer*, Harry N Abrams, 2000.

Aldington, Richard, *Life for Life's Sake*, Viking, 1941.

Anderson, Chester, *James Joyce*, London, Thames & Hudson, 1986.

Antheil, George, *Bad Boy of Music*, (first pub. 1945), Samuel French, 1990.

Attridge, Derek, ed., *The Cambridge Companion to James Joyce*, Cambridge Univ. Press, 1999.

Bair, Deirdre, *Samuel Beckett: A Biography*, Simon & Schuster, 1990.

Baker, Carlos, *Ernest Hemingway, A Life Story*, Collins, 1969.

Barnes, Djuna, *James Joyce*, Vanity Fair XVIII, April 1922. Incl. in *Djuna Barnes* below.

Barry, Alyce, *Djuna Barnes: Interviews*, Sun & Moon Press, Maryland, 1985.

Benstock, Shari, *Women of the Left Bank*, University of Texas Press, 1986.

Beach, Sylvia, *Shakespeare and Company*, Harcourt Brace, 1959.

Bowen, Zack, *Padraic Colum: A Biographical Critical Introduction*, Southern Illinois University Press, 1970.

Brown, Terence, *The Life of WB Yeats*, Gill and Macmillan, 1999.

Bruccoli, Matthew J., *Some Sort of Epic Grandeur: The Life of F Scott Fitzgerald*, Harcourt Brace Jovanovich, NY, 1981.

Bryher (Annie Ellerman), *The Heart to Artemis: A Writer's Memoir*, Harcourt Brace, 1962.

Budgen, Frank, *James Joyce and the Making of Ulysses*, (first pub. 1934), Oxford University Press 1991.

Burgess, Anthony, *Ernest Hemingway*, Thames and Hudson, 1978.

--------------------, *Here Comes Everybody: An Introduction to James Joyce for the Ordinary Reader*, London, Faber and Faber, 1965.

Cahalan, James M, *Liam O'Flaherty: A Study of the Short Fiction*, GK Hall and Co, Boston, 1991.

Cairns, David, *Berlioz: The Making of an Artist*, Penguin, 2000.

Callaghan, Morley, *That Summer in Paris*, Coward-McCann, NY, 1963.

Campbell, James, *Paris Interzone*, Vintage, London, 2001.

Carpenter, Humphrey, *Geniuses Together*, Unwin Hyman, 1987.

Charters, Jimmy, *This must be the Place: Memoirs of Montparnasse*, (first pub. 1937), Collier Macmillan, 1989.

Clarke, Austin, *A Penny in the Clouds,* Moytura Press, Dublin, 1968.

----------------, *Twice Round the Black Church*, Routledge & Kegan Paul, 1962.

----------------, *Stephen Dedalus: the Author of Ulysses*, New

Statesman XXII (Feb 23 1924), a short account of his meetings with Joyce.

Clarke, Dardis, ed., *Austin Clarke Remembered*, Bridge House, Dublin, 1996.

Colum, Mary, *Life and the Dream*, New York, 1958, rev. Dolmen Press, Dublin, 1966.

----------------, *A Little Knowledge of Joyce*, Saturday Review of Literature XXXIII, 29 April, 1950.

Colum, Padraic, *Arthur Griffith*, Browne and Nolan, Dublin, 1959.

------------------, *Portrait of James Joyce*, Dublin Magazine, VII (Apr-June) 1932.

------------------, *The Road Round Ireland*, Macmillan, NY, 1926.

Coogan, Tim Pat, *De Valera: Long Fellow, Long Shadow*, Random House, 1993.

-------------------, *Wherever Green is Worn: the Story of the Irish Diaspora*, Hutchinson (UK) 2000, Palgrave (New York) 2001.

Costello, Peter, *Liam O'Flaherty's Ireland*, Wolfhound Press, Dublin, 1996.

Cowley, Malcolm, *A Second Flowering: Works and Days of the Lost Generation*, Penguin, 1973.

--------------------, *Exile's Return: A Literary Odyssey of the 1920s*, Penguin Books, 1994 (first pub. 1934).

Crispi, Luca, *Reading and Writing Ireland's Past and Future: James Joyce (1882-2012)*, The Stinging Fly, issue 17, Vol. 2, Winter 2010-11.

Cronin, Anthony, *Heritage Now: Irish Literature in the English Language*, Brandon, 1982.

-------------------, Samuel Beckett: The Last Modernist, Flamingo, 1997.

Cunard, Nancy, *GM – Memoirs of George Moore*, Rupert Hart-Davis, 1956.

Curran, CP, *James Joyce Remembered*, Oxford Univ. Press, 1968.

Davenport-Hines, Richard, *A Night at the Majestic: Proust and the great Modernist Dinner Party of 1922*, Faber and Faber, 2007.

Drutman, Irving, ed., *Janet Flanner: Paris was Yesterday*, Harcourt Brace Jovanovich, 1972.

Dukes, Gerry, *Illustrated Lives: Samuel Beckett*, Penguin, 2001.

Eliot, Valerie and Haughton, Hugh, eds., *The Letters of TS Eliot, Vols. 1 and 2,* Faber and Faber, 2009.

Ellmann, Richard, *James Joyce*, New York, Oxford University Press, 1959. Rev. 1982.

------------------, ed., *Letters of James Joyce*, Vols. 2 and 3, New York, Viking Press, 1966.

------------------, ed., *Selected Letters of James Joyce*, New York, Viking Press, 1975.

Elvery, Beatrice, *Today we will only Gossip*, first pub. Constable, London, 1964.

Fargnoli, A Nicholas, and Gillespie Michael P, *James Joyce A to Z – the Essential Reference to the Life and Work*, Facts on File Inc, NY, 1995.

Fehsenfeld, Martha Dow and Ovenbeck, Lois More, eds., *The Letters of Samuel Beckett 1929-1940*, Cambridge University Press, 2009.

Fenton, Charles A., *The Apprenticeship of Ernest Hemingway*, Mentor, NY, 1961.

Bibliography

Ferriter, Diarmaid, *Occasions of Sin: Sex and Society in Modern Ireland*, Profile Books, London, 2009.

Finneran, Richard J, ed., *Letters of James Stephens*, Macmillan, 1974.

Fitch, Noel Riley, ed., *In transition – A Paris Anthology*, Secker and Warburg, 1990.

------------------, *Sylvia Beach and the Lost Generation*, WW Norton and Co., NY and London, first pub. 1983.

FitzGerald, Desmond, *The Memoirs of Desmond FitzGerald 1913-1916*, Routledge and Kegan Paul, London, 1968.

Ford, Ford M, *It was the Nightingale*, Philadelphia, Lippincott, 1933.

Ford, Hugh, ed., *The Left Bank Revisited: Selections from the Paris Tribune 1917-1934*, Pennsylvania State University Press, 1972.

------------, *Published in Paris: A Literary Chronicle of Paris in the 1920s and 1930s*, Collier, 1975.

Foster, RF, *Paddy and Mr Punch: Connections in Irish and English History*, Allen Lane/Penguin, 1993.

-------------, *WB Yeats: A Life*. (Vols. 1 and 2), Oxford Univ. Press, 2003.

Frazier, Adrian, *George Moore 1852-1933*, Yale University Press, 2000.

Freund, Giselle and Carleton VB, *James Joyce in Paris: His Final Years*, Harcourt Brace, 1965.

Garvin, Tom, *1922 – The Birth of Irish Democracy*, Gill and Macmillan, 1996.

Gilbert, Stuart, ed., *Letters of James Joyce*, Vol. 1, Faber, 1957.

------------------, *Souvenirs de Voyage*, Mercure de France, CCCIX (Mai-Aout 1950).

Gill, Anton, *Peggy Guggenheim: The Life of an Art Addict*, HarperCollins, 2001.

Glassco, John, *Memoirs of Montparnasse*, New York Review Books, 2007.

Gluck, Barbara, *Beckett and Joyce: Friendship and Fiction*, Associated University Presses, New Jersey, 1979.

Gogarty, Oliver St J, *As I was Going down Sackville Street*, (first pub. 1937), O'Brien Press 1995.

------------------------, *The Joyce I Knew*, Saturday Review of Literature, XIII Jan. 25, 1941. See also *They think they know Joyce*, Sat. Review XXXIII March 18, 1950.

Gordon, Luis, *The World of Samuel Beckett 1906-1946*, Yale University Press, 1996.

Gordon, W Terrence, Hamaji E and Albert J, *Everyman's Joyce*, Mark Batty, NY, 2009.

Gorman, Herbert, *James Joyce: A Definitive Biography*, Farrar & Rhinehart, NY, 1939, rev. 1948.

Gonzales, Alexander G, ed., *Modern Irish Writers: A Bio-Critical Sourcebook*, Aldwych Press, London, 1997.

Greacen, Lavinia, *Chink: A Biography*, Macmillan, 1989.

Guggenheim, Peggy, *Out of this Century*, (first pub 1946), Andre Deutsch, 2005.

Halpern, Susan, *Austin Clarke, His Life and Works*, Dolmen Press Dublin and Humanities Press New Jersey, 1974.

Hansen, Arlen J., *Expatriate Paris: A Cultural and Literary Guide to Paris of the 1920s*, Arcade Publishing, NY, 1990.

Bibliography

Hayman, Ronald, *Proust*, Minerva, 1991.

Hemingway, Ernest, *A Moveable Feast*, Penguin 1966.

Herring, Phillip, *Djuna: The Life and Work of Djuna Barnes*, Viking Penguin, 1995.

Hobhouse, Janet, *Everybody who was Anybody: A Biography of Gertrude Stein*, Weidenfield and Nicolson, London, 1975.

Holohan, Renagh, *The Irish Chateaux: In Search of Descendants of the Wild Geese*, Liliput Press, Dublin, 1989.

Hone, Joseph, *The Life of George Moore*, Gollancz, 1936.

Huddleston, Sisley, *Paris Salons, Cafés, Studios*, Blue Ribbon Books, NY, 1928.

Hutchins, Patricia, *James Joyce's World*, Methuen, 1957.

Jackson, John Wyse and Costello, Peter, *John Stanislaus Joyce: The Voluminous Life and Genius of James Joyce's Father*, Fourth Estate, 1997.

Jeffares, A Norman, and MacBride White, Anna, eds., *A Servant of the Queen: The Autobiography of Maud Gonne*, Univ. of Chicago Press, 1995.

Joyce, Stanislaus, *My Brother's Keeper*, Faber and Faber, 1958.

Kain, Richard M., *Susan L Mitchell*, Bucknell University Press, New Jersey, 1972.

Kelly, AA, *The Letters of Liam O'Flaherty*, Dublin, Wolfhound Press, 1996.

Kennedy, Michael, *Ireland and the League of Nations 1919-1946*, Irish Academic Press, 1996.

Kennedy, SB, *Irish Art and Modernism*, pub. for Hugh Lane Municipal Gallery Dublin by the Institute of Irish Studies at

Queens University Belfast, 1991.

Keogh, Dermot, *Ireland and Europe 1919-1948*, Gill and Macmillan, 1988.

Kiberd, Declan, *Inventing Ireland: the Literature of the Modern Nation,* Vintage, 1996.

-----------------, *The Irish Writer and the World*, Cambridge University Press, 2005.

-----------------, *Ulysses and Us: the Art of Everyday Living*, Faber and Faber, 2009.

Killeen, Terence, *Ulysses Unbound: A Reader's Companion*, Wordwell in assoc. with NLI, 2004.

Knowlson, James, *Damned to Fame: The Life of Samuel Beckett*, Simon & Schuster, NY, 1996.

Knowlson, James and Elizabeth, eds., *Beckett Remembered, Remembering Beckett*, Bloomsbury, 2006.

Lynn, Kenneth S, *Hemingway*, Simon and Schuster, London, 1987.

Macardle, Dorothy, *The Irish Republic*, Irish Press, 1951.

MacBride White, Anna and Jeffares, Norman A, *The Gonne-Yeats Letters 1893-1938*, Hutchinson, 1992.

MacCabe, Colin, *James Joyce and the Revolution of the Word*, Macmillan, 2002.

McAlmon, Robert, *Being Geniuses Together 1920-1930*, rev. with afterword by Kay Boyle, Doubleday, 1968. P/b edition North Point Press, San Francisco, 1984.

McCormack, WJ, *Fool of the Family: A Life of J. M. Synge*, Weidenfeld and Nicholson, 2000.

Bibliography

McCourt, John, *The Years of Bloom: James Joyce in Trieste 1904-1920*, Dublin, Lilliput Press, 2000.

Maddox, Brenda, *Nora: a Biography of Nora Joyce*, Hamish and Hamilton, 1988.

Magee, William, (John Eglinton, pseud.) *Irish Literary Portraits*, first pub.1935, repub. by Books for Librarians Press, NY. 1967.

Martin, Augustine, ed., *James Joyce: The Artist and the Labyrinth*, Ryan Publishing, 1999.

Matthews, James, *Voices: A Life of Frank O'Connor*, Gill and Macmillan, 1983.

Maye, Brian, *Arthur Griffith*, Griffith College Publications, Dublin, 1997.

Mellow, James R, *Invented Lives – F Scott Fitzgerald*, Houghton Mifflin, 1984.

--------------------, *Hemingway: A Life Without Consequences*, Hodder and Stoughton, 1992.

Mitchell, Arthur, *Revolutionary Government in Ireland: Dáil Éireann 1919-22*, Gill and Macmillan, 1995.

Mizener, Arthur, *Scott Fitzgerald*, Thames and Hudson, h/b 1972, p/b 1987.

Murphy, Patrick J, *Patrick Tuohy: From Conversations with his Friends*, Town House, Dublin 2004.

Noel, Lucie, *James Joyce and Paul L Léon: The Story of a Friendship*, The Gorham Book Martini, 1951.

Norburn, Robert, *A James Joyce Chronology*, Palgrave Macmillan, 2004.

Norris, David and Flint, Carl, *Joyce for Beginners*, Icon Books, 1994.

O'Brien, Eoin, *The Beckett Country*, Black Cat Press in assoc. with Faber and Faber, 1986.

O'Brien, James H., *Liam O'Flaherty*, Buckness University Press, New Jersey, 1973.

O'Connor, Ulick, *Oliver St John Gogarty*, Jonathan Cape, 1964.

O'Connor, Ulick, ed., *The Joyce we Knew*, Mercier Press 1966, Brandon 2004.

O'Flaherty, Liam, *Shame the Devil*, Dublin, Wolfhound Press, 1981.

Poli, Bernard J, *Ford Madox Ford and the Transatlantic Review*, New York, Syracuse Univ. Press, 1967.

Potts, Willard, ed., *James Joyce: Portraits of the Artist in Exile*, Wolfhound Press, 1979.

Powell, Jessica, *Literary Paris: A Guide*, The Little Bookroom, NY, 2006.

Power, Arthur, *From the Old Waterford House*, Ballylough Books, 2004.

---------------, *Conversations with James Joyce*, Lilliput Press, Dublin, 1999.

Putnam, Samuel, *Paris was our Mistress: Memories of a Lost and Found Generation:* first pub. Southern Illinois University Press 1947, Arcturus Books 1970.

Pyle, Hilary, *James Stephens, His Work and an Account of his Life*, Routledge and Kegan Paul, 1965.

-------------, *Red-headed Rebel: Susan L Mitchel, Poet and Mystic of the Irish Cultural Renaissance*, Woodfield Press, Dublin, 2008.

Reynolds, Michael, *Hemingway: The Paris Years*, WW Norton, NY, 1999.

Bibliography

Rielly Edward J, *F Scott Fitzgerald, a Biography*, Greenwood Press, Connecticut and London, 2005.

Rodriguez, Suzanne, *Wild Heart: A Life*, (biography of Natalie Clifford Barney), HarperCollins, 2002.

Ryan, John, ed., *Envoy magazine Vol. 5, No. 17, April 1951*, (special issue on Joyce).

Schenkar, Joan, *Truly Wilde:* The *Unsettling Story of Dolly Wilde, Oscar's Unusual Niece*, Virago Press, 2000.

Schloss, Carol Loeb, *Lucia Joyce: To Dance in the Wake*, Bloomsbury, 2004.

Schreibman, Susan, ed., *Collected Poems of Thomas MacGreevy: An Annotated Edition*, Anna Livia Press, Dublin, 1991 and Catholic University of America Press, Washington DC.

Smoller, Sanford J, *Adrift among Geniuses: Robert McAlmon, Writer and Publisher of the Twenties*, Pennsylvania State Univ. Press, 1975.

Stacton, David, *The Bonapartes*, Hodder and Stoughton, 1967.

Staley, Thomas F and Lewis, Randolph, eds., *Reflections on James Joyce: Stuart Gilbert's Paris Journal*, University of Texas Press, 1993.

Stein, Gertrude, *Paris France*, Scribners, 1940.

Stephens, James, *The Joyce I Knew*, Irish Digest XXVIII July 1947.

------------------, *James, Seumas and Jacques*. Macmillan, 1964.

Sternlicht, Sanford, ed., *Selected Short Stories of Padraic Colum*, Syracuse University Press 1984.

Souhami, Diana, *Gertrude and Alice*, Phoenix Press, London, 2000.

Tobin, Al and Gerty, Elmer, *Frank Harris: A Study in Black and White*, Haskell House, US, 1970.

Tomkins, Calvin, *Living Well is the Best Revenge*, a biography of Gerald and Sara Murphy, Modern Library, NY, 1998.

Vaill, Amanda, *Everybody was so Young: Gerald and Sara Murphy*, Warner Books, 1999.

Vance, Norman, *Irish Literature – A Social History*, Basil Blackwell, Oxford, 1990.

(Various), *Proceedings of the Irish Race Congress in Paris 1922*, Cahill and Co, London, 1922.

Walker, Dorothy, *Modern Art in Ireland*, Lilliput Press, Dublin, 1997.

Walsh, Keri, ed., *The Letters of Sylvia Beach*, Columbia University Press, 2010.

Ward, Margaret, *Maud Gonne: A Life*, HarperCollins, 1993.

Weber, Ronald, *News of Paris: American Journalists in the City of Light between the Wars*, Ivan R Dee, Chicago, 2006.

White, William, *By-Line: Ernest Hemingway*, Penguin, 1968.

Williams, William Carlos, *Autobiography*, first pub. 1948, New Directions 1967.

Wilson, Edmund, *The Shores of Light: A Literary Chronicle of the Twenties and Thirties*, Farrar, Strauss and Young, New York, 1952.

Wineapple, Brenda, *Genet: A Biography of Janet Flanner*, Univ. of Nebraska Press, 1992.

Wiser, William, *The Crazy Years: Paris in the Twenties*, New York, Thames and Hudson, 1983.

------------------, *The Twilight Years: Paris in the 1930s*, New York, Carroll & Graf, 2000.

Wolff, Geoffrey, *Black Sun: The Brief Transit and Violent Eclipse of Harry Crosby*, New York Review Books, 1976.

Yeats, WB, *Autobiographies*, Macmillan, 1961.

Younger, Calton, *Arthur Griffith*, Gill and Macmillan, 1981.

Abbreviations used:

Ellmann - in reference to *James Joyce*, OUP, 1982.

OFJJ - in reference to *Our Friend James Joyce*, Victor Gollancz, London, 1959.

A Little Circle Of Kindred Minds

Index

C

D

E

F

G

H

I

M

N

R

S